# KINGSHIP

Frontispiece

Coat-of-arms of James IV of Scotland (by courtesy of the Österreichische Nationalbibliothek)

# COSMOS

## The Yearbook of the Traditional Cosmology Society

### Volume 2

### 1986

# KINGSHIP

edited by

Emily Lyle

Published by the Traditional Cosmology Society
Edinburgh

# COSMOS 2   Kingship

A grant from the Spalding Trust towards the cost
of publication is gratefully acknowledged.


ISSN 0269 8773
ISBN 1 869960 01 7

Printed by Reprographics Unit (Drummond Street)
University of Edinburgh

# CONTENTS

# THE SYMBOLISM OF THE RAYED NIMBUS IN EARLY ISLAMIC ART

Robert Hillenbrand

The purpose of this paper is to investigate a theme which is so familiar in classical and Christian art as to have sunk to the level of a cliché, and yet is still a relatively unexplored topic in Islamic art: the nimbus (Collimet-Guérin 1961). The present study will therefore focus on the Islamic use of this time-honoured motif; and — to keep the enquiry within manageable bounds — will investigate one particular manifestation of that theme, namely the rayed nimbus. What follows does not pretend to be an exhaustive account even of this specialised version of the nimbus motif. The study of Islamic iconography is, after all, still in its infancy and thus the first task must be to map out the territory.

The few examples cited in this paper are therefore intended principally to substantiate the claims made here that the Islamic world did on occasion use the theme of the rayed nimbus in the full consciousness of its symbolic associations; that its varied visual expressions testify to repeated original and imaginative reworkings of a nuclear idea; and that in the Islamic world this idea resurfaced across such gulfs of space and time that it may fairly be regarded as a constant of Muslim royal iconography. Given the ever-present danger of over-interpretation which is the bane of studies of this kind, it is worth stating at the very outset that the conclusions reached in this paper are tentative; they make no claim to certainty. It will be enough if the material assembled here encourages would-be iconographers to examine related objects and monuments with greater awareness of their possible symbolic value.

It is worth emphasising this point, since the celebrated Islamic antipathy to religious images ought, one might think, to have prevented Islamic artists from even considering the use of the nimbus.[1] At the outset, certainly, there was no possibility of a straightforward transfer of the Christian motif into Islamic visual terms. Yet the large-scale adoption by the Muslims of the varied paraphernalia of the imperial image as developed by Rome and Byzantium did leave some scope for the secular use of the nimbus within an Islamic setting, especially if that setting had no overt religious significance. These points will be elaborated below. Thereafter, the prime purpose of this paper will be to show how the nimbus did indeed enter Islamic art in this way — by the back door, so to speak — how the religious connotations of the rayed nimbus in particular were never entirely forgotten and how they emerged in an increasingly explicit manner over the centuries, culminating in representations which at long last provided a direct Muslim equivalent to the standard use of this theme in Christian iconography.

The specific examples to be discussed here could certainly be multiplied if the purpose of this paper were to plot the development of the rayed nimbus in detail. Yet such is not the aim. Instead, this brief study will seek to highlight, by means of a few carefully selected test cases, the principal ways in which this theme was employed in early medieval Islamic art. To tease out its manifold associations in the requisite detail, quarrying the copious literary sources in the process, is a task for future research. The same desire to present the subject in its broad outlines only also dictates that the discussion of other types of halo, such as the solid gold roundel[2] or the flame halo,[3] to say nothing of still more abstract references to the theme, will be limited to a few comments *en passant*. It is worth bearing in mind, however, that each of these topics would also repay detailed investigation.

The examples of the rayed nimbus which follow have been selected to substantiate the claim made earlier in this paper that this theme repeatedly resurfaces at different times and places. Accordingly, the discussion — which, for the sake of clarity, will maintain a strict chronological sequence — will embrace in turn Umayyad Syria, 'Abbasid Iraq, Aghlabid Ifriqiyya, Umayyad Spain, and finally, late Fatimid and Mamluk Egypt — until, in Ilkhanid Iran, and very probably under Western or Byzantine influence, the rayed nimbus was at last employed in a way long standard in Christian iconography, namely around the head of a holy person. The discussion will span the eighth to the fourteenth century, and will include examples from most of these centuries, as well as a brief excursus into pre-Islamic Iran.

As the analysis proceeds, it will become apparent that these successive references to the theme of the rayed nimbus are so varied as to defy categorisation. They occur in architecture, in city planning, in mosaic, in metalwork and in painting. It would not be hard to add to this list further examples from these media, as well as others drawn from pottery, tilework and ivory carving. Finally, it should become increasingly obvious that, until near the end of the period under discussion, these versions of the rayed nimbus — for all their major differences in type, scale and medium — nevertheless have one factor in common: they all avoid the obvious expression of the theme, namely as the surround for the head of a monarch.[4] Indeed, they seem to go to the opposite extreme by expressing the idea of the rayed nimbus in deliberately obscure language. In effect, then, they have to be decoded. The implications of this finding will be examined at the end of this paper. For the time being it will suffice to note the likelihood that the disc halo was openly adopted because it could more readily be interpreted as a purely secular and honorific symbol, whereas the rayed nimbus was forced underground because its principal association was with sanctity.

It must be conceded at the outset that the notion of a rayed nimbus as a symbol of sanctity was, as noted earlier, not calculated to appeal to Muslims. Its associations were too loaded. In the Christian world of the Mediterranean it connoted either saints[5] or, more commonly, Christ himself.[6] On rarer occasions it was used for Byzantine imperial images.[7] Earlier it had been employed in the Roman world as an attribute of the gods, such as Sol or Jupiter himself,[8] or of emperors who claimed divinity and invincibility.[9] Similarly, in the art of Hatra,[10] Dura[11] and Palmyra (Colledge 1976: 41-4, 212, figs. 22-3 and pls. 19, 28, 35-6, 39 and 41) in the first two centuries or so of the Christian era it had been used for images of gods, and this custom was maintained in the Sasanian period.[12] The appearance of the rayed nimbus as an element in certain Sasanian crowns[13] continued this association with divinity while establishing at the same time the imperial connections of the theme. The use of the rayed nimbus for royal figures is also attested in Sasanian art.[14] In the Iranian world it could be seen as a visible expression of the divinely bestowed charisma of kingship, the royal glory known variously as *hvarnah-* (a word which can be transcribed in several different ways), *khvarrah*, *farrah* or *farr*.[15] This essentially conceptual image could be helped along, as it were, by actually gilding the hair of the Persian monarch, so as to create a shimmering nimbus — an idea enthusiastically taken up by certain Roman emperors who powdered their heads with gold-dust (L'Orange 1947: 33, 66, 90, and 135). Clothes were similarly treated; thus the trousers of the Sasanian monarch Hormuzd IV were covered with gold ornaments (Huart 1927: 144), while many centuries earlier the rulers of ancient Assyria had worn appliqué gold bracteates, especially rosettes, sprinkled over their clothing, a fashion recorded earlier still in the case of Mesopotamian deities (Oppenheim 1949: 180-1, 186-7, 191). The uses of the rayed nimbus in the eastern part of the Iranian world and its adjoining territories, notably the empire of the Kushans[16] and Gandhara,[17] would repay further investigation. As for the pre-Sasanian antecedents of the rayed nimbus in the ancient Near East, these are a separate and complex study;[18] they show that this symbol is of immense antiquity, and goes back almost to the very beginnings of civilisation.

Thus at the time of the Muslim conquests in the seventh century the rayed nimbus already had a long history both as a sign of divinity or sanctity and as an attribute of rulers. From the earliest days of their faith the Muslims had resolutely set their faces against any visual representation or symbol of Allah. Thus there was no possibility at all of appropriating the motif of the rayed nimbus as a reference to Allah. Since the depiction of saints is a phenomenon only of later medieval Islamic art, there remained only one possibility, namely to exploit the imperial associations of the theme in a new Muslim context. Here too, however, there were serious difficulties. Chief among these in the early decades of Muslim rule was the ingrained prejudice of the Arabs against the very idea of kingship, let alone its outward trappings. For centuries the word "king" (*malik*) functioned as a potent term of abuse. From the death of Muhammad onwards, the ruler of the Muslim community took the title of caliph (*khalifa*) — literally "successor" — or *amir al-mu'minin* ("Commander of the Faithful"). These titles had a religious flavour not to be found in the word *malik*. In theory, then, Muslim orthodoxy — especially in these crucial early years of the faith — frowned on the pomp and circumstance of royalty and looked with favour on the simple, austere lives led by the early caliphs.

It was perhaps only a matter of time before theory and practice diverged. The fifth caliph, Mu'awiya, who in 661 founded the first dynasty of Islam — named after his own clan, the Umayyads — deliberately adopted a princely lifestyle replete with ceremony and with conspicuous consumption, arguing that he had to do so in order to cut a suitable figure as ruler of the Syrians, themselves long accustomed to the splendours of Byzantine monarchy.[19] By and large later caliphs followed Mu'awiya's lead, and thus in theory the way was open to appropriate for Islam the complex royal iconography and ceremonial practice of Byzantium and, for that matter, Sasanian Iran.

In practice, however, the Muslims — unlike their counterparts in the medieval West (Schramm 1954-6; 1958) — avoided a wholesale adoption of this alien imagery and ritual. Some motifs and ceremonies, for instance, had too pronounced a Christian flavour to serve Islamic purposes. Interestingly enough, the rayed nimbus apparently fell into this category. Presumably, in the transitional stage when Byzantine and Sasanian motifs were tentatively being put to new Islamic uses, this motif was rejected — though whether because it was blasphemous, subversive or dangerously ambivalent remains uncertain. One may suspect, however, that the associations of divinity which clung to the motif emphatically disqualified it for use in the standard Roman, Byzantine, Palmyran or Sasanian manner — that is, as a halo surrounding the head of a divine, saintly or royal personage. Indeed, for a full seven centuries this obvious primary use of the theme is not encountered in the Islamic world. When, after this long lapse of time, it does turn up, its appearance is unmistakably the result of a fresh influx of Christian influence, as the context makes clear. Subsequent figures with rayed nimbi in Islamic art can also be associated with direct Western influence.[20]

If, then, there is no example of the rayed nimbus used in association with a figural image in early Islamic art, how is it possible to argue that the theme so much as survived there? The answer is simple: it went underground. Barred — probably for religious reasons — from using it in the explicit fashion adopted by earlier civilisations, Islamic artists resorted to more indirect means, and sought instead to exploit the symbolic associations of this motif. It thereby entered a new lease of life, experiencing transformations unknown in earlier cultures — cultures which, free to use the motif in its most obvious and effective way, had no need to explore more recondite methods of saying the same thing. The early Islamic variations on this theme all seek to suggest rather than display.

The earliest of the examples chosen for detailed examination in this paper is also perhaps the most fully documented one, and may therefore serve as a test case for the admittedly speculative theory that in early Islamic art the rayed nimbus was depicted implicitly rather than explicitly. It is to be found in the Umayyad palace of Khirbat al-Mafjar near Jericho, datable from c.739-44.[21] The iconography of the monuments has been elucidated in magisterial fashion by the late Richard Ettinghausen (1972: 17-65), and it will be impossible to avoid recapitulating some of his findings. Nevertheless, there remains ample scope for further investigation. The buildings in question are in all probability (Hamilton 1969) the work of the then heir-apparent to the caliphate, the playboy prince al-Walid ibn Yazid.[22] The potentially blasphemous associations of the rayed nimbus within an Islamic context make it peculiarly appropriate that precisely this theme should recur repeatedly, and — for good measure — at iconographically charged locations, in a palace and a pleasure-dome erected by a prince whose own blasphemous mockeries of the faith were an open scandal.[23] Al-Walid, perhaps alone of the Umayyad family, would have been ready to flout orthodox opinion by arrogating forbidden imagery to himself. Moreover, while he was still crown prince his fondness for Byzantine culture and ways had excited adverse comment at court (Musil 1907: 158). Yet even he, it seems, drew the line at representing himself with a rayed nimbus behind his head in the manner of Palmyran gods, Christian holy images and Byzantine emperors. Nevertheless, the radiating design is nothing short of a leitmotif at this, his favourite haunt. At the same time, it should be remembered that Khirbat al-Mafjar is not alone among Umayyad palaces in harping upon such themes, and corroborative evidence aplenty could be cited — if space permitted — from 'Amman, Mshatta, Qasr al-Hair al-Gharbi and Khirbat al-Minya. That said, Khirbat al-Mafjar offers by far the greatest wealth of evidence in this matter and is therefore the obvious choice for detailed analysis here.

There is not enough space here to investigate the manifold occurrences of rayed motifs in the palace proper; yet, for all their variety, they are no more than a prelude to the much more explicit use of radiating themes in the bath hall itself, a room which may justly claim to be the climax of the whole site. As in the palace itself, these themes are quite naturally integrated into the overall design. They make sense decoratively as well as symbolically, and are not perceived as foreign bodies.[24] For those with eyes to see, they deepen the meaning of the ensemble; for those who are not privy to the code, there is no sense of something missing. Rather is it the decorative splendour of the bath hall and the adjacent *diwan* that strikes the eye, and it takes a little time for other ideas to make themselves felt. Indeed, it could be argued that the plethora of radiating motifs, especially in the bath hall, was intended to operate well-nigh subliminally and to provide a backdrop, as it were, to the most deliberately directed versions of the radiating theme. The latter examples should therefore be envisaged as part of a wider ambience of related and mutually dependent motifs.

The outer entrance to the bath and the doorway leading from the vestibule to the main hall are enough to announce the principal axis of the building. Along that axis the major themes which evoke the idea of a nimbus are to be found. They are carefully spaced and are located with an eye to maximum effect. In the virtual absence of detailed information as to the way the upper elevation was decorated, attention must perforce be concentrated on the floors and on the first few feet of the walls above them. Nevertheless, in view of the care taken to co-ordinate the decoration in the upper reaches of the palace vestibule,[25] the bath porch interior and the *diwan*, it is unlikely that the billowing vaults and central dome of the bath hall did not make their own distinctive contribution, in the way of applied ornament, to the themes discussed in this paper. The nature of that contribution must of course remain a matter of speculation.

It will be convenient to begin with the decoration of the floor. This comprises a continuous mosaic of surpassing size and quality divided into thirty-eight colourful panels or "carpets". Pride of place incontestably goes to the great central roundel (Plate I) which occupies the space immediately below the dome; the visual correspondence between the two was assuredly intentional, and indeed the four subsidiary vaults of the elevation also found their mosaic reflection in the four roundels — the only ones of that form in the whole floor — directly below them. The principal roundel employs a Catherine wheel design which had long been a familiar feature of Roman[26] and Byzantine[27] mosaic floors; but it rises above these relatively humble antecedents on two counts, namely its size and the absence of an *emblema*. These aspects will repay a more detailed discussion.

The roundel is the biggest version of this theme which has survived from antiquity.[28] Its absolute size — the diameter is some 10 m. — is magnified illusionistically by the way it bursts the confines which strict symmetry would allot to it and thereby intrudes into the space of the adjoining "carpets". With the increase in size comes an increase in complexity, so much so that it becomes unsatisfactory to read the design as "mere" pattern. The central location of this roundel means that its size and intricacy attract maximum attention. That being so, the absence of an *emblema* is even more significant. In a Roman floor, such as the example at Delos, the centrepiece or *emblema* of such a Catherine wheel design usually depicts a god or an appropriate personification. In a Christian context the *emblema* might be a bust of Christ or a Chi-Rho monogram, thus continuing the tradition of alluding to divine or supra-human beings in this key location. An eighth-century observer habituated to these associations might justifiably have expected to see some Muslim equivalent to such themes in a mosaic which otherwise followed Romano-Byzantine models so closely and even improved upon them. That later Muslims were receptive to such ideas is proved by the frequency with which the central roundel occupying the inner surface of a dome — the morphological equivalent of the centrepiece in the floor mosaic roundel — bears the inscription *Allah*, often with rays streaming from that name.[29] Moreover, the accurate use of a Hellenistic personification of Gea in the appropriate central location, again a roundel, in a floor fresco at the Umayyad palace of Qasr al-Hair al-Gharbi proves,[30] if proof were needed, that the Umayyads were ready and able to take over this particular tradition when it suited their purposes. These reflections suggest that the absence of an *emblema* in a setting where a particularly striking one was to be expected, in keeping with the ambitious size of the mosaic and its key location, was deliberate; and, as a corollary, that the emptiness of the central roundel was itself fraught with meaning.

What factors, then, can be marshalled to elucidate this meaning? Almost eight thousand triangles are employed to define a form which has nothing triangular about it but rather recalls a rosette or lotus. These are themselves, of course, significant forms in the royal context of Khirbat al-Mafjar.[31] Prolonged study of the design, however, brings somewhat different ideas to mind. The core of the pattern, endlessly generating semi-parabolic lines in opposing directions, evokes the very essence of energy and irresistibly draws the eye towards it. The pattern also contrives to suggest the notion of whirling movement at high speed. Above all, however, the white circle at the centre of the roundel is so obviously the source of this radiating movement that the mosaic as a whole cannot fail to evoke the sun and its rays.[32] Given the emphasis on red and yellow in the rays streaming from the centre, it may be permissible to interpret the whiteness of the central roundel as an image of molten heat, an idea that would of course strengthen these solar associations. Here, then, is the most explicit reference to solar symbolism so far encountered at this site. That it may have a further royal and quasi-political dimension is suggested by its location — namely at the dead centre of the principal building at Khirbat al-Mafjar. It would be difficult to imagine a more splendid setting than this for an enthroned monarch, and the built-in associations of the blank central disc in this specific architectural context would alone suffice for that monarch to claim a connection with the heavens, even without the rays so powerfully evoked by this mosaic. By that reckoning the intended reference would be to an oculus in a dome or vault, with its attendant symbolism of two-way traffic between earth and heaven.[33] The great original of this concept is of course the Pantheon (MacDonald 1976: 88-92), but the idea was enthusiastically taken up in Byzantine architecture, notably in Ravenna where it occurs in a series of late fifth- to early sixth-century monuments: in the presbytery vault of San Vitale, the apses of Sant' Apollinare in Classe and and of the Archepiscopal Chapel, and the domes of the two baptisteries (Bovini 1956: pls. 14, 20, 25, 47 and 53). It is also found in numerous other churches from Rome (Mâle 1960: pls. 46 and 52) to Daphni (Demus 1948: pl. 7). Frequently the "oculus" was filled with sacred images, and thus the classical connotations of the *clipeus* (L'Orange 1953: 90-102) and apotheosis (L'Orange 1947) could be evoked to enrich the Christian significance. It seems likely that in the case of ribbed domes a further refinement was developed, whereby the ribs themselves functioned as rays radiating from the central medallion, which could be occupied by some appropriate solar image. At Khirbat al-Mafjar, then, the *emblema*, when it was not the caliph himself enthroned directly over that spot, can legitimately be interpreted as the sun itself or, more generally, the heavens. Once again, ambiguity is of the essence.[34]

It may not be entirely irrelevant in this connection to note that Umayyad propaganda, and specifically that of al-Walid II, harped on the divinely sanctioned nature of the caliphal office, with the concomitant right of the caliphs to the title *khalifat Allah* ("God's Deputy");[35] on the relatively rare occasions that their 'Abbasid successors used this title they toned it down to *khalifat rasul Allah* ("Deputy of the Messenger of God").[36] The same wine-bibber and libertine (as his contemporaries called him) who devised the sophisticated and hedonistic amenities of the pleasure-dome at Khirbat al-Mafjar also affixed his name to a document drawn up in the most rarefied chancery style, larded with Quranic quotations and allusions, which enjoined his provincial governors in the name of religion to take the oath of allegiance to his sons al-Hakam and 'Uthman (minors and therefore ineligible to be the subject of such oaths) as his proposed successors (Crone and Hinds 1986: 118-26). Woven into this lengthy letter is a comprehensive apologia for the institution of the caliphate, vaunting the hallowed status and responsibilities of that office and underlining the extent to which God has made the caliph His instrument, entrusting to him absolute authority over the Muslim community. The caliph, according to this document, is much more than the shepherd of his people; he is the successor to the prophets, whose line had terminated with Muhammad. To dismiss al-Walid as a mere playboy is therefore to miss a crucial dimension in his image of himself and in the image which he wished to project. Khirbat al-Mafjar, like Mshatta — which is now generally attributed to al-Walid II (e.g. Creswell 1969: I/2, 641) — exudes absolutism as well as a love of pleasure. Unfortunately Mshatta was abandoned before any of it was finished, so there is no way of telling whether the interior decoration, or for that matter the facade in its completed state, would have amplified the message of power already implicit in the architecture (Hillenbrand 1981: 71, 77-80). Khirbat al-Mafjar, too, was never entirely finished, but the bath hall was, and its integration of architecture, ornament and iconography offers the best prospect available of investigating how at least one Umayyad caliph could use art for political purposes. With this background in mind, the exegesis of the symbolism wielded so deftly in the decoration of the bath hall will make much better sense.

It remains to define the parameters within which the discussion of the great roundel might suitably proceed. Too explicit a reference to the sun or, indeed, to al-Walid himself, might have been judged too dangerous from the standpoint of Islamic orthodoxy, or perhaps too obvious to please the wilfully eccentric personality of the heir-apparent. A certain reticence, however, a teasing ambiguity in the manipulation of symbols, was — as already noted — wholly characteristic of that personality. To some extent, then, it is open to the person confronted with this mosaic to read it as simple decoration, as a reference to the sun, to the prince, to the idea of the divine, or to a combination of some or all of these ideas. In that sense the mosaic is a challenge. At all events, there can be litle doubt that it lends itself to these various interpretations; and it is the theme of the rayed nimbus that combines them all most happily.

The positioning of the central roundel seems to signpost this spot in some ceremonial sequence or procession whose original context cannot now be recovered (Ettinghausen 1972: 40). The fact that the only related design in the entire floor occurs in the so-called "royal" apse suggests that here too the prince was wont to sit enthroned, again with rays radiating from his person. Before proceeding to an analysis of the "royal" apse, however, it is worth noting briefly the design of the first mosaic "carpet" vertically laid along the principal axis.[37] This manipulates a whole battery of related themes: radiating scallops,[38] rosettes and stellar patterns. These dominate the composition. At the other end of the axis, and directly in front of the three apses in the north wall, is a long, narrow strip of mosaic — a runner, to maintain the analogy with carpets — whose principal decoration comprises a double row of rosettes. This "runner" has its direct counterpart at the opposite end of the hall just beyond the entrance threshold. Thus the principal mosaics along the ceremonial axis have their message reinforced by the subsidiary mosaics at either end. The emphasis on radiating motifs is unswerving, and this concerted emphasis is not to be found elsewhere in the bath hall. Here, then, is further evidence that motifs which are superficially neutral, and can successfully operate as such, can by conscious and directed use be made to serve as symbols.

The climax of the decoration in the bath hall, however, is not to be sought in the great central roundel but in the culminating apse which terminates the ceremonial axis at its northern end. No pains were spared to

enhance the significance which its central position along the north wall
already guaranteed (Figure 1).

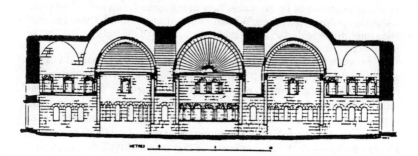

Figure 1

Khirbat al-Mafjar, bath hall: reconstruction of apses in west
ambulatory (after Hamilton)

The corresponding apses to right and left were plastered white; this apse
alone had a brightly painted archivolt and moulding above (Hamilton 1959:
320 and pl. LXXV/7). Where the flanking apses had a series of plain niches
in the lower dado, the corresponding niches in the "royal" apse were
enriched with double colonnettes. In the flanking apses this area was
crowned by a single niche on colonnettes; only in the royal apse was there a
central double niche resting on three blocks of triple colonnettes. All this
was in itself enough substantially to enrich the central apse and to
differentiate it more than adequately from its fellows. Yet it was not these
details, but rather the floor and the hood of this apse, that clinched the
special role reserved for this area and made the most explicit references to
the rayed nimbus yet encountered at this site. Since these references are
concentrated within a confined space they cannot fail mutually to enrich
each other. Once again, then, it is the location of these motifs, just as much
as their intrinsic nature, which loads them with meaning.

The more striking of the two references is assuredly the semi-dome of
the apse. Hanging from its apex was an ingeniously carved solid stone chain
about a metre long which terminated in a sugar-loaf form (Figure 2)
persuasively explained by Ettinghausen as the *qalansuwa* or royal bonnet
worn by the Umayyad caliphs (1972: 30-3).

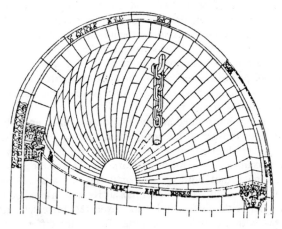

Figure 2

Khirbat al-Mafjar, bath hall: reconstruction of central apse in west
ambulatory (after Hamilton)

The form was borrowed from the Sasanians, as was the notion of
suspending royal headgear from a chain over the royal throne (Erdmann
1951: 114-7). The slight twist applied to a time-honoured prototype — in
this case, replacing the storied Sasanian crown by a *qalansuwa* — is
typically Umayyad. Perhaps there is in addition a touch of mischief in the
shrunken scale of the *qalansuwa*, described as a tall hat in the literary texts
but here measuring a derisory 50 cm., its slenderness quite dwarfed by the
cumbrous chain from which it hangs.[39] The proper proportions of chain and
headgear are neatly reversed. Given that al-Walid was heir apparent, not
caliph, at the time that the bath hall was built, the latent element of parody
is not hard to explain. The censorious reigning caliph, Hisham, could
scarcely have taken exception to the playful execution of the motif,
however much he might fume at the implied *lèse-majesté*. Perhaps, then,
this is yet another example of a trait that resurfaces repeatedly at the site: a
wilful ambiguity in the key images.

Whatever interpretation is finally adopted, the visual impact of the
hanging *qalansuwa* — especially if it were originally coloured — is
incontestable. It was surely intended to catch the eye of anyone entering the
bath hall, and its deeper meaning is as surely clinched by the backdrop
chosen for it. Centrally placed but set well over half a metre back from the
extrados of the arch, and at a substantially lower level, it would have stood
out against the semi-dome of the apse. The masonry of that semi-dome is
laid in radiating courses (Figure 1), whereas the flanking semi-domes are

built up in horizontal courses of stone. The contrast itself is striking. All the radiating lines stream from a blank semi-circle at the base and dead centre of the vault — thus creating the very image of the sun at horizon level. The *qalansuwa* is so suspended as to foster the illusion that it is itself the source of these rays. It seems justifiable to infer that a direct association is intended between the sun and the symbol of royalty, and thus by association the prince himself. It is typical of this particular patron that, despite the high seriousness of these associations, one cannot entirely discount the possibility of parody.

This theme of interlinked images and ideas is taken up with renewed force in the floor mosaic of this apse, which must be seen as a deliberate echo of the great radiating central roundel of the bath hall. No other version of this motif occurs in any of the other "carpets". This connection, it should be noted, implies that both areas — not just the apse — have royal associations. In its essence the smaller mosaic is simply a bisected version of the larger one, with the multiple rays executed in scales rather than triangles, but with an analogous palette. The major difference is in the treatment of the centre. In place of the blank disc in the great roundel, the floor of the "royal" apse has a curious composite design that conjoins the ideas of clouds, rays, fire, rosette and sun (Plate II and Figure 3).

Figure 3

The predominance of red and yellow in the colour scheme serves to intensify these associations.[40] Since the rest of the apse mosaic develops the rayed theme even more explicitly than the great central roundel, notably by a radiating cluster of straight white lines superimposed, as it were, on a ground of multicoloured intersecting curves, the layout as a whole invites the observation that the central semi-disc is the source of all the light being depicted. It thus affords an exact parallel, but in another medium, for the hood of the apse above it.

How is this unique concatenation of ideas to be decoded? The hanging *qalansuwa* renders it certain that this apse held al-Walid's throne. Even when he was not there, the *qalansuwa* — like the Sasanian crown in the absence of the emperor — symbolised his presence. For good measure, it exploited by means of the radiating masonry behind it the solar — not to say divine — connotations of monarchy. The floor mosaic uses a different medium to make the same point, for there can be little doubt that the royal throne was set well within the apse, its base probably so placed as to leave the semi-disc visible. Hamilton has convincingly explained the allegorical panel immediately adjoining the semi-disc (Plate II) as a punning reference to al-Walid's name (1978: 130-2, 135-6) — though other interpretations could be proposed (Hillenbrand 1982: 33-4) and such ambiguity may indeed have been the intention.

Thus, as with the interlocking effect of the *qalansuwa* and the radiating masonry in the elevation of the apse, so too at ground level is the royal theme not confined to a single appearance. Indeed, there are three separate references to it, each more explicit than the last: the main floor mosaic, the semi-disc and the allegorical panel. With the throne in place, only the latter two would have been fully visible; it was thus especially important that their message should come across clearly.

So much, then, for the "royal" apse and its decoration. When it is considered in tandem with the rest of the decoration along the principal axis which opens with the effigy of the caliph on the facade of the porch, it will be seen that there is a slow build-up of significant details whose cumulative effect is unmistakably to associate the ruler with a web of inter-related images in which the cognate ideas of the rosette and the rayed nimbus loom large.

In the *diwan* at Khirbat al-Mafjar — a retiring-chamber which opens off the main bath hall —the message is slightly different from that of the bath hall itself, with a marked emphasis on the exercise of absolute power and on the idea of apotheosis. Yet even here the rosette is to be found, this time in an iconographically crucial location at the apex of the dome's inner surface. This is beyond question the most splendid rosette in the entire corpus of Umayyad art.[41] Set within a huge garland comprising a series of concentric circles, some filled with fruit and foliage, and then within a double hexafoil roundel whose innermost lobes contain alternating male and female heads (a conceit still not fully explained, but perhaps carrying paradisal associations), the heart of the design features a huge blossom set amidst radiating outspread leaves. This rayed theme corresponds precisely to the centre of the dome — in other words, the very place where an oculus would mark the intersection of heaven and earth. The heads looking down into the *diwan* encourage the supposition that these represent beings from another and higher world.[42] For all that their flavour is secular rather than religious, there can be little doubt that they are an expression — couched in the teasing and unpredictable visual language so typical of this site — of the same ideas which led to the depiction of heavenly beings in similar locations in Christian churches.[43] The successively lobed and circular medallions within which these heads are set are a further reminder of the oculus concept. Given the arrangement of the garland as a whole, it is perhaps not too fanciful to suggest that the rayed rosette at its centre is a deliberate allusion to the themes exploited so intensively along the ceremonial axis in the bath hall proper.

What conclusions can be drawn from the assemblage of motifs from Khirbat al-Mafjar that have been singled out for discussion here? One might note first the consistent occurrence of certain themes in key locations. This should scotch the charge that the foregoing discussion has artificially removed these motifs from their context, which was amidst much other decoration for which, perhaps, no meaning was ever intended. It is fundamental to the arguments in this paper that the axis here described as "ceremonial" and "principal" was indeed both of these and that its decoration was carefully chosen to underline the fact. Other areas which lacked this specific function could well dispense with iconographic leitmotifs. Secondly, those responsible for the architecture and its decoration disdained mere repetition of the key themes. Instead they did their utmost to ring the changes on these themes, and their remarkable success in these efforts commands admiration. Both the radiating motif and the rosette crop up in numerous guises, on both large and small scales, and in media as varied as stone, plaster, mosaic and fresco. The protean manifestations of these two motifs, when so many others were readily available, argues that they enjoyed some special status. The third conclusion may sound paradoxical. For all that these particular themes occur so repeatedly, they are never used in the direct and unmistakable fashion that one might expect, namely in close association with a portrait of al-Walid himself, though one might note the presence of a rosette at the base of the full-length statue of this same prince at the entrance to the bath hall (Hamilton 1959: 229 and pl. LV/1). The reason is not far to seek, and some allusion has already been made to it. In Christian art there was no reason to dissemble the nimbus; it was an accepted iconographic convention whether used for Christ, saint or emperor. Yet it was precisely this traditional bracketing of the motif with Christianity that, as noted above, posed problems for Muslims who wished to avail themselves of it. For an Umayyad or early 'Abbasid caliph to have himself depicted with a nimbus would have been to invite an infuriated outcry from the orthodox. It would have branded the culprit as an unbeliever. The only permissible reference to the theme was a covert one. This was, moreover, a peculiarly sensitive issue in the Umayyad period because at that time Byzantium was still the major unconquered enemy confronting Islam. Its territories bordered Syria, and the churches which catered for the overwhelmingly Christian populace in that country would no doubt have had their fair quota of nimbed images of Christ, saints and other religious figures. It therefore behoved any Muslim to tread with care if he wished to allude to this particularly loaded concept. Hence, presumably, the restrained, allusive and at times even cryptic quality of the motifs under discussion. Each could at need be explained away as pure decoration.

Khirbat al-Mafjar, for all its subtleties of design, was still essentially a private palace and could not really affect the world outside the Umayyad court. The next test case to be considered, however, goes to the very opposite extreme, for it was deliberately intended to be as public as possible. This was the city of Baghdad, founded in 762 by the caliph al-Mansur after a long and intensive search for a suitable site.[44] Its intent is at once commemorative, propagandist, geopolitical, religious, symbolic and functional — though the exact weighting to be attached to each of these factors is of course a matter of dispute. Thus, if it can be shown that the city plan embodies the concept of the rayed nimbus, Baghdad would be without question the most grandiose and telling version of that theme in the entire canon of Islamic art.

The physical form of early 'Abbasid Baghdad will not yield its full quota of insights until its wider setting in time and space has been sketched. The 'Abbasid Revolution of 750 did much more than topple the Umayyad dynasty. It was nothing short of a seismic upheaval in Islamic history. It purported to replace the clannish, arabophile and Syrian-oriented régime of the Umayyads with a pan-Islamic government whose legality rested on blood ties with the family of the Prophet, and in which non-Arabs could take their place in the sun. It set its face resolutely against Syria, and thereby the Mediterranean and its millennially hellenised world, and turned to the east, in particular to the Iranian world, and beyond that to the Inner Asian steppelands, China and India. This momentous political re-orientation demanded some symbolic statement worthy of it. Baghdad was that statement. Sited at the extreme eastern boundaries of the arabophone world, though still within that world, and a mere stone's throw from Ctesiphon, the legendary capital of Sasanian Iran, and in the land of ancient

Babylon, its location was itself enough to finalise the break with the Graeco-Roman past and to symbolise the new balance of power. It proclaimed solidarity with the lands to the east and was pointedly anti-Umayyad. Moreover, whereas the Umayyad capital of Damascus had been landlocked, Baghdad was on the banks of the Tigris, accessible to ocean-going shipping and thus effectively an inland port whose mercantile horizons embraced the Indian Ocean and the China Sea. Baghdad, then, was the earnest of a new era: a bridge between East and West.[45]

So much, then, for the commemorative and geopolitical aspects of the new foundation. To unravel the other strands in this complex web of meanings requires an analysis of the physical form which the city took. This is not the place to adjudicate between the various reconstructions that have been proposed, and the theories as to the city's function which accompany them.[46] Happily there is general agreement on the key points, thanks to the detailed descriptions of the city given by medieval Arab historians. This is doubly fortunate since there have been no excavations on the site of the ancient city. The plan of Baghdad was circular (Figure 4). Its exterior perimeter had a triple ring of fortifications preceded by a ditch. Sandwiched between these walls and an inner ring of fortifications, complete with *intervallum*, were the living quarters of the citizens of Baghdad. According to one interpretation there was a further concentric band of living quarters within this inner ring, and the present discussion is based on that reconstruction of the precinct enclosure, reproduced in Figure 4.

The prehistory of the circular city plan has been sufficiently rehearsed in earlier scholarship to demonstrate that there is nothing startlingly original about the idea as such.[47] It is the disposition of space *within* the walls that is new (Hillenbrand 1983: 20-1); for no other known version of the circular city is so empty inside, a peculiarity that will be analysed in a moment. Although other versions of the concentric plan are described in literary sources — for example the seven-fold walls of Median Hamadan which excited the wonder of Herodotus[48] — the standard division of the interior was into four quadrants, whether in Assyrian and Viking camps (L'Orange 1953: 14-5 and figs. 7 and 9) or in Parthian and Sasanian cities. Baghdad rejects this in favour of concentrating the houses along the inner wall. Similarly, it was common enough in such plans for the palace and the place of worship to be located at the centre of the city, as witness Parthian Hatra (Safar 1952) and Sasanian Shiz (Naumann 1976: 19-24 and figs. 6-7). Hatra even has a central precinct with much open space (Herrmann 1977: 60). In Baghdad this combination operates in a new way because the empty space around it is so extensive. It is the particular achievement of Baghdad, then, to borrow freely from its varied precursors but to rework the resultant ideas in new and unexpected ways.

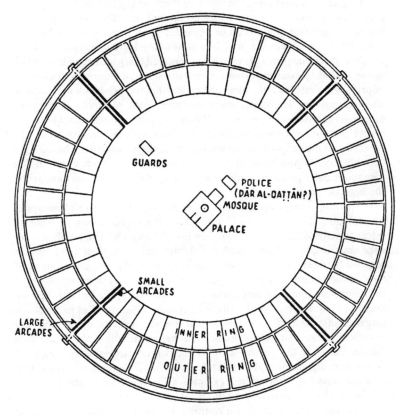

Figure 4

Baghdad: reconstruction of Round City (after Lassner)

Easily the most striking and original feature of the city is its emptiness. The paradox of a city in which domestic housing is so clearly of secondary importance has goaded some scholars into suggesting that it was not a city at all but an overgrown palace.[49] Yet the verdict of the medieval sources is unambiguous: this was indeed a city, and a city moreover that was the envy of the world (Lewis 1974: 69). Why, then, did the caliph al-Mansur expend such vast effort and money in constructing a city in which the built-up area was subordinate to the empty space? This same empty space was extremely expensive in terms of labour and materials, since it involved an immense extra outlay of bricks for the walls, to say nothing of the time required to excavate the great outermost ditch. It seems clear, therefore, that the empty space was integral to the entire conception and had its special part to play.[50] Since, too, it was concentrated around the caliph's own palace it seems a fair assumption that he regarded it in some sense as his own personal space. A chance anecdote recounting his displeasure when his nephew, the ailing prince 'Isa ibn Musa, entered this precinct on his donkey shows that al-Mansur experienced an acute sense of trespass and invasion of privacy, so much so that he issued orders that no such incident should be allowed to recur. Thereafter everyone entering the precinct — except the caliph — had to do so on foot.[51] When this proprietorial attitude to the empty precinct is considered in conjunction with its circular form, the centrality of the caliphal palace and the radial disposition of the housing for the citizenry, it is the image of the rayed nimbus that comes to mind. In that case the circular precinct would be a visual equivalent of the aura encircling the head of the ruler.

This empty space operates in still other ways. It is a powerful metaphor for isolation. The ruler is as it were under the spotlight, visible from all sides, the cynosure of attention. His inviolability and inaccessibility are alike emphasised and safeguarded.[52] At the same time there is a poignant contrast between the extreme shortage of space for the domestic housing of the common people, huddled together in sealed-off segments in the lee of the inner wall, and the conspicuous consumption of space by the caliph. In human terms, the plan of the city is so grossly self-centred as to approach megalomania, but of its psychological impact as an image of absolute monarchy there can be no doubt. The halo symbolised the more than human status of the person within it, and thus carried with it ideas of remoteness and untouchability. At Baghdad these ideas are translated into an actual landscape whose sheer extent — a distance every petitioner had to traverse on foot — drives home the point.

The radiating theme is not confined to the relationship between the great open precinct — the cold empty heart of Baghdad — and the radially disposed segments of urban housing which surround it at a respectful distance, like courtiers in attendance on a king.[53] It is also found in the palace. This apparently consisted of a great central dome — that dome which "was the crown of Baghdad, the standard of the realm and the most considerable monument of the 'Abbasid sovereignty" as a medieval Baghdadi historian said[54] — from which radiated four great archways opening onto courtyards aligned to each of the four gates (Figure 5; for alternative reconstructions, see Figures 6 and 7).[55]

Once again, then, axial symmetry is given a political edge and symbolic import. The caliph sat enthroned at the centre of this palace at a spot which asserted his control of all that went on in the city. This use of the radiating theme to suggest political surveillance is, it seems, a new dimension in this image (Hillenbrand 1983: 20).

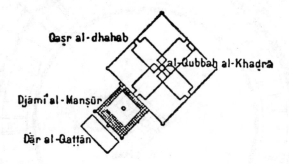

Figure 5

Baghdad: reconstruction of caliphal palace and Great Mosque (after Herzfeld)

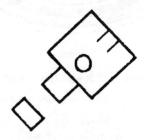

Figure 6

Baghdad: reconstruction of caliphal palace and Great Mosque (after Grabar)

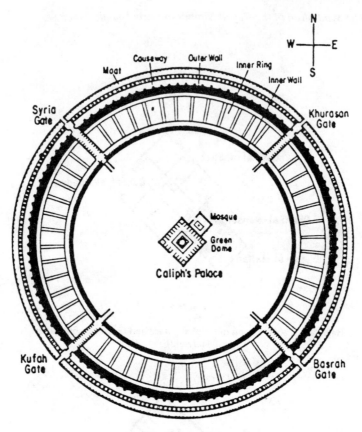

Figure7

Baghdad: reconstruction of Round City, based on Herzfeld (after Beg)

These remarks by no means exhaust the significance of this central area. The ninth-century geographer and historian al-Ya'qubi opens his account of the Muslim world with the pregnant words: "I begin with Iraq only because it is the centre of this world, the navel of the earth, and I mention Baghdad first because it is the centre of Iraq, the greatest city ... ".[56] It is therefore an acceptable inference that the centre of the city was even more precisely the *omphalos* of the world, at least according to many a contemporary Muslim. Not only were mosque and palace, the religious and secular arm of Islam, conjoined here, but there was a dome at the dead centre: the so-called *qubbat al-khadra'*. Recent research suggests that *al-khadra'* should be translated as "blue" rather than "green", and this would of course strengthen the already long inbuilt associations of the dome with the sky (Wendell 1971: 119-22). "Blue" domes are, as is well known, recorded as having dominated several Umayyad palaces,[57] but none of these could rival the portentous setting of the caliphal palace at Baghdad. The sources vary as to the date when the plan was laid out, but there is general agreement that the timing was fixed by astrologers[58] and it has been noted that the city was built under the sign of Jupiter,[59] the most fortunate planet, whose influence was believed to extend over places of worship and the staging-posts of travellers (Wendell 1971: 122). The connection with worship would fit well with the prominent location of the Friday mosque, while the connection with travel would be especially appropriate in a city which was so obviously intended to represent the wide extent of the Islamic empire. The assembling of craftsmen to the number of a hundred thousand from all over that empire (Lewis 1974: 73) to help build the city can be seen in the same light — a symbolic as well as an actual corvée. These considerations strengthen the case for regarding Baghdad as an Islamic mandala, namely a schematic representation of the whole world, a view recently propounded by Professor Wendell (1971: 122). Such ideas can be paralleled in the very different context of Sui and contemporary T'ang China, most notably in the design of the capital Chang'an, which was viewed as a micro-cosmos (Figure 8).[60]

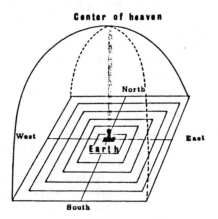

Figure 8

The Emperor of China and the capital city, Chang'an, in the cosmological order (after Seo)

The religious aspect in the planning of Baghdad, briefly mentioned in the previous paragraph, has been almost entirely neglected in earlier discussions. It does, however, play a crucial role in the interpretation of the city plan as a gigantic nimbus, for in Islamic art it is characteristic of the rayed nimbus theme that some religious significance is intended, whether explicit or implicit. In this case, the preponderant bias is surely towards the expression of secular power. Yet that message is tempered in two distinct ways. The first is the presence of the city's Friday mosque in the central plaza adjoining the palace. In this close juxtaposition al-Mansur was merely continuing a tradition domiciled in Iraq since the period of the Rashidiyyun, the Rightly-Guided caliphs, as the excavated plan of the Dar al-Imara at Kufa testifies (Kessler 1963: 36-65). The first Umayyad caliph, Mu'awiya, also had his palace adjoining the principal mosque of Damascus (Elisséeff 1965: 280). Indeed, this association is present at the very beginning of Islam, for the house of the Prophet at Medina served for worship as well as meeting the varied political and organisational needs of the community (Pedersen 1930: 316-7). Yet al-Mansur did more than simply continue a well-established tradition. The presence of the Friday mosque within the great open plaza at the centre of the city proclaimed in the most public way his allegiance to Islam. At the same time, no-one could fail to notice the diminutive scale of the mosque vis-à-vis the palace beside it. Moreover, the mathematical centre of the city lay in the middle of the throne-room at the heart of the palace. To that extent, therefore, the palace displaced the mosque. In a design where centrality and symmetry count for so much, this emphasis on the dues of Caesar at the expense of the dues of God cannot be accidental.

The other veiled reference to religion is embodied in the location of the city gates.[61] In the most obvious and convenient parallel for Baghdad, the early Sasanian capital of Firuzabad — and also in numerous other circular plans — the four gates are aligned to the cardinal points of the compass.[62] This enables the lord of the city, if he be so minded, to stake a claim to world-wide dominion. The orientation of Islamic buildings towards the cardinal points of the compass is so commonplace as to require no further comment. Why, then, should the plan of Baghdad reject this familiar pattern, with its built-in symbolic advantages? The key seems to lie in the naming of the gates: Sham, Khurasan, Basra and Kufa. A glance at a map suffices to show that these names were symbolic and presumably referred to roads that led in these directions. Thus caravans to Iran, for example, would depart from the Khurasan gate. The gates could not well have faced in the true direction of these places, or Sham (Syria) and Khurasan would have had more than a single quadrant between them, while Kufa and Basra, which are only a little more than three degrees apart, would not have had their gates separated by a full quadrant (90 degrees) of the city. Indeed, if cartographical accuracy had been the aim, another name would have had to be found for at least one of the latter two gates.

All this substantiates the accounts of the medieval sources themselves to the effect that the names were a kind of shorthand. By that reckoning Basra, the emporium for trade with India and China, would be the obvious choice of name for the gate that opened on these wide vistas. By the same token, the Kufa gate would be the point of departure for caravans to the Hijaz, and in particular the pilgrim caravan. It was precisely from Kufa that pilgrims would take the desert road to the Holy Cities. "Kufa" may thus be interpreted as shorthand for "Mecca" — though it remains a mystery why the gate was not so termed. The *qibla* of the Friday mosque, the throne-room of the palace and the Kufa gate were all, it seems, aligned roughly (not precisely)[63] to Mecca. The available data do not permit any further refinement of this line of argument, but its implications are nonetheless striking. They suggest that the entire city — and perhaps, by extension, the whole world of which it was the centre and the image — was in fact orientated to Mecca. Thus its entire political ideology should be seen *sub specie aeternitatis*. It is in this light, too, that the name of the city assumes its full significance; for Baghdad means "god-given" in Persian (Massignon 1962: 249; Levy 1929: 7-8; Le Strange 1900: 10-1), while its other name, Madinat al-Salam, or "City of Peace", has been interpreted as a deliberate echo of a term used in the Qur'an (Sura VI, 127) to refer to Paradise (Duri 1960: 894).

Discussion of Baghdad as an embodiment of the rayed nimbus would be incomplete without some reference to the Sasanian antecedents of this concept, for its closeness to the Sasanian capital of Ctesiphon suggests that it was intended to supplant the latter city. Central to the belief in the divinely ordained sovereignty of the shah[64] was the idea of the radiance which surrounded him — the *farr-i kayani*[65], otherwise known as *farr-i padshahan* or *farr-i izadi*. The heritage of this concept deserves a little further discussion here. It is fundamental to the argument of this paper that the idea of the royal *farr* survived the downfall of the Sasanians and was incorporated into the store of ideas which the Islamic world inherited from its predecessors. Supporting evidence for this assertion is abundant. One might turn, for example, to the *Shahnama* or "Book of Kings" of Firdausi (completed c. 1010), a rich repository of Sasanian lore and tradition; and references to the royal *farr* are indeed copious in that work (Wolff 1965: 602).[66] It might be argued, of course, that this is only to be expected in an epic poem devoted to Iran's pre-Islamic past.[67] For this reason it might be preferable to explore the evidence furnished by an unimpeachably Islamic source, namely the references to the *farr-i izadi* in the writings of al-Ghazali, one of the foremost theologians and political thinkers of medieval Islam. In his work *Kimiya-yi Sa'adat* he develops the image of the divine effulgence or light (*farr-i izadi*) given by God to the *sultan* — a term which he uses in this context to denote authority, no matter whether it is caliphs or sultans that exercise it. He explains the symbolism as follows:

> The sun of justice appears first in the breast [of the ruler]. Then its light falls on the people of the [royal] house. Then it penetrates to the entourage [of the ruler]. Then its rays reach the subjects. Anyone who hopes for rays without the sun is seeking the impossible. (al-Ghazali 1361 A.S.H.: I, 538)[68]

A similar emphasis on light surfaces repeatedly in the writings of al-Ghazali (Milstein 1986: 534-6, 540).

Nor was this emphasis confined to al-Ghazali. His work *Nasihat al-Muluk* ("Counsel for Kings"), which belongs to the "Mirror for Princes" genre so popular in the medieval Iranian world, contains a section which is now thought to be the work of an anonymous contemporary of his (C. Hillenbrand: in press) and which makes use of very similar ideas à *propos* the royal *farr*. This anonymous author states that in the case of sultans "kingship and the divine effulgence (*farr-i izadi*) have been granted to them by God" (Bagley 1971: 45). A little later in the same work an anecdote — the pure stuff of legend — is cited in which Aristotle is made to say that "great men owe their greatness to the divine effulgence" (Bagley 1971: 73).

Both Persian and Arabic versions of the *Nasihat al-Muluk* have survived, and they shed an interesting sidelight on the way that the notion of *farr* was understood in Islamic times. In the Arabic text, the equivalent of the Persian *farr-i izadi* is *al-zill al-ilahi* or "the divine shadow" (Bagley 1971: 73, n. 5). In this context the anonymous author quotes a *hadith* that "authority (*al-sultan*) is God's shadow on earth", thereby providing — if one may assume the reliability of this *hadith* — an Islamic confirmation of the pre-Islamic Persian idea.[69] The two phrases can be seen as the positive and negative images of the same fundamental idea. The unity of concept which seems to underlie these two very different expressions could be of quite special significance in the context of the foregoing discussion of Baghdad, suggesting indeed that the city could have been intended as a visual calque of these two ideas. Yet is this a justifiable line of argument?

Perhaps the best way of tackling this problem is to investigate how the phrase "shadow of God" is to be understood. It seems that two divergent interpretations are possible. According to one line of argument, the phrase "shadow of God" should not be interpreted as a personal reference to the ruler but, like the term *al-sultan*, as a reference to the power that he (and for that matter his entire dynasty) wields; while the word "shadow" should be understood as "place of refuge" (Goldziher 1897, repr. 1970: 134-7). The contrary argument would assert that "shadow of God" is indeed intended to refer to a given ruler.[70] After all, it was precisely al-Mansur, the founder of the Round City, who said of himself that he was "God's rule on earth" (Goldziher 1971: 67); and indeed the 'Abbasid rulers in general regarded themselves as "God's shadow on earth" (Goldziher 1971: 67). In other words, they applied the generalising tenor of the *hadith* to their own person, so that the 'Abbasid caliph himself became, in the words of al-Mas'udi, "the Shadow of God stretched out between him and his people" (Goldziher 1971: 67). It is possible, of course, that the equation of *farr-i izadi* with *al-zill al-ilahi* took place only as late as Saljuq times; but it is at least tenable to propose, on the basis of the evidence cited above, that the idea was much older and that the Round City was its crowning expression in visual form. It should not be forgotten that both palace and mosque — in other words, the very embodiment, in architectural terms, of the caliphal office itself — were located side by side at the heart of that city.

With these remarks in mind, it will be convenient to return to the vexed question of how the Sasanians gave visual expression to the notion of the royal *farr* or *\*hvarnah-*. It is well known that certain animals, notably the ram[71] and the rooster (the latter significantly found on a wall-tile at Samarra),[72] symbolised this effulgence. So too, it seems, did the successful hunt.[73] On a more abstract level, perhaps the most striking expression of this idea is the celebrated Cup of Khusrau, datable to the sixth century AD (Figure 9).[74]

Figure 9

This circular bowl made of gold and silver, precious and semi-precious stones, is set with red rosettes in concentric circles. The design is so ordered that these rosettes diminish in size as they converge on the central disc of transparent rock crystal which depicts the shah enthroned in majesty. This layout not only suggests that the shah is the source of the rays formed by the rosettes but also uses colour to make the same point. The pale silvery radiance of the central disc, a colour taken up in alternating sequence by every second rosette outside that disc, is the perfect foil for the ruby red of the other rosettes. Design and colour thus harmonise in a graceful allusion to the royal Sasanian title of "partner with the stars, brother of the Sun and Moon" (Herzfeld 1930: 128-31; L'Orange 1953: 36; Duchesne-Guillemin 1983: 886), and to the royal nimbus or *farr-i kayani*. Possibly the circular shape was itself intended in this particular context to have cosmic associations, an idea already well developed in the circular plan of Firuzabad, the first Sasanian capital, and carried still further in the celebrated cosmic throne hall of Khusrau II, the Taq-i Taqdis.[75] Even if this is going too far, it is surely permissible to view this cup as a direct conceptual ancestor of the Round City of al-Mansur.

Enough has been said to explain why the Round City of Baghdad cast such a potent spell over the minds of later Muslims. No doubt many of its subtleties were obscured by the passage of time and eventually forgotten. It is highly probable, too, that even in its golden prime they were fully understood by only a few people. That its layout was a proclamation of absolute caliphal power must, however, have been apparent to all who lived in it, while its seemingly unprecedented shape was an invitation to see it as something more than a mere city. Al-Ya'qubi describes how al-Mansur, on seeing the site of the future city, explained that this was the place where his father had foretold he would build a city "in which I must live, and in which my descendants after me will live. Kings were unaware of it before and since Islam, until God's plans for me and orders to me are accomplished" (tr. Lewis 1974: 73). The lesson was well learned by his successor, al-Mutawakkil, in the following century, who founded the city of Ja'fariyya (Abu Dulaf) and, according to al-Ya'qubi, installed himself with the words "Now I know that I am indeed a king, for I have built myself a city and live in it" (Creswell 1940: 277). Thus the city was itself an emblem of royalty. Once the notion of the Round City as a symbol had taken root, the way was clear for the further refinement of seeing in it a vast rayed nimbus where power radiated from the centre. By virtue of its superbly calibrated design, in which every detail contributes to the desired impact, Baghdad exercises a perennial fascination as a cosmic symbol of unique intensity in the Islamic world. But as a machine for living it was a woeful failure (cf. Le Strange 1900: 42-6). The 'Abbasid régime had pledged itself to remove racial, social and fiscal inequalities, proclaiming instead the brotherhood of all Muslims. Such stirring claims could not long survive the sight of the

Round City. Its inequalities were built into its very structure, and were too glaring to find favour even in a society which was only notionally egalitarian. It was, in short, unworkable and was unmasked as such within little more than a generation. Thus the symbol long outlasted the reality.

The detailed exposition of the use of the rayed nimbus and closely related themes at Khirbat al-Mafjar and at Baghdad must suffice to indicate that this concept was well established and well understood from early Islamic times onwards. Accordingly, the subsequent appearances of the motif cited below are mentioned more to indicate its popularity throughout the length and breadth of the Islamic world, and to draw attention to its often surprising transformations, than to embark on still further explorations of its meaning in an Islamic context.

The sequence, then, may profitably be resumed in Aghlabid Ifriqiyya in the ninth century, in the works of the *amir* Abu Ibrahim Ahmad in the Great Mosques of Tunis (856-63) and Qairawan (862-3). Once again, the context is royal; but now, perhaps for the first time, it is also specifically religious. Nevertheless, the two strands are inextricably linked, for according to medieval Islamic custom it was the duty of the political ruler to lead his people in prayer. For that purpose he stood immediately in front of the *mihrab*, or prayer niche. At both Tunis and Qairawan this spot was marked by a magnificent dome whose honorific purpose can scarcely be doubted, though there is room for argument as to whether the honour is intended for the ruler, for Islam or for both. In both mosques this dome is divided into twenty-four ribs, convex externally and concave within (Creswell 1940: pls. 84c and 92b). This radiating design was not an Islamic invention, for the gored dome had been used in imperial Rome, for example in Hadrian's villa at Tivoli (Smith 1956: 191), perhaps even as a royal symbol. Possibly even then it was recognised as a rayed nimbus in three dimensions. In these Muslim monuments, however, that message is intensified by the design of the squinches which carry the dome. Each bears a radiating fan motif which cannot but echo the much grander design above (Creswell 1940: pls. 84a and 92b). In each case, too, the great ribbed dome rears its profile high above the surrounding roofscape, constituting a marker of the royal presence, and of the *mihrab*, which is visible from far away (Creswell 1940: pls. 84b and 92c). Perhaps it was the same desire for an external signpost of royalty which prompted the addition, a little over a century later, of a similar but smaller ribbed dome over the central archway leading into the covered sanctuary in each of these mosques (Hill, Golvin and Hillenbrand 1976: pls. 86 and 111). This served to create an axial progression to the *mihrab*, further emphasised by the extra width of the central aisle. It is easy to recognise here the architectural vocabulary which at Khirbat al-Mafjar served purposes of largely secular glorification. The wider aisle, the singling out of specific stages along the processional way, the culminating niche with a radiating vault over it — all are there.

These ideas are taken up with renewed intensity around 965 in the enlargement of the Great Mosque of Cordoba in Spain by the Umayyad caliph al-Hakam II (Ewert: in press). The ribbed cupola of the *maqsura* or royal box in front of the *mihrab* comprises eight gadroons, each of them separated by a double serration (Figure 10).

Figure 10

At the centre of the cupola is a salient orb with a blue star. From this orb there stream eight broad rays whose deep blue ground is criss-crossed with white spots, perhaps a deliberate metaphor for the night sky. The ground colour of the entire cupola is gold and a smaller lobed medallion made up of golden rays radiates from the central disc. It is this latter feature which drives home the idea of a rayed nimbus, and the central golden orb readily suggests the sun.[76] This cupola, moreover, marks that particular spot in the mosque which was reserved for the caliph, and it thus straddles the religious and secular realms. Under that same cupola, too, was set the famous *mihrab* in which the caliph stood to lead his community in prayer. The *mihrab* at Cordoba offers further evidence on the nimbus theme; the room to which it leads is covered with a scalloped vault (Goitia 1968: pl. 28) while its celebrated mosaic facade has as its centrepiece a horseshoe arch with radiating voussoirs in constantly changing colours (Goitia 1968: pl. 22). Framed within this arch, the Umayyad ruler of Muslim Spain, whether conscious of it or not, was employing the same kind of architectural conceit and the same veiled allusions to the rayed nimbus as his remote forebear in Umayyad Syria, al-Walid II, or the 'Abbasid caliph who probably ordered the Khassaki *mihrab* at Baghdad (Creswell 1970: 36-7 and fig. 26). In Cordoba as at Khirbat al-Mafjar the key factor is the concentration of related images in a selected, significant location. Thus the ubiquity of radiating voussoirs elsewhere in the mosque — for this is the most obvious decorative cliché of the building — in no sense invalidates the suggestion that in the area of the *maqsura* this motif is employed for symbolic purposes. Equally, it is no part of the present argument to suggest that every occurrence of radiating voussoirs, ribbed cupolas and multifoil arches in Maghribi architecture must be explained *à tout prix* as an example of royal symbolism expressed through the medium of radiating designs. The gradual decline of a feature which was originally specific and meaningful into a decorative cliché devoid of any significance is a familiar process in the history of art. In the present case it might be suggested, with all possible reserve, that the conscious use, for purposes of royal symbolism, of radiating motifs in the architectural vocabulary of the Maghrib reached its high-water mark in the tenth century. Thereafter, while its occurrence may be suspected in some of the buildings of the Muluk al-Tawa'if, such as the Aljaferia in Zaragoza,[77] or in some of the great Almohad mosques such as those of Tinmal, Marrakesh,[78] Tlemcen and Taza,[79] the balance gradually altered. The increasing popularity of these features, and the tendency to use them for decorative embellishment divorced from any structural imperative, spelt the end of their usefulness as bearers of symbolic meaning.

So far the examples of radiating motifs have been drawn from largely or even exclusively secular contexts, and the notion of sanctity, which in the Western tradition is almost inseparable from the rayed nimbus, has been relegated to secondary status. That this was not always the case in the Islamic world is illustrated by a sequence of examples from Fatimid Egypt. All of them, it seems, occur on *mihrabs* or at least on niches which face Mecca. They feature a radiating design which, when it occurs in roundel form, often has a central disc; while the same theme in a niche-hood has a central half-disc at the base.[80] In both types the clear visual implication is that the source of the rays is the disc or half-disc.[81] This area often bears a sacred name,[82] usually Allah but sometimes Muhammad or 'Ali[83] (Figure 11).

It seems clear that a double symbolism is intended here: the idea of a solar disc or semi-disc whose rays stream forth, and — pursuing this image somewhat further — the idea that Allah, 'Ali or Muhammad is the source of spiritual light (Milstein 1986: 533-6). The association between light and the prayer niche had long been familiar and was commonly symbolised in two ways, often found together. One was the depiction of a hanging lamp within the *mihrab* niche; the other consisted of a relevant quotation from the Qur'an. This was usually Sura XXIV, 36-7:

Figure 11

a   Cairo: *mihrab* in mausoleum of Muhammad al-Hasawati
b   Cairo: side *mihrab* in Mashhad of Sayyida Ruqayya
c   Cairo: main *mihrab* in Mashhad of Sayyida Ruqayya

God is the Light of the heavens and the earth; the likeness of His Light is as a niche wherein is a lamp (the lamp in a glass, the glass as it were a glittering star) ... . Light upon Light; (God guides to His Light whom He will).

The Fatimid examples under discussion, such as those on the facade of the Aqmar mosque (1125; see Creswell 1952: pls. 82c and 83c-d) and on the *mihrab* of the Mashhad of Sayyida Ruqayya (1133; see Williams 1985: pls. 7-10), were therefore able to exploit the long-familiar associations between *mihrabs* and light (R. Hillenbrand: in press) and, using them as a point of departure, to attempt new variations on that theme. In retrospect it is merely strange that these explicit references to the rayed nimbus were not encountered earlier. The unique status of the written word in Islamic iconography[84] encourages the further suggestion that the name in the disc or half-disc does duty for an image, and thus the rays which surround that name can be interpreted as the rays of a nimbus. Here, then, finally, is an authentically Islamic equivalent to a Christian image depicting the nimbed bust of a holy personage.

It is of course true that in Fatimid architecture, and in the Ayyubid and Mamluk buildings which take up its ideas, the rayed niche-hood was something of a leitmotif. In an evolutionary sequence which has been carefully plotted by Creswell (1952: pls. 109-14), these niches multiplied to form the distinctive Egyptian stalactite vaulting (*muqarnasat*). Sometimes, as in the apex of the entrance arch to the mausoleum-*madrasa* of Sultan Hasan (1356), the *muqarnas* system can be seen to develop from a rayed semi-circle (Dodd and Khairallah 1981: I, fig. 36); and when, as in that very case, the accompanying inscription is Sura XXIV, 36-7, it is tempting to conclude that the intention is to refer to a rayed nimbus. Nevertheless, the ubiquity of the *muqarnas* theme in medieval Islamic art should enjoin extreme caution on any attempt to propose a specific connection with the rayed nimbus in such vaults. As with all vaults, the association with the heavens was latent, and, no doubt, a more directed reference to the theme of the rayed nimbus was occasionally made. Nevertheless, it seems safest to accept that most *muqarnas* vaults were erected with no *arrière pensée* of this kind.

The penultimate example also comes from Egypt, although it is representative of a whole body of work from Syria and the Jazira as well as Egypt itself. In some respects it is a natural continuation of the Fatimid niches just discussed; in others it reverts to the earlier symbolism of the rosette. The examples in question are all metalwork objects, and thus the scope of the enquiry broadens significantly. Yet, like architecture, these objects had a political function, for they were prominently inscribed with the names of *amirs*, viziers and other notables and their rich decoration symbolised the conspicuous consumption of their owners. A whole series of these objects bears, as Dr J.W. Allan has recently shown,[85] groups of interrelated solar symbols; and the discussion earlier in this paper has demonstrated how closely the idea of the rosette, for example, was linked to that of the rayed motif and thereby to the rayed nimbus itself. An early and well-known example of this series is a cylindrical box datable to the thirteenth century and now in the Victoria and Albert Museum (no. 320-1866). By way of introduction to the whole group of these objects it will be worth recapitulating here the findings of Storm Rice and Dr Allan. The former refrains from suggesting a provenance any more specific than "the Eastern lands of the caliphate" (1950b: 632); the latter attributes it to the Jazira (1982: 27). Understandably enough, neither feels able to suggest a specific patron for the piece. Its cylindrical body bears successive bands depicting a benedictory inscription, a floral border, a Christian ordination scene and a frieze of animals passant. It is, however, the lid of the box — literally and metaphorically the crown of the object — that is significant in the present context (Figure 12).

Figure 12

Most of the lid is taken up by a large central roundel at whose heart is a twelve-pointed star enclosing a six-petalled rosette. At the periphery of the roundel six similar stars, each with only eleven points, wheel in stately motion and at regular intervals around the central star, all this against a background of interlaced strapwork. Once again, an apparently minor detail — the number of points in the stars — emerges as significant by virtue of its location. The number twelve, besides its inherent suitability for designs in which geometrical symmetry and harmony are important, has for millennia had symbolic associations. Eleven, by contrast, may here justifiably be interpreted to signal incompleteness. The eleven-pointed stars, therefore, are in a double sense satellites of the twelve-pointed star. The meaning of the composition is further clarified by the inscription which encircles the rim of the lid. Storm Rice identified it as a quotation from the apology and panegyric composed for the king of Hira, Nu'man b. Mundhir, by the sixth century poet al-Nabigha al-Dhubyani (1950b: 631-2):

> Don't you see that God has granted you a degree of power[86] which makes all the kings (grovel at your feet)? For you are a sun; the kings, stars. When the sun rises no star will be seen.

This revival of pre-Islamic poetry some seven centuries later is apparently unique in Muslim metalwork and calls for some explanation. It is at least conceivable that a poet from the Days of Ignorance was selected because it was realised that the idea expressed in these lines skated perilously close to blasphemy. They would need less defence coming from a Jahiliyya poet than from a Muslim one, and their sense would remain intact. Here at last, then, is clear textual evidence to the effect that a Muslim ruler could apply solar symbolism to himself.[87] Dr Allan has cited numerous other contemporary metal objects, especially from the Mamluk domains, which rework solar symbols of various kinds into new combinations — two candlesticks from Siirt, which intensify the royal and solar symbols by using gold inlay for them alone, a *kursi*, a Qur'an box and several others (1982: 24-6, 62-8). Beyond any doubt, however, the *pièce de résistance* among these objects is the incense burner of the Mamluk sultan al-Malik al-Nasir Muhammad ibn Qala'un, now in the Nuhad es-Said collection (Plate III).

The cylindrical body, carried on three feet, has a monumental domed lid with double finial. On both the body and the lid the major band of decoration carries the titles of the sultan, while the arabesques of the four lesser bands are regularly interrupted by plain roundels with a central horizontal band reading "Glory to our lord the sultan" in a layout deliberately reminiscent of Mamluk heraldic blazons. The underside of the object (Allan 1982: 89, below) is largely taken up by a large ten-lobed medallion, each lobe filled by a whirling rosette like a Catherine wheel, itself crowned by a kind of fleur-de-lis. At the centre is a ten-petalled rosette with a central orb. Of equal interest is the internal incense tray (Allan 1982: 89 above), whose complex ensemble of motifs — ducks, lotuses, rosettes, and six-pointed stars — has been persuasively explained by Dr Allan as a group of solar images (1982: 88). The sunken part of the tray is surrounded by a veritable pallisade of seventy-three rays. Its centre, too, in common with other Mamluk objects for royal use, like the basin made for Hugh IV de Lusignan, King of Jerusalem and Cyprus, carries a rayed rosette (Rice 1956: 390, fig. 1), and this fashion continued in Ilkhanid Iran (Melikian-Chirvani 1982: pls. 57, 71, 76a, 86a).

Yet it is of course the main body and lid of the incense burner that draw the eye like a magnet, and here the focus of attention is assuredly the pair of superposed multilobed roundels which occupy the centre of the body and lid respectively, extending in each case to the full height of all four decorative bands and spreadeagled across most of what might be termed the main facade (Allan 1982: 88). The examples cited earlier in this paper have pointed to the connection between the multi-lobed roundel, or bisected versions of it, as solar emblems, whether used two-dimensionally as applied decorative motifs or three-dimensionally in architecture. In the incense burner the equivalence is complete, for the body of each roundel is taken up by a circular *naskhi* inscription sounding a sonorous roll-call of the sultan's titles. The Mamluk epigraphic fashion for reducing the scale of the horizontal elements in the Arabic alphabet while greatly exaggerating the length of the shafts is here turned to brilliant account. The ascenders fan out from the central disc — another epigraphic roundel like those in the narrow bands — for all the world like the rays of the sun. That conceit is intensified by the choice of gold for the inlay in which the letters are executed. Thus the reflecting rays blaze forth with redoubled power. The words "Glory to our lord the sultan" [88] at the centre of these epigraphic rays invite the conclusion that the sultan is himself the sun. Here then is an Islamic re-interpretation of the hoary equation of the ruler with the sun, as shown for example in the winged disc of Ahura Mazda depicted on Achaemenid monuments (L'Orange 1953: 86, fig. 60; cf. Root 1979; Kuhrt 1984: 158; Dalley 1986: 85, 92-5, 99-101).

In the case of the piece under discussion it is surely no accident that the artist has so composed these radial inscriptions that the sultan's personal names — Muhammad and Qala'un respectively — are lifted out of the ruck of his titles and placed closer to the centre of the "solar disc", and thus in a specially favoured position. Since the titulature of the time could be expanded or condensed at will, as is shown by buildings and objects alike, the artist could easily have composed radiating inscriptions to include the sultan's name along with his titles. That he chose to single out the sultan's name, as it were in capitals, is of a piece with the self-glorifying tenor of these royal objects. After all, the titles were the common property of successive rulers; but the monarch's personal name was his alone.

Radiating epigraphic roundels of this kind occur on other pieces of Mamluk metalwork, such as the basin of Hugh IV de Lusignan, mentioned earlier (Figure 13). It is characteristic of their design that these shafts should radiate from a central disc which bears some symbolic reference to the person being honoured. This detail of design encourages the equation of this disc with the ruler's head, and thus allows the radiating ascenders to function as a rayed nimbus. Indeed, the Bobrinski "kettle" or bucket of 1163 (Ettinghausen 1943; Figure 14a), a thirteenth-century penbox in

Figure 13

Inscription on brass basin made for Hugh IV de Lusignan (after Rice)

Bologna (Figure 14b) and an inkwell from Iran datable c. 1200 (Figure 14c) all show a seated ruler with a rayed nimbus. On the penbox he is at the centre of a huge roundel containing the images of the six planets and the twelve signs of the zodiac;[89] and nimbed sun-faces are also known in the metalwork of this period.[90]

Yet this direct representation of the ruler with a rayed nimbus remained exceptional, and it was the more symbolic versions of the theme which carried the day. Perhaps the most outstanding example in this category, representing as it does the most harmonious blending of decorative themes and symbolic motifs, is a circular fourteenth-century Mamluk mirror signed by Muhammad al-Waziri (Plate IV; see Rice 1950a: 370-3 and Aga-Oghlu 1930).

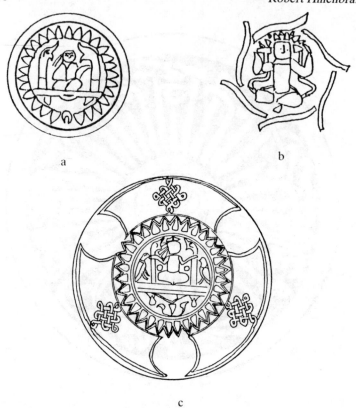

a

b

c

Figure 14

a  Detail from the Bobrinski bucket
b  Detail from penbox in Bologna
c  Detail from an Iranian inkwell, c. 1200

At its dead centre is a brief epigraphic formula of the kind already mentioned. From this radiates a centrifugal inscription like those on the incense burner of Sultan Qala'un. In the inner circular border each cardinal point is marked by a rosette, while in the outer border are disposed the twelve signs of the zodiac. The outermost rim is marked by a border of serried rays. Very literally this ensemble could be read as a mirror of the world; but that world is under the dominion of the sultan, whose epigraphic image occupies the centre, in the place of the sun itself. In medieval Islamic literature this association was a commonplace of panegyric;[91] but it may be doubted whether the literary expressions of this theme were ever as neatly dove-tailed — complete with planets, zodiacal signs, solar rays, rosettes, lotuses, scallop-shells and epigraphic roundels — as their visual counterparts in the metalwork of the twelfth to fourteenth centuries.[92]

The last example to be cited brings the wheel full circle. It is to be found in the illustrated *Jami' al-Tawarikh* of Rashid al-Din, produced at Tabriz in north-west Iran and containing an inscription dated 1306. In the scene where Moses and the Children of Israel stand on the banks of the Red Sea watching the Egyptians drown (f. 8b), Moses is shown with a gold-rayed halo (Talbot Rice 1974: 19 and pl. 11). It must be emphasised that this is the only occurrence of the motif in all the seventy remaining pictures of the Edinburgh manuscript, even though these illustrations include another four scenes from the Moses cycle, a lengthy series of images covering the life of Muhammad, and several depictions of Old Testament prophets; nor does a rayed nimbus occur in the companion volume of the text, now in Switzerland (Gray 1978). It seems fair to conclude from this that the halo used on folio 8b is a borrowed feature. The most convenient parallel for the scene as a whole — though not for the halo itself — is certainly the familiar Byzantine composition of the same subject.[93] The principal difference between the Islamic and the Byzantine version is that the latter is commonly a two-tier composition. Faced with a narrow oblong picture space, the Islamic artist simply conflated the two tiers into one. Yet the matter does not end there. In the Byzantine model, Moses is young and beardless; nor does he have a halo. The Islamic painting, on the other hand, shows him as a bearded, mature man with a delicately painted halo comprising multiple gold lines. In the other Moses scenes, for which no illustrated Old Testament prototype suggests itself, the artists probably had to draw on their own imaginations, in which the rayed halo had evidently not yet lodged. It is noticeable, too, that the form of the halo is not one which recommended itself to later Islamic painters, who preferred the solid gold roundel type — as did Byzantine artists — or the flame halo of east Asian derivation.[94] Only in the paintings of Mughal India does the rayed halo become popular,[95] almost certainly through the agency of Western European art. It seems reasonable to assume that in Ilkhanid Tabriz, a busy mart thronged by European ecclesiastics, ambassadors and merchants, contemporary Western missals and devotional pictures were available, and that the rayed halo given to Moses on folio 8b reflects some such source.

This paper has ranged very widely in time and space and has investigated a wide variety of media. It has suggested that the concept of the rayed nimbus was widely diffused in Islamic art and that artists drew impartially on western and eastern sources as well as on their own imaginations in devising suitable vehicles for the idea. It was characteristic of their approach to hint at the concept rather than express it in direct visual terms. In this they differed sharply from their counterparts in the West, probably for religious motives. This need to dissemble could plausibly account for the remarkably varied expressions of the rayed nimbus theme described in this paper. The nature of Islamic iconography made it inevitable that the connotation of sanctity which is so dominant in Western uses of the rayed nimbus should be relegated to a secondary role in favour of projecting a message of secular authority. Yet that notion of sanctity is never far away, and it resurfaces in the most unexpected guises. It is a timely reminder of the joint heritage shared by Christian and Islamic art.

ACKNOWLEDGEMENT

It is a pleasure to thank Ruth Hillenbrand for executing the drawings reproduced in Figures 3 and 10.

NOTES

1  For a general account of the place of the nimbus in Islamic art, see Milstein 1986: 533-52, especially 536-41. This study came to my notice (through the kindness of Dr Milstein) only after the present paper was complete, and it was therefore impracticable to incorporate its findings into the body of this paper, though some reference to it is made in the notes. In the event, it deals principally with the period after 1300, so that there is very little overlap.

2  This disc type, unlike the flame halo or the rayed nimbus, suffered such a general depreciation in Islamic art, especially in painting and metalwork, that it offers a somewhat forbidding prospect for research. For the ultimate *reductio ad absurdum* in the demeaning of this motif, see the execution of al-Hallaj as depicted in the manuscript of al-Biruni's *Kitab al-athar al-baqiya 'an al-qurun al-khaliya* (Edinburgh University Library, ms. Arab 161, f. 94a). Of the seven people in the scene, which include a pair of executioners, only one — al-Hallaj himself — is without a halo: clear evidence that the halo, though debased, is not entirely meaningless. For an illustration, see Soucek 1975: 127. The literature on the disc halo in Christian art is of course extensive. For an introduction to the subject, see Stephani 1859; Krücke 1905 (well summarised in Strzygowski 1906); Künstle 1928: I.25-9; Leclercq 1935.

3  For the origins of this motif, see Tavernor-Perry 1907: 22, and Milstein 1986: 538-9.

4  The disc halo, on the other hand, could be used for this purpose from an early date in Islamic art, as witness the post-Sasanian dish in the Hermitage of a monarch seated cross-legged on a carpet (Orbeli and Trever 1935: pl. 18). Buddhist connections have been suggested for the feature of clusters of tiny punched depressions adorning the surface of the halo (Bahrami 1952: 15 and fig. g). Cf. also the Buyid medal in the Freer Gallery of Art, in which the monarch has a disc halo both on the obverse, with its enthronement scene, and on the reverse, which shows him riding out with his falcons (Bahrami 1952: pl. I, 1a and 1b).

5  The literary references to the radiance which suffused the faces of certain early Christian saints are abundant (L'Orange 1947: 96 and cf. 98; Cormack 1985: 67). The extant visual examples which bear on the theme of this paper are, however, somewhat ambivalent in that the saints in question actually have a conventional disc halo set within a larger rayed semi-circle: e.g. a mosaic of St Demetrius in his church at Thessalonica (Grabar 1968: pl. 193) and St Menas on an ivory

possibly dating to the seventh century (Weitzmann 1979: no. 517). Cf. the discussion in note 7 below. It should also be said that in the early centuries of Christian art the conventions governing the use of the halo were not yet fixed (Leclercq 1935: 1303).

6   One of the earliest examples is the Christ Helios depicted in the mosaics of the mausoleum of the Julii below St Peter's in Rome and dating to the early fourth century (Lassus 1967: colour pl. 13). For later examples, see the depiction of Christ in the Rossano Gospels (Grabar 1966: pls. 228-32), in the chapel of San Venanzio, San Giovanni in Fonte, Rome, of seventh-century date (Grabar 1968: pl. 322 — pace the remarks of Leclercq 1935: col. 1298), and a seventh-century censer from Constantinople (Weitzmann 1979: no. 562). Perhaps the most instructive example of all was the mosaic depicting a colossal bust of Christ with a nine-rayed nimbus at the apex of the triumphal arch of San Paolo fuori le Mure in Rome (Leclercq 1924: col. 261-2, fig. 4852). For all that, there can be no question that this form of halo had already fallen into disfavour before Iconoclasm, perhaps because its pagan antecedents were too evident. It is perhaps worth drawing attention to the rayed mandorla sometimes used to enclose the entire figure of Christ, as in the famous sixth-century Transfiguration mosaic in the Monastery of St Catherine in the Sinai desert (Lassus 1967: colour pl. 46), or in the Vision of Ezekiel, a mosaic of the early fifth century at Hosios David, Thessalonica (Grabar 1966: pl. 141). The large-scale aureole found in these mosaics is clearly related to the rayed nimbus encircling the head (Grabar 1968: 117 — who adds, interestingly enough, that "this nimbus probably comes originally from Mazdean Persia").

7   Here too the evidence is ambivalent; clearly artists hesitated to invest Byzantine emperors with the rayed nimbus in its most obvious form, preferring (as in the Islamic world) to suggest it. See for example a marble relief from Venice (Grabar 1936: 21; Lampros 1930: pl. 96, with the suggestion that it is Alexius Comnenus) and the well-nigh identical plaque in the Dumbarton Oaks collection (L'Orange 1953: 108, fig. 81), in which the entire background of the standing imperial figure consists of concentric rays.

8   For Sol, see Weitzmann 1979: 130, fig. 20; Brenk 1977: pl. 345. Cf. too the Helios figures on coins (L'Orange 1947: fig. 14a-d and L'Orange 1935: 328 and fig. 4b, d, e, g, h, j, k, l; see also L'Orange 1935: 330-1 for the suggestion that the origins of this type are to be sought in Syria) and in the floor mosaics of synagogues at Hamat Tiberias, Beth Alpha, Na'aran and Husefa (M. Dothan, in Weitzmann 1979: 374-5 and Avi-Yonah 1981: 396-7 and pls. 60-1). As for Jupiter, his origins as the old Italian sky-god automatically associated him with various heavenly phenomena; in his character of Jupiter Lucetius,for instance, he was the god of the light of the sky.

9   For a discussion of the rayed crown and its solar connotations, see L'Orange 1935: 331, 336-7 and fig. 5e and f, and L'Orange 1962: 27-31 and fig. 10; cf. also Weitzmann 1979: no. 59. The deliberate manipulation of light in some of the state appearances of the emperor is described at length by Ammianus Marcellinus (Rolfe 1950: 245). For an early imperial use of this theme, cf. the aureole of seven rays, each about 7 m. long, which encircled the head of Nero's Colossus in Rome, an image later changed to a likeness of the Emperor Titus as the sun (Tavernor-Perry 1907: 20).

10  E.g. for solar deities (Safar and Mustafa 1974: pl. on 276) and for two of the Hatra Triad of deities: Brmryn (pls. on 105, 106 and 115) and Mrn or Shamash (pls. on 113 and 178). A typical image of the god Brmryn (pl. on 113; colour pl. in al-Salihi 1978: 35) shows him with a halo of twelve rays; it would be interesting to investigate the astral and zodiacal associations of the number of rays depicted

in such haloes.

11  E.g. the god Iarhibol (Perkins 1973: 102 and pl. 42) or the solar deity in the Nemesis relief (Perkins 1973: 90 and pl. 36).

12  Cf. the rock relief of the solar deity Mithra at Taq-i Bustan (Ghirshman 1962: pl. 233), a radiate bust of the same god on an intaglio (pl. 298) and the goddess depicted on a capital found at Isfahan, whose radiating disc combines the properties of the rayed nimbus and the flame halo (Herzfeld 1941: 330 and fig. 413). Solar deities with rayed nimbi are represented on several Sasanian seals (Harper 1978: 149). A radiating nimbus was of course a standard component of the iconography of Mithra in the Roman world too (S.R. Zwirn, in Weitzmann 1979: nos. 173-4; Hinnells 1975: pls. 13a, 15d, 18b and 19b). For further comments on the relationship of Mithra to aspects of light and sun see Gershevitch 1975: 68-75, 82-3; for a brief summary of the role of Mithra in Iranian religion see Hinnells 1973: 76-89. A *drachm* of Khusrau II bears on the reverse a bust of Anahita with a rayed (or flame?) nimbus, and similar busts are known on a *dinar* of the same monarch and on a Hunnish imitation of such coins; this was minted in Kabul in 728 (Göbl 1983: pls. 28/6, 30/8 and 32/6 respectively). Cf. the very similar nimbus encircling the head of Asha, one of the Amesha Spentas (the aspects or "children" of Ahura Mazda), set above a fire altar on another intaglio (Ghirshman 1962: pl. 299).

13  Such as that of Bahram I (Goetz 1938: 2234, fig. 745j) or Narseh (Sarre and Herzfeld 1910: pl. XLI and fig. 104), though the latter example is attested only by a rock relief and not by Narseh's coins; indeed, the relief appears to copy the crown of Bahram I, his elder brother (215-6). Such radiating crowns are also known in later Roman art, e.g. a coin of Alexander Severus minted in Asia Minor (B. Narkiss, in Weitzmann 1979: no. 350).

14  E.g. a stucco plaque from Chal Tarkhan / Eshqabad showing a stag-slayer, a theme with clear Mithraic connotations (Harper 1978: 116); its date is immediately post-Sasanian, as is presumably that of two further fragmentary royal images in stucco, both surrounded by an unmistakable rayed nimbus (Kröger 1982: 56 and pl. 93/5 and 7). One might also note the implications of the rays streaming from the central bust of the ruler on the medallion bowl in the Freer Gallery (Harper 1981: 26 and pl. 4). For a general discussion of the rayed nimbus in Sasanian art, see Thompson 1976: II, 10 ff.

15  Hertel 1931; Bailey 1943: 1-78; Duchesne-Guillemin 1963; Boyce 1975: 66-8; Yarshater 1983: 345-6; Frye 1984: 216-7, with further bibliography.

16  Lukonin 1969: pl. 21; Hinnells 1973: 50 for a Kushan coin depicting Asha Vahista (the third Amesha Spenta) with a radiant nimbus. Cf. too Rosenfield 1967: 197-201.

17  Cf. Marshall 1973: 104 and fig. 142, as well as figs. 62 (the Boddhisattva's head-dress), 100 and 140; and Tavernor-Perry 1907: 22, fig. III.

18  See, for example, its use for a Babylonian relief found at Khafaje and depicting a creature variously described as a female demon (Moortgat 1969: 87, pl. 211); a fiery cyclops (Frankfort 1970: 113); and a solar being (Postgate 1977: 93). The sun-god was often depicted with rays springing from his shoulders (Frankfort 1970: 79, 90 and 112, and figs. 83[B] and 96[B]); so were certain Mesopotamian goddesses (Prinz 1915: 143-4 and pl. XIII/4-5).

19  Cf. Lammens 1908, summarised in Lammens 1932. For the flavour of the state which Mu'awiya kept, see the extracts from (unnamed) original sources quoted by Schroeder 1955: 204-11; cf. Grabar 1977: 56 and 60.

20  Notably in Mughal India, for example in paintings of Jahangir (Gascoigne 1971: 129, 130, 139 and 178). One of these depicts a Western monarch — James VI of Scotland and I of England — in the same picture (pl. 129).

21 The basic publication is Hamilton 1959.

22 For brief biographies of him, see Gabrieli (1935), 1-26; Derenk 1974: 27-47; and Hillenbrand 1982: 10-35.

23 For typical examples, with references, see Hillenbrand 1982: 16.

24 These remarks are intended to be applied particularly to the rosette, at first sight an innocuous and bland motif. For a discussion of its pre-Islamic antecedents and possible significance at Khirbat al-Mafjar, see Ettinghausen 1972: 36-40. Cf. too Oppenheim 1949: 191 with its comment that the rosette has been "known since the oldest periods for its numinous value"; Frankfort 1970: 37, 40, and figs. 32-3, 153 and 180; and Postgate 1977: 145. Rosettes were used just as profusely at the late Sasanian site of Taq-i Bustan as at Khirbat al-Mafjar; see, for example, Sarre and Herzfeld 1910: 210, fig. 98 (also reproduced in Herzfeld 1920: pl. LXV and there located at a different part of the reliefs). Cf. also the shield of the equestrian figure at that site, which bears a central rosette from which rays stream forth (Porada 1965: colour plate on 207). That the motif still retained some of its ancient power into Islamic times in Iran, and specifically retained its associations with kingship, is well illustrated by a post-Sasanian silver dish in the Hermitage (Sarre 1922: pl. 110). It depicts a ruler reclining on a couch while being serenaded by musicians. Hovering in splendid isolation directly over his head is a concentric lobed rosette displaying strongly marked diagonals in the Sasanian manner. A winged figure bearing royal insignia floats to the left of this rosette. A much smaller rosette, probably a space-filler like the three heart-shaped motifs scattered at random throughout the composition, is placed above the monarch's foot.

25 I hope to take up elsewhere the discussion of the architecture and decoration of this area, since it would unbalance the present paper to investigate this material in detail.

26 It is found from Delos in Greece to Ampurias in Spain; for a typical example at Beit Jibrin in Palestine, see Avi-Yonah 1981: pl. 149.

27 See Hamilton 1959: 335 for eight examples of this type in the Levant.

28 For earlier discussions of this roundel see Hamilton 1959: 335-6; Ettinghausen 1972: 39-40 and Brisch 1973: 179.

29 E.g. a gallery vault in the mausoleum of Öljeitü at Sultaniya in north-west Iran, of early fourteenth-century date (Seher-Thoss 1968: pl. 42).

30 Schlumberger 1946-8: 93-6 and pl. B.

31 For the rosette, see note 24 above. For the lotus, see the discussion of the Mithra relief at Taq-i Bustan in Herzfeld 1920: 63 and fig. 15; and, for an even earlier example, the tomb of Cyrus at Pasargadae, which dates to the sixth century BC. Here a composite lotus rosette occupies the place of honour just below the peak of the gable: see Stronach 1971; 1978: 35-7. A closely related design occurs on a glass dish of the 2nd-1st century BC from Alexandria or Asia Minor (Lukonin 1977: 119; cf. in general Ward 1956).

32 Compare, in a Christian context, the radiating pattern, executed in marble and mosaic, of the church of San Vitale in Ravenna, executed c. 540, with further radiating motifs inside the individual segments thus created (Brenk 1977: pl. 43).

33 For an extensive investigation of this relationship see Lehmann 1945 and, in the special context of the eastern Iranian world, Soper 1947: 225-6, 230-2.

34 Thus the dome of the central church of the twelfth-century Panto-crator monastery in Constantinople bears a radiating stellar or rosette design (Cormack 1985: fig. 81). Other churches in the capital which employ similar ideas include Haghia Sophia itself — though here the original roundel is lost and only the forty radiating ribs remain (Lassus 1967: colour plate 47) — and

the Kahrie Cami (Underwood 1966: Vol. 2, pls. 42 and 66).
35  Or perhaps "the deputy appointed by God", as is suggested by Watt 1971: 571.
    For cogent arguments in favour of interpreting the phrase *khalifat allah* in an
    even more "removed" sense as the person consecrated by God as the *khalifa* of
    the Prophet see Goldziher 1897, repr. 1970: 137-9.
36  Although tradition asserts that the first to use this title was the first caliph
    himself, Abu Bakr (Watt 1971: 572; Crone and Hinds 1986: 19-20). Crone and
    Hinds, however, suggest the possibility that this title was essentially a fabrication
    of the 'Abbasid *'ulama'* (1986: 16-23).
37  This is labelled no. 25 by Hamilton (1959: 328-9, 331-2 and pls.
    LXXIX and XCI).
38  Cf. the use of the same theme as a halo on the consular diptych of Anastasius
    (Weitzmann 1979: plate on p. 98).
39  It is of course possible that the stone *qalansuwa* was swathed in material or
    enclosed in a wooden shell to make it seem bigger.
40  This Umayyad mosaic bears a striking resemblance to a Roman floor mosaic
    from Verulamium / St. Albans (Wheeler 1957: 39, colour plate). The latter,
    however, depicts a scallop-shell and thus at once raises the question whether the
    analogy with the Umayyad mosaic is at all relevant. As Wheeler demonstrates,
    however, the scallop had a network of symbolic associations in the ancient
    world, among them sanctity (1957: 47). Hence, perhaps, its popularity for
    portraits of the deceased in a whole series of early Christian sarcophagi (Brenk
    1977: pls. 73, 75b, 77 and 83). The appropriateness of the motif for the
    decoration of a niche or semi-dome is too obvious to require analysis; but when
    one recalls the sacred associations of the scallop in early Christian iconography
    (see N.P. Sevcenko in Weitzmann 1979: 589) it comes as no surprise that such a
    motif is so often found directly behind the head of a sacred personage (e.g. in a
    fifth-century ambo from Thessalonica illustrated in Grabar 1966: pls. 263-5).
    Hence the term "shell halo" fittingly applied by S.R. Zwirn to the portrait of
    Anastasius on his diptych (Weitzmann 1979: 97); cf. the close-up detail in
    Grabar 1968: pl. 159. Finally, it is worth noting the occurrence of a motif very
    similar to that of the apse mosaic at Khirbat al-Mafjar in a piece of
    (unfortunately) re-used stone sculpture in a window at the Fenari 'Isa Cami in
    Istanbul, datable c. 930 (Krautheimer 1965: 265 and pl. 146B).
41  Especially well reproduced in Grube 1967: 33, fig. 6.
42  The notion of a heavenly realm peopled by personalities or allegories whose
    busts gaze down on those below was frequently expressed in the decoration of
    late antique ceilings (Lehmann 1945: 4-6 and figs. 3, 29 and 42).
43  E.g. the dome mosaic of St. Mark's in Venice, where a ray issues from the
    central figure of Christ to each of the Twelve Apostles (Demus 1948: pl. 8).
44  The care taken over this process, and the legends which grew up around it,
    signal the peculiar importance which was attached to Baghdad from the very
    beginning (Lassner 1970: 121-33; Levy 1929: 14-7).
45  In this context it is worth drawing attention to the suggestion made by Wendell
    that the moving spirit behind the entire foundation was not al-Mansur at all,
    but his vizier Khalid b. Barmak, whose Persian extraction and sympathies can
    be assumed to have given him a special propensity for this task (1971: 123-7).
46  See Creswell 1940: 4-17 for a discussion of these; and Lassner 1970: 132-3,
    138-54.
47  The origins of the plan are clearly analysed by Creswell 1940:
    18-22.
48  Quoted by L'Orange (1953: 10) with commentary.
49  Lassner 1965: 95; it is a theme to which he returns consistently in his later

writings (e.g. 1970: 143).

50  Among the Sasanian parallels for this idea that spring to mind, two deserve particular emphasis. First, one might cite the aura of empty space that surrounds the equestrian figure at Taq-i Bustan, a figure spotlighted by the sunshine which does not penetrate to the crowded investiture scene occupying the upper tympanum (Sarre 1922: pl. 84). This aura of empty space around the king recurs in numerous rock reliefs (Sarre and Herzfeld 1910: pls. V, XXXIX and XLII). The second is the 'Imarat-i Khusrau at Qasr-i Shirin, also of the late Sasanian period, where the throne-room is preceded by a vast open esplanade which has been expensively and laboriously raised on a platform some 8 m. high (Reuther 1938-9: 539-42, figs. 153-4).

51  Lassner 1970: 144-5, with useful commentary.

52  Al-Mansur's obsession with security is well documented; for example, alarmed at the quantity of strangers frequenting the markets of Baghdad, he had these markets removed outside the city limits (Nöldeke 1892: 131).

53  Huart 1927: 145 notes that in the Sasanian court a curtain separated the ruler from his household; it was placed ten cubits from the ruler and a further ten cubits from the position occupied by the highest classes of the state.

54  Levy 1929: 24, translating al-Khatib al-Baghdadi (ed. 1904: 11).

55  This description follows the interpretation of Herzfeld (Sarre and Herzfeld 1920: II, 134-6) and Creswell 1940: 30-1, which has long remained the standard one. It is only proper to point out, however, that this view has been challenged, notably by Oleg Grabar 1959: 101-2, on the grounds that the literary evidence could be interpreted differently, namely as a description of a longitudinally arranged plan (see also Beg 1985, from which Figure 7 is taken). More recently Professor Grabar has expressed his view as follows: "the palace was arranged around a court, an iwan of unknown shape, and two domed rooms" (Ettinghausen and Grabar 1987: 78). Figure 6 represents his necessarily cautious attempt to give an architectural form to the ambiguous literary evidence; but it should be remembered that al-Khatib's text is too delphic on this point to allow any definite conclusions. For that reason it seems justifiable that the hitherto canonical interpretation of the palace's appearance should be allowed to stand in the present paper (Figure 5). It is, after all, probable that — given the obsession with axiality, symmetry, centrality and symbolic meaning which the plan of Baghdad exudes — the caliph would indeed have had his throne room at the mathematically central point of the city. In that event, a centralised palace of the kind envisaged by Herzfeld (and, following him, Creswell) would certainly constitute the most appropriate climax for a city which had claims to world dominion built into its very design.

56  Lewis 1974: 69, translating al-Ya'qubi, *Kitab al-buldan*.

57  Grabar 1959: 103-7; Wendell 1971: 117-20; Lassner 1970: 133-6.

58  Lassner 1970: 232; cf. the pregnant remarks on this matter by Massignon 1962: 249-50.

59  According to al-Khatib al-Baghdadi 1904: 3, tr. Lassner 1970: 46, one of the astrologers said he "looked into the horoscope of the city which was for Jupiter in Sagittarius". Cf. Schroeder 1955: 278.

60  Seo 1986: 160-1; Wheatley 1971.

61  For an introduction to the problems posed by these gates see Wendell 1971: 116-7.

62  For an aerial view of Firuzabad, see Ghirshman 1962: fig. 160; on these cities in general, see Creswell 1940: 18-22, and Wendell 1971: 103-5. Cities with gates facing each of the four principal points of the compass included Hatra and Darabgird.

63  The appellation *al-zawra'* ("the crooked" or "the oblique") which was applied
    to the western half of the town was perhaps an allusion to the *qibla* (Le Strange
    1900: 11) — though Levy says the term was applied "to the eastern half of the
    town lying on the left bank" (1929: 8).
64  Browne 1928: 71, citing a rock inscription of Ardashir I vaunting his "spiritual
    origin from the gods" (*minu chitri min yaztan*), and 128.
65  On this term see Christensen 1944: 31, 146 and 508. The Arab historian
    al-Tha'alibi in his history of the Sasanian kings defines it as the divine majesty
    which kings can reflect (al-Tha'alibi 1900: 7). Cf. too the quotations furnished
    by Ettinghausen 1972: 42-3; Widengren 1959; and, above all, the references
    cited in note 15 above.
66  Such references of course occur in the works of other Persian poets too. A
    particularly significant example is found in Anvari's panegyric of Rukn al-Din
    Qilich Tamghach Khan, son-in-law of Sultan Sanjar, whom he terms "Khusrau
    with the *farr* of Afridun" (Melikian-Chirvani 1984: 293).
67  For the role of the *Shahnama* in moulding Islamic ideas about kingship in Iran,
    see Buckler 1935: 19-21.
68  I am grateful to my wife for this translation.
69  Bagley 1971: 45; cf. Goldziher 1971: 67. The nature of the Arabic language
    allows a crucial ambiguity to creep in here, for *al-sultan* could as easily mean "the
    Sultan himself" as the abstract notion of "authority" or "government". This
    *hadith*, in other words, was susceptible to a radical change of meaning in the
    course of the centuries.
70  Goldziher 1971: 67. It will be noted that Goldziher himself seems to espouse
    both points of view.
71  Widengren 1965: 312-3; Erdmann 1969: 86-7, with a reference to Shapur II
    wearing a golden and bejewelled ram's head instead of a crown; and
    Ettinghausen 1972: 42-3, who notes that the ram, mountain sheep and ibex are
    sometimes regarded as synonymous. This would, incidentally, place in a new
    light the presence of ibexes upholding the royal name on the controversial Alp
    Arslan salver (Pope 1938-9: pl. 1348).
72  Kröger 1982: 35 and pl. 75/2.
73  For the use of the nimbus in association with the successful hunt, see Kröger
    1982: 37 and 56.
74  The major study of its significance is Herzfeld 1920a. For a colour plate, see
    Ghirshman 1962: pl. 277; see also L'Orange 1953: 75.
75  For the Taq-i Taqdis, the famous revolving throne of Khusrau II, and the cosmic
    throne hall in which it was set, see L'Orange 1942: 295-8; Herzfeld 1920b;
    Reuther in Pope 1938-9: 555-6; Ackerman in Pope 1938-9: 775-8, 878-9;
    Melikian-Chirvani 1975: 31-2; and Naumann 1976: figs. 8-9 for the radiating
    (nimbed?) design of the Berlin salver which is often thought to depict that
    structure.
76  These points are best illustrated by a colour plate; see Goitia 1968: pl. 19.
77  Ewert 1978. Ewert's patient and meticulous researches over the past two
    decades have done more than the work of any other scholar of Islamic art to
    document the theory that a particular architectural form (in this specific case,
    networks of intersecting and interpenetrating arches) could be used in the
    medieval Islamic world to express meaning.
78  For these two mosques see Ewert and Wisshak 1984: pls. 26-7 and 55.
79  For these two buildings see Marçais 1955: 194 and 259.
80  Cf. Weitzmann 1979: 647.
81  It will be remembered that this is the theme of both the mosaic and the radiating
    masonry in the throne apse at Khirbat al-Mafjar.

82   Williams 1985: 45-6, 51-2 and pls. 7-10, 15 and 18. Note the ribbed dome above the *mihrab* in, for example, the *mashhad* of Sayyida Ruqayya, dated 1133 (Creswell 1952: pl. 87a).

83   It is conceivable that some residual memory of the Sasanian heritage of the *farr-i izadi* may be operative here, for 'Ali's son al-Husain was believed to have married Shahrbanu, the daughter of the last Sasanian king Yazdagird III (Boyce 1967).

84   Most recently explored by Dodd and Khairallah 1981: I, 1-18.

85   Allan 1982: 15-16, 23-9; cf. Melikian-Chirvani (in press) and al-Biruni's description of how, on the day of Nauruz, the mythical king Jamshid "rose ... like the Sun, the light beaming forth from him, as though he shone like the Sun. Now people were astonished at the rising of two Suns" (L'Orange 1953: 87).

86   Or "has given you a shape which" (Rice 1950b: 632).

87   For a detailed discussion of this topic, see Baer 1981 and 1983.

88   The notion of "glory" (*'izz*) is of course peculiarly well fitted to dovetail with the image of the nimbus; the English word "glory", like its Persian equivalent *farr*, can itself be used to denote a nimbus.

89   Discussed in Baer 1981: 13 and 1983: 259.

90   See Allan 1986: 139; significantly, this is a candlestick, which may well explain the presence of four other radiating themes on it.

91   See the examples cited in Baer 1981: 17 and 1983: 271-2.

92   Similar themes recur quite frequently in the luxury ceramics of this period (Pope 1938: pls. 656A, 712-3 and Atıl 1973: no. 40).

93   Grabar 1953: 169; Talbot Rice 1959: pl. XXI.

94   Cf., for example, the *Mi'rajnama* dated 1436 in the Bibliothèque Nationale, Paris (Séguy 1977: *passim*). Significantly enough, this form appears to enter Islamic miniature painting at almost exactly the same time as the rayed nimbus. Like the rayed nimbus in the *Jami' al-Tawarikh*, moreover, it is used in a context which bespeaks a full awareness of its import. Just as the rayed nimbus in that manuscript stands out because it is the only time that a halo occurs in any of the illustrations, so too is the impact of the flame halo in the Biruni manuscript of 1307 intensified by its sparing use. While the solid gold roundel occurs dozens of times as a halo in this manuscript, the flame halo is reserved for the angel Gabriel (f. 141b) and for the Prophet Muhammad (ff. 161a and 162a; see Soucek 1975: figs. 22, 24 and 25. There is perhaps a hint of the same theme in the *Jami' al-Tawarikh* image of Alexander entering the land of fog and wearing a rayed helmet; see Talbot-Rice 1974: 81-2, pl. 22.). It is tempting to associate the simultaneous introduction of both the unambiguous and Christian rayed nimbus and the Far Eastern flame halo with that openness to foreign influences and non-Islamic faiths which characterised early Ilkhanid Iran. That same openness was responsible, it seems, for the birth of a specifically Islamic religious iconography, as can be seen precisely in the Biruni and *Jami' al-Tawarikh* manuscripts.

95   Cf. the examples cited in note 20 above, or the portrait of Aurangzib in the Chester Beatty Library in Dublin, to cite only a few examples among many.

REFERENCES

Ackerman, P. (1938-9). Sasanian Jewelry. In Pope (1938-9), pp. 771-8.
—— (1938-9). Some Problems of Early Iconography. In Pope (1938-9), pp. 831-5.
Aga-Oghlu, M. (1930). Ein Prachtspiegel im Topkapu Sarayi Museum. *Pantheon* 6, 454-7.
Allan J.W. (1982). *Islamic Metalwork. The Nuhad Es-Said Collection.* London: Sotheby.
—— (1986). *Metalwork of the Islamic World. The Aron Collection.* London: Sotheby.
Atıl, E. (1973). *Ceramics from the world of Islam.* Washington: Smithsonian Institution.
Avi-Yonah, M. (1981). *Art in Ancient Palestine. Selected Studies collected and prepared for publication by H. Katzenstein and Y. Tsafrir.* Jerusalem: The Magnes Press, The Hebrew University.
Baer, E. (1981). The Ruler in Cosmic Setting: A Note on Medieval Islamic Iconography. In *Essays in Islamic Art and Architecture. In Honor of Katharina Otto-Dorn*, ed. A. Daneshvari (Malibu: Undena Publications), pp. 13-19.
—— (1983). *Metalwork in Medieval Islamic Art.* Albany: State University of New York Press.
Bagley, F.R.C., tr. (1971). *Ghazali's Book of Counsel for Kings ("Nasihat al-Muluk").* London: Oxford University Press.
Bahrami, M., ed. G.C. Miles (1952). A Gold Medal in the Freer Gallery of Art. In *Archaeologica Orientalia in memoriam Ernst Herzfeld* (Locust Valley, New York: J.J. Augustin), pp. 5-20.
Bailey, H.W. (1943). *Zoroastrian Problems in the Ninth-century Books.* Oxford: Oxford University Press.
Beg, M.A.J., ed. (1985). *Historic Cities of Asia — An introduction to Asian cities from antiquity to pre-modern times.* Kuala Lumpur: Percetakan Bat Huat Seng.
Bovini, G., tr. G. Scaglia (1956). *Ravenna Mosaics.* Greenwich, Connecticut: New York Graphic Society.
Boyce, M. (1967). Bibi Shahrbanu and the Lady of Pars. *Bulletin of the School of Oriental and African Studies* 30, 30-44.
—— (1975). *A History of Zoroastrianism* I. Leiden: E.J. Brill.
Brenk, B. (1977). *Spätantike and frühes Christentum.* Frankfurt-am-Main: Propyläen Verlag.
Brisch, K. (1973). (co-author) Omayyaden. In *Die Kunst des Islam*, eds. B. Spuler and J. Sourdel-Thomine (Berlin: Propyläen Verlag), pp. 139-45, 153, 171, 177-86.
Browne, E.G. (1928). *A Literary History of Persia. I. From the Earliest Times until Firdawsi.* Cambridge: Cambridge University Press.
Buckler, F.W. (1935). Firdausi's "Shah-namah" and the "Genealogia Regni Dei". *Journal of the American Oriental Society* 55, Supplement 1, 1-21.
Christensen, A. (1944). *L'Iran sous les Sassanides.* Copenhagen: E. Munksgaard.
Colledge, M.A.R. (1976). *The Art of Palmyra.* London: Thames and Hudson.
Collimet-Guérin, P. (1961). *Histoire du nimbe des origines aux temps modernes.* Paris.
Cormack, R. (1985). *Writing in Gold. Byzantine Society and its Icons.* London: George Philip.
Creswell, K.A.C. (1940). *Early Muslim Architecture* II. Oxford: Oxford University Press.

—— (1952). *The Muslim Architecture of Egypt. I. Ikhshids and Fatimids A.D. 939-1171.* Oxford: Oxford University Press.

—— (1969). *Early Muslim Architecture. Umayyads. A.D. 622-750.* I/2. Oxford: Oxford University Press.

Crone, P. and M. Hinds (1986). *God's Caliph: Religious authority in the first centuries of Islam.* Cambridge: Cambridge University Press.

Dalley, S. (1986). The god Salmu and the winged disk. *Iraq* 48, 85-101.

Daremberg, C., E. Saglio and M. Pottier (1877-1919). *Dictionnaire des antiquités grecques et romaines, d'après les textes et les monuments.* IV, 84-5, s.v. "Nimbus". Paris: Hachette.

Demus, O. (1948). *Byzantine Mosaic Decoration. Aspects of Monumental Art in Byzantium.* London and Henley: Routledge and Kegan Paul.

Derenk, D. (1974). *Leben und Dichtung des Omaiyadenkalifen al-Walid ibn Yazid. Ein quellenkritischer Beitrag.* Freiburg im Breisgau: Klaus Schwarz Verlag.

Dodd, E.C. and S. Khairallah (1981). *The Image of the Word. A Study of Quranic Verses in Islamic Architecture.* I. Beirut: The American University of Beirut.

Duchesne-Guillemin, J. (1963). Le Xuarənah. *Annali dell' Istituto Orientale di Napoli* 5, 19-31.

—— (1983). Zoroastrian Religion. In *The Cambridge History of Iran. 3(2). The Seleucid, Parthian and Sasanian Periods,* ed. E. Yarshater (Cambridge: Cambridge University Press), pp. 866-908.

Duri, A.A. (1960). Baghdad. In *Encyclopaedia of Islam* (2nd ed.). I. (Leiden: E.J. Brill), pp. 894-908.

Elisséeff, N. (1965). Dimashk. In *Encyclopaedia of Islam* (2nd ed.). II. (Leiden: E.J. Brill), pp. 277-91.

Erdmann, K. (1951). Die Entwicklung der sasanidischen Krone. Exkurs I: Die hängende Krone. *Ars Islamica* 15-6, 114-7.

—— (1969). *Die Kunst Irans zur Zeit der Sasaniden.* Mainz: Florian Kupferberg.

Ettinghausen, R. (1943). The Bobrinski "Kettle", Patron and Style of an Islamic Bronze. *Gazette des Beaux-Arts* 24, 193-208.

—— (1972). *From Byzantium to Sasanian Iran and the Islamic World.* Leiden: E.J. Brill.

Ettinghausen, R. and O. Grabar (1987). *The Art and Architecture of Islam, 650-1250.* Harmondsworth: Penguin.

Ewert, C. (1978). Spanisch-Islamische Systeme sich kreuzender Bögen. III. Die Aljaferia in Zaragoza. 3 vols. Berlin: Walter de Gruyter and Co.

—— (in press). Eastern-Oriented Traditionalism in Western Islamic Architecture: from the Caliphate of Cordoba to the Almohads. In *The Art of the Saljuqs in Iran and Anatolia,* ed. R. Hillenbrand (Costa Mesa, Cal. : Mazda Publishers).

Ewert, C. and J.P. Wisshak (1984). *Forschungen zur almohadischen Moschee. Lieferung 2: Die Moschee von Tinmal (Marokko).* Mainz: Verlag Philipp von Zabern.

Fehérvári, G. (1972). Tombstone or Mihrab? A Speculation. In *Islamic Art in the Metropolitan Museum of Art,* ed. R. Ettinghausen (New York: The Metropolitan Museum of Art), pp. 241-54.

Frankfort, H. (1970). *The Art and Architecture of the Ancient Orient.* Harmondsworth: Penguin.

Frye, R.N. (1984). *The history of ancient Iran.* Munich: C.H. Beck.

Gabrieli, F. (1934). Al-Walid ibn Yazid. Il califfo e il poeta. *Rivista degli Studi Orientali* 15, 1-64.

Gascoigne, B. (1971). *The Great Moghuls.* London: Jonathan Cape.

Gershevitch, I. (1975). Die Sonne das Beste. In Hinnells (1975), pp. 68-89.
al-Ghazali, ed. H. Khedivjam (1361 A.S.H.). *Kimiya-yi Sa'adat*. Teheran: Markaz-i intisharat-i 'ilmi va farhangi.
Ghirshman, R., tr. S. Gilbert and J. Emmons (1962). *Iran. Parthians and Sassanians*. London: Thames and Hudson.
Göbl, R. (1983). Sasanian Coins. In *The Cambridge History of Iran*. 3 (1). *The Seleucid, Parthian and Sasanian Periods*, ed. E. Yarshater (Cambridge: Cambridge University Press), pp. 322-39.
Goetz, H. (1938-9). The History of Persian Costume. In Pope (1938-9), pp. 2227-56.
Goitia, F.C. (1968). *La Mezquita de Cordoba*. Granada and Florence: Albaicin / Sadea.
Goldziher, I. (1897, repr. 1970). Du sens propre des expressions Ombre de Dieu, Khalife de Dieu, pour désigner les chefs dans l'Islam. In *Gesammelte Schriften* IV, ed. J. Desomogyi (Hildesheim: Georg Olms Verlagsbuchhandlung), pp. 133-40.
––––––– (1971). *Muslim Studies (Muhammedanische Studien)* II, ed. S.M. Stern, tr. C.R. Barber and S.M. Stern. London: George Allen and Unwin, Ltd.
Grabar, A. (1936). *L'empéreur dans l'art byzantin: Recherches sur l'art official de l'empire d'Orient*. Paris: Les Belles Lettres, for La Faculté des Lettres de l'Université de Strasbourg.
–––––––, tr. S. Gilbert (1953). *Byzantine Painting*. Geneva: Skira.
–––––––, tr. S. Gilbert and J. Emmons (1966). *Byzantium. From the death of Theodosius to the rise of Islam*. London: Thames and Hudson.
––––––– (1968). *Christian Iconography: A Study of its Origins*. Princeton: Princeton University Press.
Grabar, O. (1959). Al-Mushatta, Baghdad and Wasit. In *The World of Islam: Studies in Honor of P.K. Hitti*, ed. R.B. Winder (London: Macmillan), pp. 99-108.
––––––– (1977). Note sur les cérémonies umayyades. In *Studies in memory of Gaston Wiet*, ed. M. Rosen-Ayalon (Jerusalem: Institute of Asian and African Studies, The Hebrew University of Jerusalem), pp. 51-60.
Gray, B. (1978). *The World History of Rashid al-Din. A Study of the Royal Asiatic Society Manuscript*. London: Faber and Faber.
Grube, E.J. (1967). *The World of Islam*. Feltham: Paul Hamlyn.
Hallade, M. (1963). Indo-Iranian Art. In *Encyclopaedia of World Art*. (New York: McGraw-Hill), III, cols. 2-18.
Hamilton, R.W. (1959). *Khirbat al Mafjar. An Arabian Palace in the Jordan Valley*. Oxford: Oxford University Press.
––––––– (1969). Who built Khirbat al Mafjar? *Levant* 1, 61-7.
––––––– (1978). Khirbat al Mafjar: The Bath Hall reconsidered. *Levant* 10, 126-38.
Harper, P.O. (1978). *The Royal Hunter. Art of the Sasanian Empire*. New York: The Asia Society.
––––––– (1981). *Silver Vessels of the Sasanian Period. Volume One: Royal Imagery* (with a technical study by P. Meyers). New York: The Metropolitan Museum of Art, in association with Princeton University Press.
Herrmann, G. (1977). *The Iranian Revival*. Oxford: Elsevier, Phaidon.
Hertel, J. (1931). *Die awestischen Herrschafts- und Siegesfeuer. Mit Text, Übersetzung und Erklärung von Yašt 18 und 19. Abhandlungen der sächsischen Akademie der Wissenschaften, Philosophisch-historische Klasse* 41, No. 6.
Herzfeld, E. (1920a). *Am Tor von Asien. Felsdenkmale aus Irans Heldenzeit*. Berlin: Dietrich Reimer.
––––––– (1920b). Der Thron des Khosro. Quellenkritische und ikonographische Studien über Grenzgebiete der Kunstgeschichte des Morgen- und Abendlandes.

*Jahrbuch der Königlichen preuszischen Kunstsammlungen* 41, 1-24, 103-47.
—— (1930). Die sasanidischen Quadrigae Solis et Lunae. *Archaeologische Mitteilungen aus Iran* 2, 128-31.
—— (1941). *Iran in the Ancient Near East.* London and New York: Oxford University Press.
Hill, D., L. Golvin and R. Hillenbrand (1976). *Islamic Architecture in North Africa.* London: Faber and Faber.
Hillenbrand, C. (in press). Islamic orthodoxy or Realpolitik: al-Ghazali's views on government. *Iran* 26.
Hillenbrand, R. (1981). Islamic art at the crossroads: East versus West at Mshatta. In *Essays in Islamic Art and Architecture. In Honor of Katharina Otto-Dorn*, ed. A. Daneshvari (Malibu: Undena Publications), pp. 63-86.
—— (1982). *La dolce vita* in early Islamic Syria: the evidence of later Umayyad palaces. *Art History* 5, 1-35.
—— (1983). Some Observations on the Use of Space in Medieval Islamic Buildings. In *Islamic Architecture and Urbanism*, ed. A. Germen (Dammam, King Faisal University), pp. 17-30.
—— (in press). Quranic epigraphy in medieval Islamic architecture. In *Festschrift for Dominique Sourdel*, ed. L. Kalus (Paris).
Hinnells, J.R. (1973). *Persian Mythology.* Feltham: Paul Hamlyn.
——, ed. (1975). *Mithraic Studies. Proceedings of the First International Congress of Mithraic Studies.* I-II. Manchester: Manchester University Press.
Huart, C., tr. C.K. Ogden (1927). *Ancient Persia and Iranian Civilization.* London: Kegan Paul, Trench, Trubner.
Kessler, C.L. (1963). A preliminary report on excavations at Kufa during the third season (tr. of M.A. Mustafa). *Sumer* 19, 36-65.
Al-Khatib al-Baghdadi, ed. G. Salmon (1904). *L'Introduction topographique à l'histoire de Baghdadh d'Abou Bakr Ahmad Ibn Thabit al-Khatib al-Baghdadhi.* Paris.
Krautheimer, R. (1965). *Early Christian and Byzantine Architecture.* Harmondsworth: Penguin.
Kröger, J. (1982). *Sasanidischer Stuckdekor (Baghdader Forschungen, 5 ).* Mainz: Verlag Philipp von Zabern.
Krücke, A. (1905). *Der Nimbus und verwandte Attribute in der frühchristlichen Kunst. (Zur Kunstgeschichte des Auslandes, Heft 35).* Strassburg: J.H. Ed. Heitz.
Kuhrt, A. (1984). The Achaemenid concept of kingship. *Iran* 22, 156-60.
Künstle, K. (1928). *Ikonographie der christlichen Kunst.* Freiburg-im-Breisgau: Herder.
Lammens, H. (1908). *Etudes sur le règne du calife omaiyade Mo'awiya I.* Beirut: Université de Saint Joseph.
—— (1932). Mu'awiya. In *Encyclopaedia of Islam.* (1st ed.). III. (Leiden: E.J. Brill), pp. 617-21.
Lampros, S.P. (1930). *Leukoma Byzantinon Autokratoron.* Athens: Ekdotikas Oikos "Eleutheroudakis".
Lassner, J. (1965). Why did the Caliph al-Mansur build ar-Rusafah? — A historical note. *Journal of Near Eastern Studies* 24, 95-9.
—— (1970). *The Topography of Baghdad in the Early Middle Ages.* Detroit: Wayne State University Press.
Lassus, J. (1967). *The Early Christian and Byzantine World.* London: Paul Hamlyn Ltd.
Leclercq, H. (1924). Galla Placidia. In F. Cabrol and H. Leclercq, *Dictionnaire d'archéologie chrétienne et de Liturgie.* Paris: Librairie Letouzey et Ane, VI,

cols. 247-75.
———— (1935). Nimbe, *ibid.*, XII, cols. 1272-1312.
Lehmann, K. (1945). The Dome of Heaven. *Art Bulletin* 27, 1-27.
Le Strange, G. (1900). *Baghdad during the Abbasid caliphate from contemporary Arabic and Persian sources*. Oxford: Clarendon Press.
Levy, R. (1929). *A Baghdad Chronicle*. Cambridge: Cambridge University Press.
Lewis, B., ed. and tr. (1974) *Islam from the Prophet Muhammad to the Capture of Constantinople. II. Religion and Society*. New York: Harper and Row.
L'Orange, H.P. (1935, repr. 1973). Sol invictus imperator. Ein Beitrag zur Apotheose. *Symbolae Osloenses* 14, 86-114, repr. in *Likeness and icon. Selected Studies in Classical and Early Mediaeval Art* (Odense: Odense University Press), pp. 325-44.
———— (1942, repr. 1973). Domus aurea — der Sonnenpalast. *Serta Eitremiana*, pp. 68-100, repr. in *Likeness and icon*, pp. 292-312.
———— (1947). Apotheosis in Ancient Portraiture. Oslo: H. Aschehoug and Co., for the Instituttet for Sammenlignende Kulturforskning.
———— (1953). *Studies in the iconography of cosmic kingship*. Oslo: H. Aschehoug and Co., for the Instituttet for Sammenlignende Kulturforskning.
———— (1962, repr. 1973). Kleine Beiträge zur Ikonographie Konstantins des Grossen. *Skrifter utgivna av Svenska Institutet i Rom* 4, 22. *Opuscula Romana* 4. (Lund), pp. 101-5; repr. in *Likeness and icon*, pp. 23-31.
Lukonin, V.G. (1969). *Kul'tura Sasanidskogo Irana*. Moscow: Izdatel'stvo "Nauka".
———— (1977). *Iskusstvo drevnego Irana*. Moscow: Iskusstvo.
MacDonald, W.L. (1976). *The Pantheon: Design, Meaning and Progeny*. Cambridge, Mass.: Harvard University Press.
Mâle, E. (1960). *The early churches of Rome*, tr. D. Buxton. London: E. Benn.
Marçais, G. (1955). *L'architecture musulmane d'Occident. Tunisie, Algérie, Maroc, Espagne et Sicile*. Paris: Arts et Métiers Graphiques.
Marshall, J. (repr. 1973). *The Buddhist art of Gandhara. The story of the early school. Its birth, growth and decline*. Karachi: Department of Archaeology and Museums, Ministry of Education, Government of Pakistan.
Massignon, L. (1962). Le symbolisme médiévale de la destinée de Baghdad. In *Bagdad. Volume spécial publié à l'occasion du mille deux centième anniversaire de la fondation*. (Leiden: E.J. Brill), pp. 249-50.
Melikian-Chirvani, A.S. (1975). Recherches sur l'architecture de l'Iran bouddhique I. Essai sur les origines et le symbolisme du stupa iranien. *Le Monde iranien et l'Islam* III, 1-61.
———— (1982). *Islamic Metalwork from the Iranian World. 8-18th centuries*. London: H.M.S.O.
———— (1984). Le *Shah-Name*, la gnose soufie et le pouvoir mongol. *Journal Asiatique* 272 (3-4), 249-337.
———— (in press). The Light of the World. In *The Art of the Saljuqs in Iran and Anatolia*, ed. R. Hillenbrand (Costa Mesa, Cal.: Mazda Publishers).
Milstein, R. (1986). Light, Fire and the Sun in Islamic Painting. In *Studies in Islamic History and Civilization in Honour of Professor David Ayalon*, ed. M. Sharon (Jerusalem and Leiden: Cana and E.J. Brill), pp. 533-52.
Moortgat, A., tr. J. Filson (1969). *The Art of Ancient Mesopotamia. The Classical Art of the Near East*. London and New York: Phaidon.
Musil, A. (1907). *Kusejr 'Amra*. Vienna: Verlag der K.K. Hof- und Staatsdruckerei.
Naumann, R. and E. (1976). *Takht-i Suleiman. Ausgrabung des Deutschen Archäologischen Instituts in Iran*. Munich: Prähistorische Staatssammlung im Selbstverlag.

Nöldeke, T., tr. J.S. Black (1892). *Sketches from Eastern History*. London and Edinburgh: A. and C. Black.

Oppenheim, A.L. (1949). The Golden Garments of the Gods. *Journal of Near Eastern Studies* 8 (3), 172-93.

Orbeli, J. and K. Trever (1935). *Sasanidskii Metall*. Moscow and Leningrad: Academia.

Pedersen, J. (1930). Masdjid. *Encyclopaedia of Islam*. (1st ed.). III (Leiden: E.J. Brill and London: Luzac and Co.), pp. 315-76.

Perkins, A. (1973). *The Art of Dura-Europos*. Oxford: Clarendon Press.

Pope, A.U., ed., with P. Ackerman (1938-9). *A Survey of Persian Art from Prehistoric Times to the Present*. Oxford and London: Oxford University Press.

Porada, E. (1965). *Ancient Iran. The art of pre-Islamic times*. London: Methuen.

Postgate, J.N. (1977). *The First Empires*. Oxford: Elsevier, Phaidon.

Prinz, H. (1915). *Altorientalische Symbolik*. Berlin: Karl Curtius.

Reuther, O. (1938-9). Sasanian Architecture. [A]. History. In Pope (1938-9), pp. 493-578.

Rice, D.S. (1950a). The Blazons of the "Baptistère de Saint Louis". *Bulletin of the School of Oriental and African Studies* 13, 367-80.

―――― (1950b). The Brasses of Badr al-Din Lu'lu'. *Bulletin of the School of Oriental and African Studies* 13, 627-34.

―――― (1956). Arabic inscriptions on a brass basin made for Hugh IV de Lusignan. In *Studi Orientalistici in onore di Giorgio Levi della Vida* (Rome: Istituto per l'Oriente), II, 390-402.

Rolfe, J.C., tr. (1950). *Ammianus Marcellinus*. Cambridge, Mass.: Loeb Classical Library.

Root, M.C. (1979). *The King and Kingship in Achaemenid Art: Essays on the Creation of an Iconography of Empire*. Leiden: E.J. Brill.

Rosenfield, J.M. (1967). *The Dynastic Arts of the Kushans*. Berkeley and Los Angeles: University of California Press.

Safar, F. (1952). Hatra and the First Season of Excavation. *Sumer* 8, 3-16.

Safar, F. and M.A. Mustafa (1974). *al-Hadra. Madinat al-shams*. Baghdad: Directorate General of Antiquities.

al-Salihi, W. (1978). *Hatra*. London: The Iraqi Cultural Centre.

Sarre, F. (1922). *Die Kunst des alten Persien*. Berlin: Bruno Cassirer.

Sarre, F. and E. Herzfeld (1910). *Iranische Felsreliefs. Aufnahmen und Untersuchungen von Denkmälern aus alt- und mittelpersischer Zeit*. Berlin: Ernst Wasmuth A.-G.

―――― (1920). *Archäologische Reise im Euphrat- und Tigrisgebiet*. II. Berlin: Verlag von Dietrich Reimer (Ernst Vohsen).

Schlumberger, D. (1946-8). Deux fresques omeyyades. *Syria* 25, 86-102.

Schramm, P.E. (1954-6). *Herrschaftszeichen und Staatssymbolik* 1-3. Stuttgart: Kohlhammer.

―――― (1958). *Sphaira, Globus, Reichsapfel*. Stuttgart: Kohlhammer.

Schroeder, E. (1955). *Muhammad's People. A tale by anthology*. Portland, Maine: The Bond Wheelwright Company.

Séguy, M.-R. (1977). *The Miraculous Journey of Mahomet. Miraj Nameh*, tr. R. Peavear. New York: George Braziller.

Seher-Thoss, S.P. and H.C. (1968). *Design and Color in Islamic Architecture. Afghanistan. Iran. Turkey*. Washington, D.C.: Smithsonian Institution Press.

Seo, T. (1985). The urban systems of Chang'an in the Sui and T'ang Dynasties. In Beg (1985), pp. 159-200.

Smith, E.B. (1956). *Architectural Symbolism of Imperial Rome and the Middle Ages*. Princeton: Princeton University Press.

Soper, A.C. (1947). The Dome of Heaven in Asia. *Art Bulletin* 29, 225-48.
Soucek, P.P. (1975). An Illustrated Manuscript of al-Biruni's *Chronology of Ancient Nations*. In *The Scholar and the Saint*, ed. P. Chelkowski (New York: New York University Press), pp. 103-68.
Stephani, L. (1859). *Nimbus und Strahlenkranz in den Werken der alten Kunst*. In *Mémoires de l'Académie des Sciences de Saint-Petersbourg*, VIe série, *Sciences politiques, histoire, philologie*, 9.
Stronach, D. (1971). A Circular Symbol on the Tomb of Cyrus. *Iran* 9, 155-8.
——— (1978). *Pasargadae*. Oxford: Oxford University Press.
Strzygowski, J. (1906). Review of A. Krücke, *Der Nimbus und verwandte Attribute in der frühchristlichen Kunst*. *Byzantinische Zeitschrift* 15, 694-6.
Talbot Rice, D. (1959). *Kunst aus Byzanz*. Munich: Hirmer Verlag.
——— (1974). *The Illustrations to the "World History" of Rashid al-Din*. Edinburgh: Edinburgh University Press.
Tavernor-Perry, J. (1907). The Nimbus in Eastern Art. *Burlington Magazine* 12, 20-3 and 95-6.
al-Tha'alibi, ed. and tr. H. Zotenberg (1900). *Histoire des rois de Perse par Al-Tha'alibi*. Paris.
Thompson, D. (1976). *Stucco from Chal Tarkhan / Eshqabad*. Warminster: Aris and Phillips.
Underwood, P.A. (1966). *The Kariye Djami*. Bollingen Series, 70. New York: Pantheon Books.
Ward, W.E. (1952). The lotus symbol: its meaning in Buddhist art and philosophy. *Journal of Aesthetics and Art Criticism* 11, 135-46.
Watt, W.M., ed. C.E. Bosworth (1971). God's Caliph. Qur'anic Interpretations and Umayyad Claims. *Iran and Islam: In memory of the late Vladimir Minorsky*, (Edinburgh: Edinburgh University Press), pp. 565-74.
Weitzmann, K. (1979). *Age of Spirituality. Late Antique and Early Christian Art, Third to Seventh Century*. New York: The Metropolitan Museum of Art in association with Princeton University Press.
Wendell, C. (1971). Baghdad: *imago mundi* and other foundation-lore. *International Journal of Middle East Studies* 2, 99-128.
Wheatley, P. (1971). *The pivot of the four quarters: a preliminary enquiry into the origins and character of the ancient Chinese city*. Edinburgh: Edinburgh University Press.
Wheeler, R.E.M. (1957). A Symbol of Ancient Times. In *The Scallop: Studies of a shell and its influences on humankind*, ed. I. Cox (London, The Shell Transport and Trading Company, Limited), pp. 33-48.
Widengren, G. (1959). The Sacral Kingship of Iran. *Numen*, Supplement 4 (Leiden: E.J. Brill), pp. 424-55.
——— (1965). *Die Religionen Irans*. Stuttgart: Kohlhammer.
Williams, C. (1985). The Cult of the 'Alid Saints in the Fatimid Monuments of Cairo. Part II: The Mausolea. *Muqarnas* 3, 39-60.
Wolff, F. (1965) *Glossar zu Firdosis Schahname*. Hildesheim: Georg Olms Verlagbuchhandlung.
Yarshater, E. (1983). Iranian common beliefs and world-view. *The Cambridge History of Iran. 3(1). The Seleucid, Parthian and Sasanian Periods*, ed. E. Yarshater (Cambridge: Cambridge University Press), pp. 343-58.

Plate I   Khirbat al-Mafjar: central medallion of floor mosaic in ball hall
(after Hamilton)

Plate II    Khirbat al-Mafjar: floor mosaic in central apse of west ambulatory in bath hall (after Hamilton)

Plate III   Incense burner of Sultan Qala`un (after Allan)

Plate IV    Mamluk mirror in Topkapi Saray (after Ettinghausen)

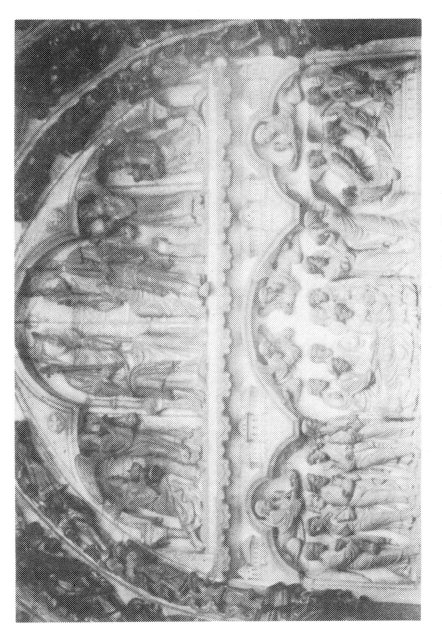

Plate V  Laon: tympanum (photo. Nicolas Wyatt)

Plate VI    Turone: Coronation of the Virgin (after Verdier)

Plate VII   Filippo Lippi: Coronation of the Virgin (after Marchini)

Plate VIII   Lucchese master: Coronation of the Virgin (by courtesy of the
Pinacoteca Nazionale, Lucca)

# THE ICONOGRAPHY OF THE CORONATION OF THE VIRGIN

Rosemary Muir Wright

The Coronation of the Virgin was one of the great theophanies of late Medieval, early Renaissance art, perhaps the greatest, for it offered a vision, at once mystical and yet convincing, of the agents in Salvation, presented, in some examples, in circumstances of the utmost royalty. It allowed for representations of the ultimate glory of the Heavenly Jerusalem, and of the theological issues enshrined in the symbolic act of the Coronation itself. An examination of the evidence from the twelfth century to the early sixteenth century reveals development in the iconography, responsive (as one would expect) to changes in formal expression, with the rediscovery of perspectival space and rounded form characteristic of the Renaissance in Italy, and it also reveals the sensitivity of patrons to the shifting emphasis of doctrine. The iconographic sequence can be discussed in three parts which I shall call "The Imagery of the Crowned Queen", "The Origins and Development of an Active Coronation", and "The Coronation as an Abstract Theme for Debate".

The Coronation itself is prefigured in the imagery of a crowned Queen seated along with Christ, in the manner of the Byzantine synthronos. Here the Virgin is to be identified with the figure of the Church, united and crowned with Christ in the ultimate glory of the Heavenly Jerusalem.

Then a more advanced type of the Coronation develops in which Christ actively crowns his mother, even while they retain their positions as a seated pair on a joint throne. The Virgin is represented as the Bride of Christ, the betrothed Sponsa of the *Song of Songs*. This active Coronation represents the culmination of the Virgin's divine purpose by her bodily reception into Heaven, and symbolises the unique privilege accorded to Christ's mother of a double assumption, both spiritual and corporeal. With the tendency towards a more realistic portrayal of religious subject-matter in Renaissance Italy, the awkwardness of crowning from equivalent seated positions must have proved irksome and a solution was found by moving the Virgin from the throne itself to a kneeling position on the ground, to receive the crown from the hands of Christ, or God the Father, who remained seated.[1]

Such representations stress the narrative aspect of the glorification of Mary. In the course of the fifteenth century, in a manner similar to other visionary themes, the Coronation assumed a more symbolic meaning. The image of crowning now hung suspended above the earth-bound figures who acted either as witnesses to the Divine mystery or forcefully discussed its import amongst themselves.

## The Imagery of the Crowned Queen

It may be that the origins of the theme of the Coronation can be traced to the twelfth century window of the old Church of Notre Dame in Paris presented by Abbot Suger of St Denis in 1150 (Mâle 1966: 152). Emile Mâle attributed the invention of the image of Christ crowning his mother Queen to Suger himself, believing that the original window, now destroyed, showed the Virgin crowned and seated on Christ's right hand. However, two contemporary representations in England suggest that the theme was more generally known (Verdier 1980: 17, n. 3). The tympanum of the south door of Querington Parish Church in Gloucestershire suggests two figures sharing a throne, one of whom is Christ, bearded and haloed. He appears to bless or perhaps even crown the veiled female figure seated on his right. The relief sculpture on a badly damaged capital from Reading Abbey in Berkshire, represents two figures seated on the same carved throne, similarly disposed to those at Querington. Christ blesses or crowns a veiled female figure who turns towards him, hands crossed on her breast in a posture of ardent submission.[2]

Without claiming the specific influence of the one over the other, it is clear that the imagery of the seated pair, the Synthronos, appeared in the first half of the twelfth century concurrently in England, France and Italy. Also the enthronement of the Virgin as Queen of Heaven may precede the imagery of the actual crowning, following the evidence from England. In such a presentation, Christ blesses the Virgin, rather than lays a crown upon her head.

The earliest clear evidence of an iconographic scheme after Suger's lost window for Notre Dame is the tympanum of the Cathedral of Senlis, begun in 1153 only two years after Suger's death and commissioned by his friend the Bishop of Thibaut.

It may be that this rendering echoes Suger's original invention for the Notre Dame window (assuming that it did represent a Coronation). At Senlis, Christ is enthroned with a crowned female figure on whom he appears to confer Divine Grace, by the blessing of his right hand. This female figure may represent Ecclesia, the personification of the Church Triumphant (Verdier 1980: 117, n. 12), for she carries the attribute of Ecclesia, the open book, in her right hand, while holding a sceptre, now partially destroyed, in her left (see Figure 2).

Seated on the same high backed throne, Christ turns towards her and blesses her. Despite the destruction of his right hand, it is clear that the gesture is one of benediction, not coronation: indeed the figure to his right

Figure 1

Doorway of the Cathedral of Senlis

Figure 2

Tympanum of the Cathedral of Senlis

is already crowned. Probably he too would have held some emblem of authority in his left hand. It is interesting to note the gesture by which the figure of Ecclesia grasps the folds of her mantle, in the manner of ancient philosophers. Such a gesture assimilates Ecclesia to that of Wisdom, a figure also identified with the Virgin. "He created me from the beginning before the world and I shall never fail." (*Ecclesiasticus* 24: 9) The Virgin, likewise, was so created, in the mind of God, before time. The Senlis portal stresses this lineage, for the restored statues in the doorway under the figure of Ecclesia recall the way of the Church, through sacrifice, priesthood and baptism. At the left of the entrance stands John the Baptist, then Aaron, Samuel, Moses and, innermost, Abraham with Isaac (Katzenellenbogen 1963: 110-1). On the curves of the archivolts, figures representing the Kings of Judah, David and Solomon, recall the ancestors of the Virgin. This association of the Church Triumphant with the Virgin is made explicit in the lintel reliefs; that on the left, under the figure of Ecclesia, depicts the Death of the Virgin, while that on the right, her awakening by the angels from her tomb in anticipation of her assumption. There is a subtle distinction between the two events. In the scene of the Virgin's death, the apostles lay her on the tomb, while two angels lower a crown above the image of her assumed soul. This assumption of the spirit is distinguished from the assumption of the body in the right-hand lintel relief, for in this tablet of the awakening, the Virgin's eyes are already open and an angel brings to her the crown. Thus the connection is explicit between Mary's Assumption in body and spirit and her glorification at the right hand of her Son, as Queen of Heaven. The Senlis portal (1160-1170) represents the glorification of Mary, rather than her actual coronation, although that development is clearly not far off.

Senlis inspired other great portals of France, such as those at Chartres and Laon, and Notre-Dame de Paris. In all of these representations, the seated pair is the iconographic type, Christ blesses, rather than crowns, the setting is the Heavenly Jerusalem and the Virgin is already crowned.

In the Coronation portal of Laon (Plate V), dating from the last decade of the twelfth century, the Virgin and Christ are seated in a more intimate relationship, each gazing intently towards the other. The Virgin carries a flowering rod, or sceptre, in her right hand, while raising her open left hand towards Christ, who rests a closed book on his left knee. The flowering rod recalls the flowering staff of Aaron, as a sign of God's choice, for his rod broke into almond blossom when it was left overnight in the tabernacle (*Numbers* 17.1-8). The image of Mary as the Holy Ark was deliberately elaborated in the popular apocryphal account of her life in the *Book of James*, in circulation from as early as the second century. It is possible that the flowering sceptre could be interpreted further in an immaculist sense, over and above the New Testament usage as a symbol of the Virgin Birth of

Christ, as when Gabriel carries a flowering staff, then a lily, at the Annunciation. Joseph's election as the husband of the Virgin was revealed by his rod breaking into flower before the High Priest. Indeed, Mary's perfect purity is a thread that runs through all twelfth century Coronations. Accordings to d'Ancona, in her survey of the iconography of the Immaculate Conception, the representation of Mary already crowned was so infused with the idea of her unique election, that the symbol could be readily adapted to Immaculate Conception imagery when required (D'Ancona 1957: 15, 28). Such associations are present in the tympanum at Laon, for in three of the archivolts are figures from the genealogy of Mary, the tree of Jesse, as at Senlis. Verdier (1980: 122) has noted that the third person in the second left-hand arch of the archivolt is Bathsheba. Again the reference is to a moment of royal choice, for at the Coronation of Solomon as King of the Israelites, Solomon set his mother Bathsheba on his throne, at his right hand (*1 Kings* 2: 19): "And the king rose up to meet her, and he bowed himself unto her, and sat down on his throne, and caused a seat to be set for the King's mother; and she sat on his right hand."

The last band of figures at Laon represents the prophets as they appear in the stained glass of Jesse Tree windows, including most probably the lost window for Notre-Dame de Paris. Indeed the link with Suger's original creation for that window may be the window of the Enthronement, at Angers Cathedral of about 1180. The first Bishop of Angers, Bishop Ulger, was associated with Suger. The positions of Mary and Christ, the veil and diadem of the Virgin, the naturalistic setting of the enthronement at Laon, all recall the uppermost medallion in the window at Angers.

The liturgical aspect of the Laon tympanum emphasises the aspect of the Church Triumphant. Two angels stand on either side of the throne, swinging censers, while on the outermost edge two candle-bearers bow on one knee in a gesture of obeisance, the proskynesis of the Byzantine rite. This is a Greek ceremonial attitude of prostration, introduced into Western art by John VII in a painting for the Basilica of S. Maria in Trastevere, in which he so bowed at the feet of the Virgin in Majesty. A further Byzantine detail is the elaborate curved back throne, with relief patterns suggestive of richness. The Laon synthronos is clearly set in heaven; wavy clouds frill under the base of the tympanum above the lintel and froth between the angels on the innermost band of the archivolt, reinforcing the idea of the location as the Heavenly Jerusalem of the *Book of Revelation*. This is made more explicit by the manner in which these angels bear the symbols recorded in that vision, namely the sun, crowns, palm branches, perfumes, a crescent moon, censers and the book with seven seals. Mary is therefore seen as the new Jerusalem, "coming down from God out of heaven, prepared as a bride adorned for her husband" (*Revelation* 21.2).

The Laon Queen is veiled under her diadem. This bridal appearance of the Church at the Last Day is symbolised in the Virgin as Bride of Christ. Maria Regina is joined therefore to the former single figure of the Majestas Domini to form a new iconographic type, the seated pair of the royal enthronement, now clearly linked by the narratives of the lintel reliefs to the death and assumption of the Virgin. The Old Testament is linked with the New in Christ, represented as the Bridegroom or Sponsus, united to his Church in fulfilment of the promise made to the patriarchs (*Hosea* 2.19): "And I will betroth thee unto me for ever; yea, I will betroth thee unto me in righteousness, and in judgement and in loving kindness, and in mercies." As in France, so in Italy, in the twelfth century themes of enthronement and assumption are integrated. In an example comparable to the tympana, the apse mosaic of Santa Maria in Trastevere in Rome by Cavallini (Figure 3), the iconography also reveals Byzantine influence. Immediately a distinction is apparent between the French examples and the Italian version.

Figure 3

Enthronement. Mosaic of the Apse of Santa Maria in Trastevere, Rome, by Cavallini.

Christ and the Virgin are seated facing the spectator, both hold visible texts, and Christ's right arm is curved protectively around the Virgin's shoulder. Moreover, the Virgin was not crowned in the original mosaic, but wore a veil capped by a net of pearls. The later restorations have accorded her a diadem hung with rows of pearls like that worn by the figure of Maria Regina in the eighth century icon in the same church. The heavenly crown, as distinct from the earthly diadem, is held above the head of Christ by a

Divine Hand in the Cavallini mosaic. Mary's earthly regality, as similar to the Queen/Empress of the icon, is explicitly suggested by a robe of cloth of gold, sumptuously adorned, thus recalling the 10th verse of *Psalm* 44 (or *Psalm* 45.13-4 in the Authorised Version):

> *Astitit regina a dextris tuis in vestitu deaurato circumdata varietate.* (The Queen is brought to your right hand in a raiment variously wrought of gold.)

> The king's daughter is all glorious within; her clothing is of wrought gold. She shall be brought unto the king in raiment of needlework.

Christ's distinctive gesture, by which Christ draws Mary to himself, recalls that by which the saints are received into Paradise by their sponsors in Roman and Etruscan funerary art. Marina Warner, in her study of the cult of the Virgin Mary, cites the supportive evidence of the conch mosaic of San Prassede, introduced by Paschal I (814-24), in which the young female saints Prassede and Pudenziana, robed in bridal splendour of cloth of gold, are ushered towards Christ by the other saints with a similar fatherly gesture (Warner 1978: 122). The bridal aspect is made explicit by the texts introduced in the Cavallini mosaic, which indicate a new emphasis, possibly to be accredited to the influence of St Bernard in the commissioning of the decoration. This is the inspiration of the *Song of Songs*, rather than *Revelation*. On Christ's codex are the words *"veni electa mea et ponam in te thronum meum"* (come my chosen one and I will set thee upon my throne). These words, which should read *"ponam te in tronam meam"*, are the opening lines of one of the responses for Matins in the Office of the Assumption. The phylactery of the Virgin reads: *"Laeva ejus sub capite meo et dextera ejus amplexabitur me."* (His left hand should be under my head and his right hand should embrace me.) This verse, repeated twice in the *Song of Songs* (2.6 and 8.3), serves as the antiphon for Matins in the Office of the Assumption, the eighth century *Liber Pontificalis*, attributed to Pope Gregory the Great. Thus Christ's gesture could also relate to the descriptions of the *Song of Songs*. In particular one of the first exegetists of the *Song of Songs*, Robert de Saint-Laurent, likened this description to the Virgin being enfolded in the glory of the Father. *"Et dextra ejus amplexabitur me, id est gloria Patris in qua ipse est, totam circumdabit et implebit me, cum de praesenti saeculo eduxerit et assumpserit me."* (And he will embrace me with his right hand, he who is the glory of the Father himself and he will surround me completely and fulfil me, when he shall have led me forth from the present generation and taken me to himself.) That the source of this nuptial imagery should be St Bernard's influence, is supported by the eighty-six sermons written by St Bernard which expounded on the *Song of Songs* in such a manner as to create a mystical sequence in which the Christian soul is transfigured by love.

In Santa Maria in Trastevere, the former figure of Ecclesia is overtaken by that of the Virgin, triumphantly assumed and embraced by Christ, thus prefiguring the soul's promised union with Christ in love.

The *Song of Songs* is crucial in the interpretation of the imagery of the Coronation. Attributed to Solomon, it is a book composed of several love lyrics, a text of the most sensuous and evocative analogies. The Shulamite — beloved of the King — was likened by Ambrose to the Virgin, the Church and every Christian soul, and thus the Canticle was seen as the love of Christ for his Church (Warner 1978: 26, n.4).

This idea was fully developed by St Bernard whose sermons on the *Song of Songs* (1135-53) absorbed the former image of Ecclesia into the new, evocative, transfiguring image of the Virgin as Sponsa. St Bernard's love of the Virgin was an intensely personal one, and his eloquence changed the remote, majestic figure of authority into a personal, beloved, gentle and merciful mother and betrothed. Because of the nature of the new devotion, namely private prayers made in a spirit of internal contemplation, and because of the geographical spread of the Cistercian order, itself dedicated to the Virgin's honour, the language of St Bernard in such prayers made familiar the emotive imagery of the *Song of Songs* to a very wide and willing audience. The Marian interpretation of the Canticle is particularly significant for the manner by which the Assumption is linked to Mary's Coronation. St Bernard had introduced into the first and second nocturnes of the Cistercian office of the Assumption lessons taken directly from the Canticles (Verdier 1980: 95).

> Happy indeed were the kisses he pressed on her lips when she was nursing and as a mother delighted in the child in her virgin's lap. But surely will we not deem much happier those kisses which in blessed greeting she receives today from the mouth of him who sits on the right hand of the Father, when she ascends to the throne of Glory, singing a nuptial hymn and saying ... Let him kiss me with the kisses of his mouth. (Quoted Warner 1978: 131)

As the Virgin had obscured the Glory of Christ by her flesh, so Christ would illuminate the Virgin with his splendour.

Such lyrical evocation of Mary's reception into Heaven must have encouraged a shift in the iconography from the synthronos type of glorification to an active coronation in which Christ crowns his mother.

## The Origins and Development of an Active Coronation

During the course of the thirteenth century, veneration of the Virgin found increasing support in the liturgical texts for the Feast of her Assumption, and in particular in the sermons of Bonaventure, by which the Virgin's heavenly triumph was represented by her Coronation, as the culminating event. This reinforcement of the importance of the Virgin in the Western tradition must be seen within the context of the scholastic debate over the exact nature of Mary's conception. St Thomas Aquinas (c. 1226-74) emphasised the theory of Sanctification, by which the Virgin, sanctified in the womb of Anne, was therefore on a level with John the Baptist with whom she shared an intercessory role for mankind at the Last Judgement. This more limited role was denied by the supporters of the Immaculate Conception as promulgated by Duns Scotus (1266?-1308), who affirmed that Mary's conception was Immaculate, Mary having been preserved from original sin by a special Act of God, on account of her role as Mother of Christ. Through the merits of Christ, she was rendered unique among women and came to exert an active role in the salvation of men. These arguments were fiercely mounted by the opposing orders, the Dominicans following the line of Aquinas, that no one, even Mary, could have been redeemed before the Redemption, and the Franciscans endorsing the belief in the Immaculate Conception. This latter position was supported by the weight of popular devotion to the Virgin of the times. Marina Warner indicated that the Franciscan position may have been more attractive to popular piety, because of the less intellectual nature of their beliefs. She mentions that "the Franciscans, whose less intellectual strain of piety kept them closer to the groundswell of popular feeling, endorsed the Immaculate Conception against the Black Friars" (Warner 1978: 242), and this "groundswell of popular feeling" may well account for the emergence of the scene of active crowning of the Virgin in the thirteenth century, perhaps representing the most up-to-date image to illustrate her increasing importance as mediatrix between man and God.

It is possible that the visual motif of an active crowning may have come from West Germany. The double portal of Strasbourg Cathedral (1225-30) makes explicit the idea of the Virgin's Triumph in body and soul; for in the tympanum of the left hand door is the dormition, and, on the right, the coronation, in which Christ both blesses and crowns his mother. Below, on the low relief sculptures of the consoles of doors are the funeral of the Virgin and the assumption of her body by the angels, respectively, which complement the scheme of the tympana above. The triumph of the Virgin is linked with the figure of Solomon, "Bridegroom and Judge", which is set between the two portals. Flanking the double portals are the figures of the Church on the left and the Synagogue on the right, thus emphasising the final concordance of the former opposition of the Old and New Testaments, in the Judgement and Coronation. The latter idea should be seen from the eschatological perspective of the return to Christ of the Shulamite bride of the *Song of Songs*. Unusually, at Strasbourg Christ crowns the Virgin seated on his left, a scheme also evident at Dijon, Bourges and Metz in the mid thirteenth century. It is the *Golden Legend* of

Jacobus which spells out the Virgin's place as being on Christ's right, her proper place for Eternity. In Bonaventure's third sermon on the Assumption, he discusses Mary's enthronement on Christ's right (Bonaventure 1901: 694-5). As Strasbourg predates both writers, the scheme may have been conditioned, as in other Italian and thirteenth century manuscript examples, by compositional factors.

The accent at Strasbourg is on the double assumption of the Virgin, responsive possibly to the writings of a German nun, Elisabeth of Schonau (d. 1164), who described how she had seen a vision of the Virgin rising bodily into heaven. Manuscripts of Elizabeth's visions were widely circulated after her death, securing a firm hold on popular imagination by the fourteenth century, especially as the vision included her reception in the heavens by a masculine figure bearing the banner of the cross. Jacobus may have drawn on such visionary writings for his own account of Mary's assumption. Jacobus, as Archbishop of Genoa from 1292 to 1298, was also the author of scores of sermons on the virtues and intercessory powers of the Virgin. The value of his text, the *Golden Legend*, lies in the sources from which he has made his synthesis, so critical for thirteenth century representations of the theme.

In addition, twelfth century sermons on the assumption such as those of Isaac de Stella (d. 1169) must have encouraged Jacobus in his analysis of the assumption. In Isaac's commentary on the Assumption, the ascension of the body of the Virgin may have been treated as that of her final reception as Queen of Heaven, by ending in an actual Coronation. This idea may be echoed in Nicholas of Clairvaux who, in writing of the Assumption in 1176, stresses the honour and dignity appropriate to the Virgin, who was received by Christ to preside with him on his throne. He stresses that it is not only the angels who go forth to meet her, but Christ himself. A further stimulus for an active crowning may have been that Isaac de Stella associated the bride of the *Song of Songs* with Esther. He wrote that just as Esther had left her apartments to plead with King Ahasuerus to spare her people, so the bride of the *Song of Songs* left the valley in response to her King's call. The Virgin likewise interceded with Christ in Heaven for mankind. Isaac thus made clear the identification of these types, by using the words formerly attributed to the action of Ahasuerus, to describe Christ's welcome of his mother into Heaven (Verdier 1980: 96). "*Cuijus faciem majestatis nec mater ejus toleraret nisi et rex in signum clementiae virgam auream porrescerit.*" (For his mother would not have sustained the face of his majesty if the king had not extended to her as a sign of his mercy, a golden sceptre/rod.)

As Isaac de Stella had linked Esther to the woman who climbs from the desert of the *Song of Songs*, so later the author of the *Golden Legend*, Jacobus da Voragine (d. 1298), made the heavenly reception of the Virgin analogous to that of the Shulamite Bride of the *Song of Songs*. In the *Golden Legend*, the author gives to Christ a similar invocation to that of Solomon as he calls to himself his mother's soul, so bringing alive her body from the tomb (Jacobus 1969: 451).

> "Come from Libanus, my spouse, come from Libanus. Come: thou shalt be crowned!" and she responded "Behold, I come, for in the head of the book it is written of me that I should do Thy will, O my God; for my spirit hath rejoiced in God my Saviour ... ." "Come my chosen one, and I shall place thee upon my throne for I have desired thy beauty!" and she answered, "My heart is ready, O Lord, my heart is ready!"

This imagery of the *Song of Songs* is evident in early thirteenth century French tympana, possibly following the German precedent, although in England in a niche sculpture above the central door of Wells Cathedral, soon after 1220, there is a Coronation in which Christ himself crowns his mother. Verdier notes that in the tympana of Mouzon (before 1231) and Moutiers-Saint-Jean, after 1250, as at Villeneuve l'Archevêque of c. 1240, the Virgin similarly receives her crown from Christ.

In her study of the Pesaro altarpiece of Giovanni Bellini, Carolyn Wilson explored the development and significance of Coronation iconography, and made reference to French and German miniatures as early as 1200 which showed Christ holding the crown on the Virgin's head with his right hand (Wilson 1977: 34, n. 2). It seems likely that the small format of the miniature enforced the compression of the imagery, resulting in a new symbol, incorporating the joint enthronement and the crowning. This active version would become more explicit as it was elaborated in large-scale relief sculpture or facade and apse decoration. If one turns to look, therefore, at the evidence from Italy, one might expect to see the imagery of active crowning following a parallel course, especially if the Franciscans can be held responsible for the spread of this imagery in the course of the thirteenth century.[3]

It should be noted that the popularity of the theme of Mary as Queen of Heaven in Franciscan thought was expressed in the poetry of Jacopone, in particular the dramatic laude, *Donna del Paradiso* (Van Os 1970: 671-6), and by the addition of the older hymns of the *Salve Regina* and the *Regina Coeli* to the service of Compline.

Franciscan evidence would offer a precedent for an active Coronation in the Upper Church of St Francis in the 1280s. This scene, if examined in the nineteenth century drawing by Ramboux, reveals a joint enthronement, not a crowning (Nelson 1985: 562, fig. 23). Mary, following Bonaventure, is however seated on Christ's right surrounded by a Heavenly host. This much damaged fresco, attributed to Cimabue, may have a bearing on the setting of the rose window in the Cathedral of Sienna, dated 1285-7, usually attributed to Duccio, but possibly by Cimabue himself. The common feature is a high backed, low benched throne. However the artist of the Siennese design has represented Christ as turning inward towards her, holding the crown on her head with both hands, a position which becomes typical in subsequent Tuscan examples. Adoring angels flank this cosmati-work throne, while Evangelist symbols occupy the side compartments of the stained glass roundel. These latter features also occur in a mosaic, ascribed to Gaddo Gaddi, on the interior facade of the Cathedral of Florence above the entrance door. This lunette dated around 1300, introduces Christ's double gesture of blessing with his right hand and crowning. He holds the crown on Mary's head with the left hand, while the Virgin bends forward submissively, thus following the shape of the lunette.

The motif of Christ's hand on the crown may have its origin in the great apse mosaic of c. 1296 in St. Maria Maggiore in Rome, by Jacopo Torriti (Figure 4).

Figure 4

Coronation. Mosaic of the Apse of Santa Maria Maggiore, Rome, by Torriti.

This decoration was ordered by the Franciscan Pope; Nicholas IV (1288-92); consequently one might expect the iconography to conform to Franciscan types, in particular the elaborate throne, which provides a setting for the figures, which suggests the architectural evocation of the palace of Heaven. Below this throne, and within an aureole of blue and green concentric circles ornamented with gold stars, hang the signs for the sun and moon. Christ, himself uncrowned according to Byzantine tradition, crowns his mother. The Virgin's crown is an elaborate diadem of imperial origin, though she herself is more youthful and delicate in feature than the prototype of the Cavallini mosaic (Lawrence 1924-5: 157).

The cosmic force of the imagery surrounding the enthroned couple lifts the event outside time, for the aureole rises into the vault of the apse above a cluster of angels as into the celestial spheres. The vault of heaven is the backdrop to many subsequent representations of the Coronation, for this Triumph of the Virgin necessarily has to be set in heaven. This heavenly locale acts as the magnetic source for the assumption, the liturgical theme with which the mosaic is explicitly linked.

Running along the edge of the curve of the apse, above the wavy waters of Jordan, are inscriptions from the antiphons for the Office of the assumption; and the association with the assumption liturgy and the *Song of Songs* is made explicit by the text on Christ's open book: "*Veni electa mea et ponam in te thronum meum.*" (Come my chosen one and I will set thee on my throne.) This type of coronation conforms to the imagery of Bonaventure (cf. Bonaventure, trans. Brady 1978: 167), who measured the extent of the radiance of Mary's triumph by examples of the sun and moon: "When the light of the moon will be like the light of the sun and the light of the sun will be seven times greater like the light of seven days." (*Lignum Vitae*) The sermons of Bonaventure, especially his third sermon on the Assumption (Bonaventure 1901: 694-5), describe Mary's integral assumption in body and spirit and her royal place in the heavenly city. In particular, he discusses Mary's enthronement on Christ's right. Moreover, the final chapter of Bonaventure's *Lignum Vitae*, a treatise on the Tree of Life, describes the heavenly state of the Blessed, in which Mary and Christ jointly govern the Heavenly Paradise. Verse 44 describes Jesus as the adorned spouse. This imagery of the Sponsus is linked to that of Ahasuerus by Bonaventure in his fourth sermon on the assumption, in which he discusses the triumph of Esther and Mordecai's dream.

> *Fons parvus crevit in fluvium maximum et in solem lucemque conversus est et in aquas plurimas redundavit. Esther est quam rex accepit uxorem et voluit esse reginam.* (A little fountain became a river and there was light, and the sun, and much water. This river is Esther, whom the king married and made queen.)

The river of the waters of life was applied in the *Song of Songs* to the Virgin herself (*Song of Songs* 4.15): "A fountain of gardens, a well of living waters, and streams from Lebanon." The river imagery is continued in *Esther* 22.1: "*Fons hortorum, puteus aquarum viventium quae fluerunt impetu de Libano.*" (The fountain of the gardens, the well of living waters which flow directly from Lebanon.)

In the Torriti mosaic, the river of life flows under the feet of the apostles, the angelic choirs and the ring of heaven itself, decked with bird life and bathing figures. This river refers also to that of the *Book of Revelation*, as the river which rushed forth from the throne of God and the

Lamb. The river "*splendidus tamquam crystallus*" (gleaming as if of crystal), was a symbol of Christ. In the grand cosmic setting of the Torriti mosaic, several themes are drawn together, Virgin Queen, Gate of Paradise and the Apocalyptic visions of the Heavenly Jerusalem.

It is likely that there were thirteenth century adaptations of the active Coronation in small devotional panels, as the Coronation was a particularly suitable subject for altar decoration, reinforcing the idea of Mary's participation in the triumph of the Church, to link the earthly realm to the divine, as did the celebration of the Eucharist on the altar itself. An early representation has been found in the work of Guido da Siena from the 1270s (Coor-Achenbach 1957: 328). In Guido's painting, Christ crowns the Virgin with his left hand, while holding an open book on his knee. The Virgin, unusually, is turned outwards with upturned open palms in the manner of an *orans*. This active Coronation is closely analogous to Torriti's crowning scene (Figure 4), in the shape of the crown and the inscription, similarly taken from the office of the Feast of the Assumption.

Developments in the first half of the Trecento suggest that artists found this formula difficult to adapt to a more naturalistic mode of vision; one solution was to avoid the awkward gesture of Christ's arm crossing over his body in the act of crowning, by turning him slightly in space, to suggest a three-dimensional throne and by implication a physical setting for the event itself, despite its heavenly nature. It seems possible that the changes effected by Giotto in the treatment of religious themes were extended to the subject of the Coronation of the Virgin. The rediscovery of pictorial space meant that the Coronation could take place within an area of described recession, such as a raised platform, on which the throne was set, as a solid volume slanting back into space. In the Coronation of the Virgin in S. Croce, Florence, by the Master of the Stefaneschi altarpiece, this raised platform is approached by a marble step before which four angels kneel, looking up, as Christ lays the crown on the Virgin's head with both hands. This polyptych in the Baroncelli Chapel, of that church, displays two features common to Trecento Coronations, namely the raised dais and the intricate Gothic ornamentation of the Throne, which is pedimental in shape and decorated with crochets. Witnesses to the scene are assembled in the side panels on the level of the angels, sharing the same floor. The sense of space created by the sharp recession of the seat of the high backed throne, allows the artist to set the Virgin into the throne on a diagonal axis. Thus her body can be made to incline submissively towards Christ who seems seated just a little farther back. The awkwardness formerly created by Christ's raised left hand in the act of crowning is avoided. This artist has raised the right arm in a parallel gesture, so that the two arms overlap. There is a movement in space, created by the inclination inwards, and reinforced by the conviction of the figures as solid volumes, their limbs thrusting through the draperies across their knees. The physical presence of the coronation does not, of course, change the celestial nature of the event which is indicated by the ecclesiastical architecture of the throne, establishing the setting as that of the Court of Heaven. The throne may acquire renewed symbolic force as the physical conviction of the scene increases.

A small panel by Vitale da Bologna, now in the Pinacoteca, Bologna (Figure 5), illustrates perfectly the minimum requirements for a coronation in a single panel, which restricts the spatial ambience, offered in the polyptych by the lateral panels.

Figure 5

Coronation. Pinacoteca, Bologna, by Vitale da Bologna.

Here again, the emphasis is on the joint throne, set back into depth, ornamented with architectural mouldings and panels, and overhung by an elaborate cloth of honour which falls behind and under the figures, thus isolating them. The heavily patterned cloth across the seat of the throne, renders redundant the usual Byzantine-type cushion which is now relegated to the floor as a footstool on which the figures rest their feet. A clearly articulated step separates the throne base from the floor and this is further decorated by panelled inlay. Adoring angels, now badly damaged, are squeezed in at the top of either side of the throne back. Christ crowns his mother with both hands in the manner of the Baroncelli polyptych. Vitale's painting is of particular interest as he presents Christ beardless and dressed in white as the bridegroom, the Sponsus of the *Song of Songs.* Christ himself is crowned and lays a crown, now lost, on his mother's inclined head. Mary's submissive gesture and her size make it easier to perform this action, as her head is lower than Christ's, at a level with Christ's hands. This lyrical little panel may be dated 1353, and suggests the more humane approach to divinity made popular by Giotto, with the accompanying formal changes in the attempt to suggest real space.

The spatial setting indicating a platform before the throne is more pronounced in a tiny coronation by Turone, now in the Museo di Castelvecchio in Verona (Plate VI). This is a fascinating panel, echoing the rounded forms and dignified behaviour of Giotto's figures, and in the delicacy and poetic vision of the angel musicians, looking forward to Fra Angelico. In this case the ecclesiastic character of the throne is quite pronounced and parallels the shape of the panel itself. A similar relationship between the throne and the tabernacle of the frame may be seen in the fifteenth century example of the Pesaro altarpiece by Giovanni Bellini who has reworked the Gothic frame into an "Albertian" Renaissance scheme. Again, Christ leans forward to crown his mother, but in the Turone example the Virgin has been removed from the throne itself to a kneeling position at Christ's feet. The sense of volume in the figures is so pronounced that it is possible for Christ to lean forward and lay the crown on her head. This must be one of the earliest instances of a kneeling Virgin, dated around 1360. This kneeling position may reflect contemporary emphasis on humility as indicated by Millard Meiss (1951: 150, n. 75). While a logical development of the idea of the submission of the Virgin to receive her crown, the kneeling position may also be associated with the visions of St Bridget of Sweden (d. 1373), a member of the Franciscan Tertiaries. Her vision of the Virgin kneeling in adoration before her newly born child was extremely influential in nativity scenes. This obeisance at the birth of her son could be seen as prefiguring her submission before him at her coronation. The Turone panel associates the Coronation with the Trinity, an iconography relatively common in the Venetian school. The importance of the Trinity in the Turone polyptych, of which this panel constitutes a pinnacle scene, can be linked to sermons of Nicolas of Clairvaux in 1176. Moreover, a hymn composed by Innocent III for the Assumption grants to God the Father the role of presenting the crown and gold sceptre to Mary (Verdier 1980: 104, n. 117). In this variant the image of God the Father is to be interpreted as a Trinity image, represented by the iconography of the "mercy seat" or "Throne of Grace". In such representations, God is seated on his throne in a receptive pose to await his crucified Son. This "mercy seat" type would be appropriate to the imagery of *Psalm* 44, especially that of the Queen at the throne (44.2): "Thou art fairer than the children of men; grace is poured into thy lips: therefore God hath blessed thee for ever."

The move towards more immediate experience was halted after the middle of the fourteenth century. A new composition, more reminiscent of the Torriti mosaic, appeared. This form stressed the visionary, supernatural character of the coronation as opposed to the more humane and rational understanding of the early years of the century. Millard Meiss suggested that the re-emphasis of the celestial location was associated with the wave of penitence and fear of judgement following the waves of the Black Death. According to Meiss (1951: 27), in such an atmosphere the Church asserted its doctrinal authority and this ritualistic mood was reflected in art.

> The ritualistic character of paintings of sacred history in the third quarter of the fourteenth century is bound up with an expression of the authority of the enduring Church.

Such a character would have been indicated by the dominance of the figures of Christ and the Virgin, set well above the adoring angels, either in the air or at the top of steps, to emphasise the lowliness of the attendants who would be compressed against the picture plane. Such an environment is clearly supernatural for even if the figures of Christ and the Virgin are still set on the shallow space of the throne platform, they now tower above the other figures. Space is reduced to a shallow passage between forms. The drapery of the throne would become more resplendent as would be the garments of both figures. The remoteness of such a type of late Trecento group is suggested in the panel in the National Gallery, London, ascribed to Agnolo Gaddi. Dating from the 1370s the Gaddi Coronation emphasises the heavenly remoteness of the scene, which occupies the upper half of the picture field with any accompanying figures arranged below. The throne in some representations even gives way to the cloth of honour alone, or to the purely symbolic celestial circle used by Venetian masters.

It was left to the fifteenth century to evolve an image which would assert the heavenly setting, yet render it convincing in terms of human perceptions. Visionary, yet actual, remote yet accessible — these dualities are always present in the evolution of the Coronation iconography, as they are in the imagery of Mary herself.

Two possibilities of development seemed to offer themselves. The first responded to the renewed naturalistic outlook at the beginning of the fifteenth century, which was based on the achievement of the early fourteenth century and such spatial concerns as were evident in the Turone panel and Baroncelli chapel examples. This can be demonstrated by the Coronation of Lorenzo Monaco, now in the National Gallery in London.

Figure 6

Coronation by Lorenzo Monaco. National Gallery, London.

Here, the great throne is set on a marble tiled floor, whose pattern emphasises the spatial recession to the base of the throne, towards which two ranks of attendant saints converge on either side. Before the throne steps, the choir of angels kneel in a half circle describing clearly an area before the heavenly throne for the worshipper. As in the Senlis tympanum example (Figure 1), two angels swing censers. Despite the triptych format this floor extends across the three panels, establishing a unified ground plane for the figures. This work may have been for the Camaldolese Monastery of Saint Benedetto fuori della Porta a Pinti, outside Florence. The second possibility, which acknowledges the new realism of the Renaissance, uses it in the service of the vision of the Heavenly Jerusalem itself, enforcing the credibility of the celestial event by the credibility of its setting even if in the sky. A similar painting to the London Coronation also by Monaco reflects this second type. This is the Uffizi Coronation of 1414, where the supernatural iconic look of the late Trecento panels is already softened. Here the tiled floor is replaced by arched bands of graded blue studded with gold stars, like a cosmic rainbow. The members of the Heavenly Court rise in rows around the Coronation, suggestive of the infinite space of the Empyrean. This court, described in the *Golden Legend*, follows the description of Gregory the Great in his Homilies on the Gospel (Jacobus 1969: 457): "With joy the heavens have taken up the Blessed Virgin this date, the Angels rejoicing, the Archangels jubilating, the Thrones exalting, the Dominations psalming, the Principalities making harmony, the Powers playing upon the harp, the Cherubim and Seraphim hymning and leading her to the supernal throne of the divine majesty." The rows recall the hierarchies of angels described by Dionysius the Areopagite, relating the nine orders of angels to the nine spheres of the geometric model of the universe. In the Uffizi painting, there is a foursided domed baldachin, an allusion to the palace of heaven as the new Jerusalem (Wilson 1977: 69, n. 2). In both the Uffizi panel and the London version Monaco has clothed the Virgin in radiant white, as the Bride of the *Song of Songs*. As the Uffizi painting was the high-altarpiece of the Camaldolese Church of S. Maria degli Angeli in Florence, the more celestial type was preferable, emphasising the cosmological significance of the event, in the Torriti tradition (Figure 4). On the other hand, a more private and personal altarpiece, as for a monastic setting, might favour the more immediate ground setting of the London type (Figure 6). As artists rationalised the effects of three-dimensional pictorial space, so their opportunities widened. The world of the invisible could be rendered as convincingly as the world of everyday perception, without thereby losing its sacred character.

The most breathtaking illusion created by this rational spatial organisation is Masaccio's Trinity (1426-7) in S. Maria Novella. The power of Renaissance perspective to lock the beholder's gaze both enforced the meditation on the idea behind the image and ensured its conviction as a palpable reality. The complex doctrine of the Trinity is explicitly linked by means of two interlocking perspective schemes to its role in Redemption. The fresco is to be read vertically, from tomb, through the donors, by means of the intercessors, the Virgin and St John, through the Crucified Christ to the redeeming arms of God the Father, whose searing gaze seeks out the spectator standing in the aisle and forces him to turn to engage with the perspective plan. Thus a liberation of formal means allows for an extension of meaning: as with the Trinity image, so in the Coronation images of the new century, there could be presumed to be a relationship between artistic representations and ideas formulated by theologians.

One of the Florentine artists of the Quattrocento most likely to be responsive to renewed doctrine and the inherited visual traditions is Fra Angelico, a Dominican Observant working in the Cloister of San Marco. He uses the new spatial discoveries of his day, now codified by the writings of Alberti, in 1435, to serve both settings for the Coronation which had been indicated by Lorenzo Monaco.

In the Coronation of the Virgin, now in the Uffizi, painted 1434-5, Fra Angelico has done away with Monaco's schematic arcs of tinted blue. Instead he offers fluffy clouds which hang suspended in the golden air, gleaming on their inner edges from the light of the central vision.

**Figure 7**

Coronation by Fra Angelico. Uffizi, Florence.

The theophany is clearly lifted to the ethereal realm. The Virgin now seated as co-redemptrix is crowned by Christ above a cloud-bank of angel heads. It is as if the heavens have opened in a blaze of burning light to reveal the circles of the Blessed, miraculously supported on tiny puffs of cloud against the gilded Empyrean. Again, the device of rounded, volumetric form is applied to the design, making it possible to see circles of space, lunging in concentric rings, inwards to the heavenly vision (Meiss 1963: 140). Towards this beatitude, the worshipper is drawn by the space left in the ranks of the blessed and indicated by the penitent Magdalen. Once this position is taken up, the worshipper must logically be absorbed in that burst of refulgent gold paint, streaming from the Coronation itself.

The visionary aspect is rendered in the frescoed cell in the Convent of San Marco, where the medium encourages luminous colour and whiteness to replace the gold of the Uffizi type, but in his Louvre Coronation of the Virgin dated after 1450 (Figure 8) Angelico set the scene on a physical base with an entirely architectural setting.

Figure 8

Coronation by Fra Angelico. Louvre, Paris.

A squared floor recedes to the base of the steps of the throne. On this kneel the adoring Saints, identifiable by their attributes and leaving space for the worshipper between their ranks in the centre along the main orthogonal. From this zone of palpable substances, the viewer is forced to shift his ground to a higher plane, described by a second perspective scheme culminating in the head of the kneeling Virgin, whose position helps to define the spatial pyramid described by the forms. Angelico has also reintroduced the more natural seeming pose of a Virgin who kneels to receive her crown. The synthronos type, while well suited to didactic non rational images, was an awkward form to render more humanly. The best that could be done, without removing her from the common throne, was to make her incline awkwardly before the blessing Christ. Here she kneels and her kneeling posture is appropriate to the ritual of divine blessing as enacted in Church ceremonial such as the consecration of a nun (Warner

1978: 128). Nine zones of the Heavenly Powers are indicated and the throne itself is canopied and decorated in the traditional ecclesiastical manner, with the gold-threaded backcloth and the rolled cushion of the Byzantine tradition.

It should be noted that iconographic invention and formal invention go hand in hand. Iconography can never be divorced from stylistic possibility. Pope-Hennessy stresses in his monograph on Fra Angelico (1974: 34-5) that the formal solution to the isolation of the crowning group by setting them in a heavenly radiance was not possible in the artistic climate of 1450.

The twin possibilities of the ground plan and the ethereal types develop quickly, possibly with the renewed enthusiasm for the theme in the second half of the fifteenth century. Marina Warner suggested that encouragement for the veneration of the Virgin increased in times when the Church was confident and self assertive. With the restoration of Martin V after the period of the Councils, the Papacy was set on its task of re-establishment and entrenchment both spiritually and politically. When Sixtus IV, a Franciscan, came to the papal throne, the veneration of the Virgin reached new heights by his formal institution in 1476 of an Office and Mass for the Feast of the Immaculate Conception. As the doctrinal arguments concerning the latter increased, so the image of the Coronation became widespread. In some cases, the Coronation was used as a symbol for the new doctrine itself. In the face of such controversy regarding the moment of Mary's sanctification and its import, the earlier iconography of the Coronation, in stressing the nuptial element in the glorification ritual, might have seemed confusing. The theogamy of mother and son might have become awkward in the light of the new emphasis on Mary's unique role among womankind. The Sponsa imagery is now superseded by that of the image of the Daughter of God. Mary is crowned by God the Father, in his role as the Trinity itself, identifiable by the prominence of his pointed tiara inset within three coronets.

The substitution of God the Father, perhaps emphasising the idea of Mary's origin in God, occurs in the large tripartite Coronation in the Uffizi by Fra Filippo Lippi (Plate VII). The link with Immaculist belief is underlined by the setting of the *Hortus Conclusus*, the closed garden. As a token of her absolute virginity the garden, sealed by a door or gate, often encircled by a palisade, was a favourite symbol of the Virgin. St Bernard had likened her to a garden of delight (Hirn 1912: 449): "*Hortus deliciarum. Nobis est sacratissimus tuis uterus, O Maria.*" (A pleasure garden for us is thy most holy womb, O Mary.)

In the 1447 Coronation, Lippi reveals the flowery shrubs of this garden ringing round the court of Heaven. The Virgin turns inward to receive the crown from the Trinity figure of God the Father, the ends of whose stole are borne by angels. Angels in the assembled company wear wreaths of red and white roses, symbols of the rosary, and bear Easter lilies as attributes of the Virgin. Mary herself kneels to receive her crown as a nun takes the veil. In an ancient form of the ritual the nun was crowned with a garland. The celebrant's words keep alive the symbolism of the Bride (Warner 1978: 128): "Receive this sign of Christ on your head, that you may be his wife, and if you remain in that state, be crowned for all eternity."

On the other hand Fra Filippo Lippi's great Apse Fresco (Figure 9) in the Cathedral of Spoleto, 1468, is perhaps the most magnificent spectacle of the heavenly Coronation.

Figure 9

Coronation by Fra Filippo Lippi. Apse Fresco, Cathedral, Spoleto.

The Virgin, resplendent in rich robes, kneels low before the patriarchal figure of God the Father. From her, curving tongues of light radiate outward within the rings of the halo like the aureole which encircles the Coronation. This vision is suspended in the great vault of heaven above a landscape of low hills. In the Empyrean hang the sun and moon. The host of heaven adore on great arcs of cloud above the rim of the half apse. This shift to a crown laid on the Virgin by God the Father, enthroned as the Trinity, instead of Christ, may indicate the change of emphasis in the Coronation itself. Now the Virgin's mystical union with Christ, and her early association with Ecclesia, have been overtaken by the idea of her unique election as part of God's plan before the creation, in his work of redemption. The new focus on Mary, veiled yet in royal robes, associates the moment of her Glorification with her unique conception, an article of belief which was vigorously debated in the second half of the fifteenth century. The focus on the Trinitarian aspect of God the Father designates this special role accorded to her from the Beginning. The *Golden Legend* recorded how Gregory in his Homilies stressed her welcome by the Trinity itself: "The most ineffable Trinity Itself applauds her with unceasing dance, and since Its grace flows wholly into her, makes all to wait upon her."

The ceremonial of Coronation imagery therefore appears to reflect the new procedure of the Renaissance painters — namely to visualise the scene as it might have appeared to earthly sight. Associations derived from traditional symbolism are married to those connected with the actual rituals of Church ceremonial, of consecration and religious festival. Once the artists mastered the techniques of depicting figures set on a circular ground plan, then it was possible to represent crowds convincingly, reinforcing by their position the idea of celestial hierarchies. Coronation iconography must also have borrowed motifs from sacred representations held as spectacles in churches to celebrate a particular feast. These *rapprasentazione* were often quite elaborate affairs, operating with complicated machinery which involved lowering and raising actors on tiny platforms. Illuminated candles, rolling cloud banks, the starry heavens, even the hand of God could be seen to move across the setting. Carefully made crowns, even the tiara of God the Father, may have been treasured stage-props. It is also likely that the Coronation imagery in Northern Europe was affected by royal ceremonial itself. The portal at La Ferte Milon introduces the image of angel attendants carrying the train of the Madonna. In fact Marina Warner (1978: 115) has pointed out how much the royal image of Mary depends on the court ceremonial of the late Middle Ages.

There appear to be two difficulties, however, facing artists in treating this theme, namely the ambiguity of the Virgin's coronation by the Father rather than the Son and the increasingly rational portrayal of a visionary spectacle. The first difficulty is resolved by the Trinitarian coronation being made more explicit. The three persons are represented by the separate forms of God the Father, the Dove, and Christ, rather than by the single representation of God wearing the Triple Tiara, and seated on his throne. Such a Trinitarian type is that of Gentile da Fabriano's Coronation c. 1400, now in the Brera, Milan, a painting originally from the Franciscan Convent at Valle. In this representation, the seated figures of Christ and the Virgin are topped by a frontal image of God the Father, who encloses their heads with out-reaching arms. Between them hovers the dove. This type of Coronation is common in Venetian altarpieces, from where it seems to take root in Northern Italy in the first half of the fifteenth century. The solution of the second difficulty was to reduce the Coronation scheme to its essential components, then to suspend such elements in the air, above the heads of the earth-bound figures. In this scheme, the visionary abstract nature of the Coronation is made apparent, while at the same time the concrete quality of the representation is left unimpaired.

## The Coronation as an Abstract Theme for Debate

The rationalism of Renaissance imagery may have forced a split in the means of representation, such as to reject any portrayal suggestive of a physical happening in favour of a symbolic usage. The change in portrayal may also be linked to developments in the ecclesiastical allegory itself, as more attention came to be paid to the concept of Mary's priesthood by her participation in Christ's sacrifice. On offering Christ in the temple, Mary was seen to have understood the sacrificial function of that presentation, as of course did Simeon, the high-priest (*Luke* 2.22): "And when the days of her purification according to the law of Moses were accomplished, they brought him to Jerusalem to present him to the Lord." This function was further underlined by her own passion at the foot of the cross. As a co-sacrificer with Christ, so she was seen as celebrant of the mass, the link between the Church on Earth and that in Heaven. This role occasioned much debate. The theme of the Pieta, or an image of the risen Christ, came to be associated with Coronation scenes.

The narrative version of the Coronation amidst a heavenly court not only had failed to establish the abstract nature of what was being portrayed but had begun to look old-fashioned. In keeping with the evolution of Marian symbols in general by the end of the Quattrocento, the symbol of the Coronation was suspended above the earth in such a way as to emphasise both its central importance and its mystical nature. The first stage in this visionary development was to adapt the iconography to the compositional type of the Virgin in Glory. The next was to present it as topic for debate. In the latter type, the symbolic crowning influences the saints who appear below on the earth, stimulating them to argument. From passive witnesses to the truth of Mary's glorification, they become active disputants, testifying for the Church. This type of arrangement originating late in the fifteenth century is called a disputa type. The scheme lent itself to different theological themes as these came under discussion.

Such a visionary type is Botticelli's Coronation now in the Uffizi, dated about 1491 (Figure 10). The upper half of the panel presents the Coronation in a radiance of light, ringed by cherubim and dancing angels treading air. In this instance, the Virgin is crowned by God the Father, once again arrayed as the Trinity wearing the Papal tiara, and recalling Fra Filippo Lippi's similar figure at Spoleto (see Figure 9). The radiance of the Coronation scene helps to emphasise the other-worldly, visionary aspect.

Figure 10

Coronation by Botticelli. Uffizi, Florence.

This is emphasised by the explicit references to Dante's vision of the Primum Mobile in the *Divine Comedy*. In his illustration to Canto XXVIII of the *Paradiso*, Botticelli renders the host of tiny heavenly figures in sparkling rings of energy similar to the radiant coronet of rose bearing angels in the Uffizi Coronation, which may be dated 1491, close to the Dante drawings themselves (Clark 1976: 24).

From choir to choir their hymn of praise rang free
to the Fixed Point that holds them in fixed place,
as ever was, as evermore shall be.    (Canto XXVIII, trans. John Ciardi)

Below, on earth, stand four saints who ponder on, and gesticulate towards, the symbol in the sky above their heads. The sky against which the abstract rings of clouds and angels is set, is, however, the natural sky and those standing below on the ground are clearly earthly witnesses, not celestial worshippers. Indeed, it could be argued that the Coronation is symbolic, a theme for meditation and reflection — not an actual but an internal vision — a theme which unites those figures through time and place.[4] The Coronation is therefore a symbolic device to draw attention to issues of faith, understood by patron, artist and spectator alike. Some kind of challenge is extended out towards the viewer, who is directed by gaze, gesture and eye-catching detail to the significant points. A resolution of 29th April 1490 provided for alms to be given to the Priors of San Marco in return for masses said for the souls of dead members of the Guild of Goldsmiths and its benefactors. The saints in the altarpiece are St John the Evangelist, St Augustine, St Jerome and St Eligius "the patron saint of the Goldsmiths". As is usual, episodes from the saints' lives are depicted in the predella below. The monumental character of Botticelli's altar may be enforced by the didactic theme. The saints are specifically chosen for their contribution to the doctrine of the Virgin. It may be that this painting offers evidence for a new type of altarpiece in which saints are witnesses on earth of, or even champions for, some particular aspect of the Virgin or Christ. This particular type of commission would have demonstrated the patron's own championship of a theological position. With the development of Franciscan preaching and revivalist waves within the Church, theologians and church dignitaries associated with lay patrons to create propaganda for their own point of view. The altarpiece, as the focus of worship, was the obvious vehicle for the transmission of these ideas.

A more explicit version is that attributed to the Luccese Master of the Immaculate Conception in the Pinacoteca of Lucca (Plate VIII). In the Lucca painting, possibly derived from a prototype common to the Botticelli also, the image is suspended centrally above the saints. But here the Trinity image is a composite one. The Virgin is crowned by her Son, while above and between them is the image of God the Father, venerable and holding his attribute of the open book displaying the symbols of Alpha and Omega. The dove hovers below the Father. Christ himself is presented as young and beardless, the bridegroom of the *Song of Songs*. The Virgin is attired in a rich brocade mantle reminiscent of earlier types. The two central Saints are St Elizabeth of Hungary and St Louis, King of France, who were both believed to witness the celestial event. Symeonides comments (1953: 27-9): "By giving them the central positon in the lower row of our Coronation, the master may have wished to note their role as kingly personages witnessing the heavenly crowning." A more exact interpretation would seem to be that these saints bear witness through their lives to their recognition of the significance of Christ's marriage to, and coronation of, his mother. Like the celebrants' invocation to the newly consecrated nun — they too are crowned for all eternity. Though they themselves do not argue, they need not. Their presence itself is a testimony to the truth of the vision, which of course is not actual, but internal.[5]

An interesting tailpiece is the recent discovery of an altarpiece in Faenza, by Jacopo Bertucci (Gibbons 1968: 357-62).

Figure 11

Coronation by Jacopo Bertucci. Pinacoteca, Faenza.

In this elaborate composition, many themes are drawn together with the typical dexterity of "Maniera" painters. The heavenly Coronation is set above arguing saints who point out its significance in a highly emotional manner. The Coronation itself is charged with undirected emotion for the Virgin is crowned by Christ the Son and God the Father, wedged in the point of the diamond formed by their respective cloud banks. The conviction of a grand cosmic drama suggested by the radiant circles of Angelico has gone. In its place is a highly charged argument full of import.[6]

The cosmic nature of the theme is reinforced in the Paradiso designed by Tintoretto for the Ducal Palace in Venice, particularly in his coloured modello for the full-scale composition. This painting establishes the Coronation of the Virgin as part of the limitless heavens in a manner which brings to mind the writing of Thomas of Citeaux (Verdier 1980: 96): "A Virgin descended to earth, ascended to the heavens, a Queen reigns over the angels, She is received by the Son, ... espoused to the air." It also suggests the cosmological model of Dante in his vision of the three circles of the Trinity, with Christ in the reflected circle, as the ultimate perfection of truth in light. Like Dante's vision, the Coronation of the Virgin could be seen as both concrete and yet of cosmological importance. It constituted a reality to those who believed in the theophany. One might see relevance in Anderson's assessment of the Dante vision when applied to the Coronation (Anderson 1983: 404):

> In any case, it was the truth and the experience of ultimate reality in Dante's vision that makes the fundamental truth of the poem independent of any cosmological system he could have chosen to enfold it, and it was the change in his consciousness, brought about by the inner transformation of love and mystical experience, that so altered his perception of the outer world that he could look into the heart of the universe, even in Florence at Easter in the year 1300.

NOTES

1 Such a scenario may reflect actual ceremonial such as the crowning of monarchs.
2 Verdier acknowledges that this figure may represent Ecclesia, whose coronation as bride of Christ reflects Byzantine iconography on coins and ivories of the coronation of the Emperor by Christ.
3 See Echols 1976 for a list of Quattrocento coronations.
4 Such an internal vision must be assumed to be represented by Fra Angelico's Cell Coronation in San Marco.
5 The connection between the empty tomb of the Assumption and the coronation above in Raphael's Oddi Coronation (Vatican Museum, Rome) of c. 1503, may be evidence of a similar integration of the earthly event with its spiritual consequences. To the apostles and the spectator, the spiritual contemplation of the empty tomb affords the internal vision of its triumphant sequel in the coronation — a truth rendered as concrete as the events which precede it.
6 That a quite specific argument is intended in many such altarpieces of the disputa type is demonstrated by the recent publication of documents regarding the contract for a coronation altar in the Musée di Villa Giunigi, Lucca (Archivo di

Stato di Lucca, A.S.L. notari 1230. Ser Pietro Lupardi, ff. 436r-437v; see Tazartes
1987:36).

REFERENCES

D'Ancona, Mirella Levi (1957). *The Iconography of the Immaculate Conception in
the Middle Ages and Early Renaissance.* New York: College Art Association of
America. Monographs on Archaeology and Fine Arts 7.
Anderson, William (1983). *Dante the Maker.* London: Hutchison.
Bonaventure, St (1901). *Opera Omnia* 9. Florence.
─────, trans. Ignatius Brady (1978). *The Tree of Life.* New York.
Clark, Sir Kenneth (1976). *The Drawings by Sandro Botticelli for Dante's Divine
Comedy.* London: Thames and Hudson.
Coor-Achenbach, Gertrude (1957). The Earliest Italian Representation of the
Coronation of the Virgin. *Burlington Magazine* 99, 328-31.
Echols, Mary Tuck (1976). The Coronation of the Virgin in 15th Century Italian
Art. Ph.D. thesis, University of Virginia.
Gibbons, Felton (1968). Jacopo Bertucci of Faenza. *Art Bulletin* 50, 357-62.
Hirn, Yrjo (1912). *The Sacred Shrine.* London: Macmillan.
Jacobus da Voragine (1969). *The Golden Legend.* New York: Arno Press.
Katzenellenbogen, Adolf (1963). *Iconographic Novelties and Transformations in
the Sculpture of French Church Facades c. 1160-1190. Studies in Western Art, I,
Romanesque and Gothic Art.* Princeton, N.J.: Princeton University Press.
Lawrence, Marion (1924-5). Maria Regina. *Art Bulletin* 7, 150-61.
Mâle, Emile (1966). *L'art religieux du XII siècle en France.* Paris.
Marchini, Giuseppe (1979). *Fra Filippo Lippi.* Milan.
Meiss, Millard (1951). *Painting in Florence and Siena after the Black Death.* New
York: Harper and Row.
───── (1963). *Masaccio and the Early Renaissance: The Circular Plan. Studies
in Western Art II. Acts of the Twentieth International Congress of the History
of Art.* Princeton, N.J.: Princeton University Press.
───── (1974). *Painting in the time of Jean de Berri: The Limbourgs and their
contemporaries.* New York: Thames and Hudson.
Nelson, Robert S. (1985). A Byzantine Painter in Trecento Genoa: The *Last
Judgment* at S. Lorenzo. *Art Bulletin* 67, 548-66.
Van Os, H.W. (1970). Kronung Mariens. *Lexicon der Christlichen Ikonographie:
Rome, Freiburg, Basel, Vienna.* Vol. 2, OL. 671-6.
Pope-Hennessy, John (1974). *Fra Angelico.* 2nd ed. London: Phaidon Press.
Symeonides, Sibylla (1953). The Lucchese Painter of the Immaculate Conception.
M.A. thesis, New York University, Institute of Fine Arts.
───── (1957-9). An Altarpiece of the Lucchese Master of the Immaculate
Conception. *Marsyas* 8, 55-66.
Tazartes, Maurizia (1987). Nouvelles Perspectives sur la Peinture Lucquoise du
Quattrocento. *Revue de l'Art* 75, 29-36.
Verdier, Philippe (1980). *Le Couronnement de la Vierge. Les origines et les
premiers développements d'un theme iconographique.* Montreal: Publications
de l'Institute d'études mediévales Albert-le-Grand.
Warner, Marina (1978). *Alone of All Her Sex: The Myth and the Cult of the Virgin
Mary.* London: Quartet Books.
Wilson, Carolyn Campbell (1977). Bellini's Pesaro Altarpiece: A Study in Context
and Meaning. Ph.D. thesis, New York University, Institute of Fine Arts.

# DUNBAR'S USE OF THE SYMBOLIC LION AND THISTLE

Priscilla Bawcutt

This paper discusses two well-known Scottish symbols: one of them, the lion, is extremely ancient and widely employed throughout Europe not only in heraldry but in fable and folklore; the other, the thistle, is of comparatively recent origin and is more restricted in currency. I must stress that I am chiefly concerned with their literary use, and even more specifically with some problems arising from their use by William Dunbar in a poem usually entitled *The Thrissill and the Rois*.

Dunbar's poem celebrates the marriage of James IV of Scotland to Margaret Tudor, daughter of Henry VII, an event which took place in Edinburgh on 8 August 1503. On Henry's part the wedding was one of a series of dynastic alliances with other European powers. James IV, for his part, obtained a large dowry from the English king. Both countries, however, hoped that the marriage would end the intermittent warfare and border skirmishes between Scotland and England; as John Leslie, the sixteenth-century Scottish historian, put it: "throuch occasione of this coniunctioun a fast and perpetuall cnott betuein thame mycht be knutt" (Cody and Murison 1888-95: 2.118). Flodden shattered such hopes for a century, but the marriage ultimately led to the Union of the Crowns in 1603. *The Thrissill and the Rois* is a political poem, but it speaks of such matters in a veiled and symbolical way. It is a short poem of under 200 lines written in the allegorical tradition of *Le Roman de la Rose*. The sleeping poet dreams that the personified month of May stands beside his bed and chides him for his "slogardie", exhorting him to compose something in her honour. He ripostes:

> Quhairto, quod I, Sall I uprys at morrow,
> For in this May few birdis herd I sing?[1]                    29-30

Thereupon he is transported into an idealised garden, presided over by dame Nature, who summons an assembly of all beasts, birds and flowers to do her homage. She crowns the Lion as king of beasts, the Eagle as king of fowls, and the Thistle as king of flowers — this is clearly a triple heraldic allusion to James IV. But the climactic position in the poem is given to the Rose, which the Thistle is commanded to honour above all other flowers. Earlier the dreamer had been instructed, somewhat ambivalently, to "discryve the Ros of most plesance" (35). Now the political symbolism becomes clear: it is the "Rois both reid and quhyt ... of michty cullouris

twane" (171-2) that Dunbar celebrates, i.e. the Tudor Rose, in the person
of a thirteen-year-old princess. The poem ends with flowers acknowledging
the Rose's sovereignty, and birds greeting her:

> Welcome to be our princes of honour,
> Our perle, our plesans and our paramour.          179-80

(There is probably a pun on "perle" = Latin *"margarita"*.) The symbolism
has affinities with that of the civic pageant that was arranged for Henry VII
on his visit to York in 1486. It was then devised that a red rose and a white
should appear, "unto whome so being togedre all other floures shall lowte
and evidentlie yeve suffrantie" (see Anglo 1969: 24). Dunbar's poem is
both a greeting to the princess and a compliment to the Tudors.


## I

The Lion is given prominence in the poem (five stanzas, compared to one
for the Eagle), and his description corresponds unmistakably to that of the
lion in the Scottish royal arms:

> Reid of his cullour as is the ruby glance:
> On feild of gold he stude full mychtely
> With flour delycis sirculit lustely.
> . . . . . . . . . . . . . . . . . . . . . . . . .
> All kynd of beistis in to thair degre
> At onis cryit lawd, Vive le roy,
> And till his feit fell with humilitie;
> And all thay maid him homege and fewte,
> And he did thame ressaif with princely laitis,
> Quhois noble yre is *parcere prostratis*.          96-8, 114-9

But I must register dissatisfaction with the usual explanation of line 119 in
this account:

> Quhois noble yre is *parcere prostratis*.

Several distinguished scholars have briefly discussed this line and a closely
related passage in one of Henryson's *Fables*, where the Lion tells a
parliament of beasts:

> I lat yow wit, my micht is merciabill,
> And steiris nane that ar to me prostrait.          929-30

All essentially concur with James Kinsley's note: "Dunbar is quoting,
rather clumsily, part of a motto associated with the armorial bearings of the
kings of Scots, *'parcere prostratis scit nobilis ira leonis'*. ... The motto is

derived from Pliny, *Nat. Hist.* VIII.19, '*Leoni tantum, ex feris clementia in supplices; prostratis parcit*.' Of the lines in Henryson John MacQueen says: "he is adapting the motto of the kings of Scotland", and Denton Fox: "A reference to ... the motto attached to the royal arms of Scotland". Kinsley's note can be traced back to earlier editors of *The Thrissill and the Rois*, such as Mackay Mackenzie and G.G. Smith.[2]

My disquiet springs from the sheer absence of documentation; none of these scholars provides any supporting evidence, none refers us to heraldic treatises or to depictions of the royal arms of Scotland, whether in carvings, sculptures, or paintings. I have not myself encountered this particular saying "attached to" or "associated with" depictions of the royal arms; nor is any such motto mentioned by Charles Burnett in a recent paper on "The Development of the Royal Arms to 1603" (Burnett 1978). I must therefore respectfully disagree with Kinsley in four particulars: Dunbar's line is not strictly a motto; nor is it regularly linked with the royal arms of Scotland; Pliny may be the ultimate, but is not the immediate, source; and I consider Dunbar's use elegant rather than clumsy.

What then is Dunbar's source? Today we are most keenly aware of the lion as a type of courage or ferocity. But the idea that the lion was a beast of great nobility, that it would spare those who prostrated themselves before it is very ancient. It occurs not only in Pliny but in Ovid's *Tristia* (III.v), and also in Martial, one of whose Epigrams tells of a lion who astonishingly learnt clemency from its master, the Emperor Domitian (I.xiv). The idea is also enshrined in medieval bestiary lore, and charmingly illustrated in one twelfth-century Latin prose bestiary, which shows three prostrate men lying in front of an open-mouthed lion. (This is reproduced on the end-papers of T.H. White's *Book of Beasts*.) The general idea was thus well-known in the later medieval period; it is the formulation that is interesting here. Dunbar is half-paraphrasing, half-quoting the first line of a popular Latin distich, one so widely known that it is included in Hans Walther's great collection of medieval Latin proverbs and sententiae:

> *Parcere prostratis scit nobilis ira leonis:*
> *Tu quoque fac simile, quisquis dominaris in orbe!*[3]

> [The noble wrath of the lion knows how to spare those who are prostrate before him; do likewise, each of you who will reign in the world.]

Although Dunbar renders the first line only, I suspect that we are intended to recall the second line as well. (Compare the modern practice of briefly alluding to proverbs or quotations too well-known to give in full: "Too many cooks ...", or "Fools rush in ...".) It is impossible to say precisely where Dunbar came across this saying. In a truncated form it occurs in the Scottish writer, John Ireland; he too says that mercy is "ganand to a lord or prince", and attributes the saying to "arestotill and philosophouris". The twelfth-century chronicler, Ordericus Vitalis, who quotes the lines in full, attributes them to a wise poet (*sagax poeta*), who wrote "the book of the Wonders of the World" (*in libello de mirabilibus mundi*). This late eleventh-century poem still survives, and the lines comprise verses 104-5. Some modern scholars consider it the work of Thierry de Saint-Trond (died 1107), but in the Middle Ages it was attributed to Ovid.[4] Just possibly Dunbar may have thought that he was quoting from Ovid, but it is more likely that he regarded the lines as a sententious maxim, unattached to any great name.

How does Dunbar's employment of this maxim compare with that of other writers? Alexander Neckam puts it to pious use: the lion is a type of God, who levels the proud, but spares the humble (Wright 1863: 228). More often the maxim has a secular application, as the phrase *in orbe* would suggest. The Archpoet concludes his famous *Confessio* with a supplication to his lord, the Archbishop of Cologne — "*fac misericordiam veniam petenti* [have pity on him who seeks pardon]" — and a witty variation on the theme (Watenphul and Krefeld 1958: 76):

> *Parcit enim subditis leo rex ferarum*
> *et est ergo subditos immemor irarum*
> *et vos idem facite, principes terrarum.*[4]

[The lion, the king of beasts, spares his subjects and forgets his wrath towards those who are under him. Do ye the same, ye princes of the earth.]

Ordericus Vitalis quotes the maxim in his account of a rebellion during the reign of William Rufus. After the rebel-lords have surrendered they beg for mercy, but the king is filled with anger (*iratus*). But his counsellors plead on behalf of the rebels:

> It is most proper that, just as you conquered them in their pride and folly by your strength, you should by your graciousness spare them now that they are humbled and penitent. Temper your royal rigour with mercy ... (VIII.2; Chibnall 1973: 4.130-1).

It is a sign of the king's magnanimity that he is finally persuaded. Closer to Dunbar's time is George Cavendish's *The Life and Death of Cardinal Wolsey* (1558). Cavendish describes how, after his disgrace, Wolsey thanks the Duke of Norfolk for the generous treatment of himself and his household servants (Sylvester 1959: 115):

> And evyn as ye haue abated my glory & highe estate and brought it full lowe / so haue ye extendyd yor honorable fauour most charitably vnto me beyng prostrate byfore ye / forsothe sir ye do Right well deserue to bere in yor armez the noble & gentill lion / whos naturall Inclinacion is that whan he hathe

vanqiesshed Any best ... than wyll he shewe most clemency vnto his
vanquysht & do hyme no more harme ... therefore these verses may be
Ascribed to yor lordshyppe / ... *Parcere prostratis / scit nobilis Ira leonis / Tu
quoque fac Simile / quisquis regnabis in orbem.*

My last illustration comes from a work by Jehan le Feron, published at Paris
in 1555, and dedicated to Mary of Guise (widow of James V); its title is *Le
Simbol Armorial des Armoiries de France & d'Escoce & de Lorraine.*
Here, in a chapter devoted wholly to the various symbolic properties of the
lion occurs a brief passage on its *"clémence benigne"*, culminating in the
familiar story of how it spares those *"qui viennent a luy a mercy iouxte le
commun proverbe: Parcere prostratis scit nobilis ira leonis"* (p. 21v). Some
earlier Dunbar scholars have misunderstood the implications of this
paragraph,[5] and it should be stressed that although Jehan le Feron, like
Dunbar, is applying this saying to the Scottish lion, he specifically calls it a
"common proverb" not a motto.

It is striking but not surprising that this maxim often occurs in the
mouths of suppliants, is addressed to princes, kings, or other powerful men,
and regularly combines flattery with moral exhortation. It should be seen as
forming a small element in the widespread *speculum principis*, or "advice to
princes", tradition: *"Tu quoque fac simile, quisquis dominaris in orbe".*
The maxim is regularly linked with one specific virtue, often held to
distinguish the good ruler from the tyrant: clemency. Ancient writers, such
as Pliny and Martial, mention this virtue when they allude to this
characteristic of the lion. So too the speech to William Rufus reaches its
climax with *"Seueritatem regiam temperet clementia".* The *speculum
principis* genre was well-known in Scotland,[6] and *The Thrissill and the Rois*
partakes of this tradition. Through Nature's speech to the heraldic Lion the
poet is exhorting his own king: "Exerce justice" (106). The chief emphasis
falls on the king as the fount of justice and good law; mercy, or clemency, is
the virtue most stressed, and it is this aspect of kingship that the Lion here
particularly symbolises: "Exerce justice with mercy and conscience". If his
subjects demonstrate their allegiance in a feudal manner — "And till his feit
fell with humilitie" — then he too must fulfil his duty to his vassals.
Prostration in homage blends with the other image of the Lion's prostrate
victim. This passage reads like a much-compressed version of an incident in
Henryson's *Trial of the Fox*: here the Lion calls a parliament of all the
beasts, and they bow before him in feudal submission, falling "flatlingis to
his feit". In response the Lion proclaims his justice, stressing the
combination of "micht" and mercy:

> I lat yow wit, my micht is merciabill
> And steiris nane that ar to me prostrait.                929-30

Another of Henryson's fables, *The Lion and the Mouse*, is even more

explicitly concerned with royal clemency. There is no doubt that the mice-
subjects have acted wrongly towards their Lion-king, and deserve
punishment. Nonetheless the mice plead that he should pardon them, and
we are told that eventually the Lion

> thocht according to ressoun
> And gart mercie his cruell ire asswage
> And to the mous grantit remissioun.                    1504-6

From the thirteenth century onwards medieval Scottish kings granted
formal letters of "remission of rancour" to subjects who had trespassed but
were duly penitent. In 1487, however, an Act of Parliament criticised "the
over common granting of grace and remissions to trespassers". James III
has been praised (by Hector Boece) for his royal clemency, but condemned
(by modern scholars) for his venality in selling remissions at a high price.[7]
Medieval thinking on clemency was shaped by Seneca, who in a famous
essay addressed to Nero intended to guide the young prince into becoming
a just and merciful ruler. Henryson's phrasing here seems closely in accord
with Seneca, who praised clemency and saw anger as a feature of the tyrant:
"*Non decet regem saeva nec inexorabilis ira* [Cruel and inexorable anger is
not seemly for a king]". But Seneca distinguished *clementia*, or mercy,
from *misericordia*, or pity, which he regarded as a weak and female
emotion; clemency was guided by rational considerations: "*clementia
rationi accedit* [mercy is combined with reason]" (cf. "thocht according to
ressoun").[8] Dunbar is, of course, far less explicit than Henryson, yet he
retains the paradoxical phrase, "noble yre". Line 119 might well be glossed
by these lines of Henryson: it implies a justifiable wrath, tempered by
rational thought, and issuing in mercy.

To return to my starting-point: this line is interesting not for its
peculiarly Scottish implications — "a motto associated with the armorial
bearings of the kings of Scots" — but rather for its international
significance. It links Dunbar and his audience with the European
mainstream: with writers who, no matter how different they were in other
respects, shared the same essentially Latin culture.[9] Dunbar is using a
traditional Latin topos in a highly traditional way. What is new yet
characteristic of his time is first, his employment of the maxim within a
vernacular piece of writing, and, secondly, its heraldic application. It is the
heraldic element which links the three passages from sixteenth-century
writers (Dunbar, Cavendish, and Jehan le Feron), which are otherwise
widely disparate. Since the lion occurs as a heraldic image all over Europe
we might well expect to find similar sayings linked with the coats of arms of
other noble families. An interesting late example occurs in a surprising
place: Mrs Thrale's account of her ancestors, who, she tells us, had as their
"Atchievement the Lyon with Three Turkish crescents". Her anecdote tells

of a fifteenth-century Henry of Salisbury, who showed mercy to one of his opponents in the Wars of the Roses when he fell upon his knees, exclaiming, "*Sat est prostrasse leoni* [It is sufficient to fall prostrate before the lion]". She continues (Balderston 1951: 1.274-5):

> Those words were therefore made choice of by his Son who survived him, as a Motto to his Arms; and that Son whose name was Thomas, built himself a Seat in the Vale of Llwydd, in North Wales, and calling it Llewenny, that is *Llew* the Lyon, *anny* for us; placed a Copper Lyon on his House Top, with *Sat est prostrasse Leoni* — written round it.

Here indeed is a motto, but is the story apocryphal?


## II

> Upone the awfull Thrissill scho beheld
> And saw him kepit with a busche of speiris;
> Concedring him so able for the weiris,
> A radius croun of rubeis scho him gaif
> And said, In feild go furth and fend the laif.          129-33

The thistle is today such a familiar and decorative feature of Scottish life, that it is easy to forget how novel was its use by Dunbar. A great deal of mystery and recent myth-making surrounds the origins of the emblematic thistle. The well-known story that in the early Middle Ages a band of invading Danes trod on a thistle and revealed their presence by shrieks of pain can be traced back no further than the nineteenth century.[10] There is much uncertainty concerning the date and origins of the Scottish Order of the Thistle.[11] As to the existence of a French Order of the Thistle, said to have been created in the fourteenth century (c. 1370) by Louis II, duke of Bourbon, this is even more controversial; one French scholar says: "*l'ordre du Chardon n'a jamais existé que dans l'imagination inventive de Favyn. Aucun monument ne reproduit la figure de cet ordre, nul chroniqueur ancien n'en fait mention.*"[12] It is not my purpose, however, to investigate these particular problems. It is enough to note that an emblematic Scottish thistle undoubtedly appears on certain coins of James III (the silver groat and half-groat) in 1474, but that it is only in the reign of James IV that it becomes at all frequent. James IV's great signet bears a rampant lion surrounded by a collar of thistles, and a thistle apears on a ceremonial coin of 1513.[13] Thistles abound, above all, in the documents and decorative trappings associated with his marriage to Margaret Tudor: in the windows of Holyrood, according to the account of John Young, the English herald;[14] in the Book of Hours, now in Vienna, presented to Margaret (see Macfarlane 1960); and in the marriage contract, which may have been decorated by Thomas Galbraith, who was a fellow-courtier of Dunbar's.[15] Dunbar, however, seems to have been the first Scot to make a literary use of this pictorial heraldic image; what today may seem hackneyed was then topical and innovative.

What was the thistle's significance at this time? In the first place it was a personal badge of the Scottish king, corresponding to the red and white rose of the Tudors or the pomegranate of Catherine of Aragon. It is well-known that the vogue for such badges was at its height in the fifteenth and sixteenth centuries, especially in warfare. The historian Malcolm Vale notes that the badge (like the *impresa* in Italy, and the *devise* in France and the Low Countries) not only met the contemporary taste for allegory; it had a practical function: "Like a crest they were more easily recognisable in combat than the elaborately quartered coats of arms, with their numerous subdivisions, which fifteenth-century noble houses bore" (Vale 1981: 96). But the thistle, like the rose or the fleur de lys, rapidly also became a national badge. There is an interesting passage in the Edinburgh burgh records for 1562 which commands that the "idol" St Giles be cut from the town's standard, and a thistle put in its place (Laing 1859: xlviii). The thistle is a highly decorative image, but it is legitimate to wonder why it was chosen, since in the Middle Ages, like the nettle and the thorn, it commonly had an adverse symbolism. Biblical references are invariably pejorative: it figures in God's curse upon mankind — "thorns and thistles shall it [i.e. the ground] bring forth to thee" (*Genesis* 3.18); it regularly symbolises unfruitfulness and disorder — "Do men gather grapes of thorns, or figs of thistles?" (*Matthew* 7.16). For Shakespeare too it is an image of political chaos and anarchy: Burgundy laments that in France, "this best garden of the world", nothing thrives "But hateful docks, rough thistles, kecksies, burrs" (*Henry V*, V.ii.52).[16] But during the fifteenth century, if not earlier, the thistle also acquired a favourable significance, clearly related to its prickly properties as a plant: warlike readiness to defend oneself or one's country. Dunbar makes this clear. He calls the Thistle "awfull", i.e. awe-inspiring; "able for the weiris", and guarded by "a busche of speiris" (there is a play on the military sense of "bush"). If the Lion here symbolises one aspect of royal justice, the Thistle symbolises the duty of a king to guard his people effectively and to protect them from invasion.

Badges or devices often consisted of two parts: the picture, sometimes known as "the body", and a phrase or motto, known as "the soul". Mottoes could also exist independently of visual images, and were as popular in sixteenth-century Scotland as elsewhere in Europe.[17] Earlier I denied that line 119 alludes to a royal motto; what I suggest is that such an allusion does occur, but slightly later in the poem. Today two mottoes are connected with the royal arms of Scotland, the better-known of which is probably *Nemo me impune lacessit* [No one provokes me with impunity], which occurs on coins of James VI and was adopted as the motto of the Order of the Thistle, when it was founded in the seventeenth century. But there is another and earlier motto, which is regularly placed in a scroll surmounting the most elaborate form of the Scottish royal arms: "In Defens". This is the short version; there also occurs a fuller version, "In my Defens, God us (me) Defend". Both the shorter and longer forms of this motto occur, associated with the thistle collar, in the depiction of the royal coat of arms in the 1503 Vienna Book of Hours (see Frontispiece).[18] Other representations of the royal arms that can be dated to the early sixteenth century also contain the same motto, "In Defens": e.g. that depicted on the tower of King's College Chapel, Aberdeen, dated 1504; and the letter from James to Ferdinand of Aragon, dated 1 July 1512, which bears the impress of the great signet and contains a scroll with the legend, "In Defens".[19] In other words, the royal motto associated with James IV and the one most likely to have been known to Dunbar was "In Defens", usually in the proximity of the thistle emblem. I suggest therefore that it is this motto that lies behind Nature's instruction to the Thistle:

> In feild go furth and fend [i.e. defend] the laif.      133

There is literary evidence to show that the vogue for the thistle in heraldry did not originate in Scotland but was current in the French-speaking world by at least the middle of the fifteenth century. Antoine de la Sale, in his story of an ideal knight, *Le Petit Jehan de Saintré*, completed c. 1455, describes his hero's helmet "which had on top a large thistle-flower, with four large leaves of gold, which all covered the top of the helmet (*qui au dessus avoit une grant fleur de chardon, a quatres grans fuilles d'or, qui toutes couvroient le chief du heaulme*)".[20] At almost the same period (c. 1457) René d'Anjou composed his famous *Livre du Cueur d'Amours Espris*. At one stage in this long allegorical work the hero visits "*l'hospital d'amour*"; René describes how they see a collection of escutcheons, one of which belonged to his brother, Charles d'Anjou. This shield was placed "within a thistle-bush of which the thistles and also the leaves were very finely picked out and portrayed in gold (*en une chardonniere, dont les chardons et aussi bien les feuilles estoient moult gentement rehausseies et pourtraictes d'or*)". Underneath were some explanatory verses, in which Charles declares his allegiance to the God of Love, and continues:

> Si me viens présenter enserré de chardons,
> Que comme Amours poingt [MS: print] fort, qui y a trop fiance,
> Suys point et enserré d'amoureuse pointure.
> Pourquoy prens les chardons et porte en ma pointure.
> Et viens a l'opital et mon blazon apporte
> Pour le mectre et asseoir doulcement sur la porte.

[And I come to show myself surrounded by thistles,
Because, as Love pierces anyone cruelly, who has trusted too much in it,
I am pricked and surrounded by the amorous thorns.
Because of this I take the thistles, and wear them on my device (*lit.* painting),
And come to the hospital, carrying my blason,
In order to place and fix it gently above the door.]

It is not certain whether Charles actually used this "*blazon*" in real life; the
thistle here may be as imaginary as in another episode of the same work, in
which Cueur engages in combat with Wrath (*Courroux*): Wrath's shield
bears a device of three thistles on a thorny branch, and can be seen depicted
on folio 26v of the famous Vienna manuscript of *Le Livre du Cueur
d'Amours Espris*.[21] René d'Anjou bore many titles, one of which was Duke
of Lorraine (through his first wife, Isabella). It is interesting therefore that
the closest parallels to the Scottish use of the thistle occur in Lorraine at the
turn of the sixteenth century. Lorraine was a small duchy in a vulnerable
position on the eastern border of France and dividing the two provinces of
Burgundy. There is some controversy as to whether the employment of the
thistle (e.g. on coins and tapestries) should be credited to the second Duke
René (1473-1508), or to his wife, Philippa of Gueldres. But the nineteenth-
century French scholar, Léon Germain (1884: 207-36), argues very
plausibly that it was René II who adopted the thistle as a national symbol —
signifying heroic resistance to invasion — after his successful struggle to
preserve Lorraine's independence against Charles the Bold of Burgundy
(d. 1477). In Lorraine, as in Scotland, it was associated with defensive
mottoes, such as "*Ne mi tocquès, il point* [Do not touch me, there is a
sting]" and "*Non inultus premor* [I am not pressed, i.e. attacked, with
impunity]"; it has been the official heraldic emblem of Nancy since 1575,
when Duke Charles III authorised the town to add it to their arms.[22] I might
note, in parenthesis, that Scotland had links with both Gueldres and
Lorraine through two royal marriages: James II married Mary of Gueldres,
and James V married Mary, granddaughter of René II of Lorraine. Mary
Queen of Scots had therefore a double claim to the emblematic thistle. The
poet, Alexander Scott, was clearly aware of this — as also of Dunbar's
poem — when he addressed a New Year's greeting to her in 1562 (Ritchie
1928-34: 235):

> Welcum oure Lyone with the floure delyce
> Welcum oure thrissill with the Lorane grene
> Welcum oure rubent rois vpoun the ryce.          2-4

The Scots associated the danger of invasion primarily with England; but to
stress this in a poem addressed to a newly arrived English princess would

clearly be discourteous. Dunbar devotes far less space to the Thistle than to the Lion.

A century later, after the Union of the Crowns, the thistle again figures in verse. The Scottish poet, Alexander Craig, and the emblem-writer, Henry Peacham, were well aware of the thistle's defensive and warlike symbolism, but in the changed political context both gave it a new application. In 1604 Craig published a poem celebrating James VI's accession to the English throne, and attributed these words to the ghost of Queen Elizabeth (Laing 1873-4: 1.24):

> The Lyons now agree, and do in Peace delight,
> The Thirsel now defends and guards the Red Rose and the White ...

In his well-known *Minerva Britanna* (1612) Henry Peacham placed two emblems on adjoining pages: in the first are two Lions (representing Scotland and England) who together uphold a diadem; in the second there emerges from the clouds a hand holding a pot, and waters a bush bearing both roses and thistles. Beneath are verses beginning:

> The Thistle arm'd with vengeaunce for his foe,
> And here the Rose, faire Cythereas flower;
> Together in perpetuall league doe growe,
> On whom the Heauens doe all their favour power.

In Dunbar's poem the threefold crowning of the Lion, Eagle, and Thistle is succeeded by Nature's climactic coronation of the Rose:

> A coistly croun with clarefeid stonis brycht
> This cumly quene did on hir heid inclois.                   155-6

It seems unnecessary to posit a single explanation for this feature of the poem. It may be intended to bring to mind the actual coronation of the young queen. It may also have been prompted by the visual imagery that accompanied the wedding: a crowned lion, for instance, forms the crest in the royal coat of arms, and is depicted in the Vienna Book of Hours; and the windows of the great chamber of Holyrood were decorated (according to Young) with "a Chardon and a Rose interlassed thorough a Crowne" (Leland 1774: 4.295). Dunbar's stress on the act of crowning might indeed be linked with James IV's adoption at about this time of the arched or imperial crown in the royal arms; Burnett notes (1978: 14) that "the arched crown was adopted by the principal kings of Europe at the end of the fifteenth century to establish a suitable distinction between independent monarchs and the petty sovereigns of minor states". But Dunbar had one definite, and Scriptural, source of inspiration. When Nature addresses the Rose, saying she is without "spot or macull", and continuing, "Cum, blowme of joy, with jemis to be cround" (153), she is directly quoting two well-known verses addressed to the Bride in the *Song of Songs* (4.7-8): *"Macula non est in te. ... Veni ... sponsa mea ... veni coronaberis"*. The same verses were quoted in a wedding pageant devised to greet Margaret's sister, Mary Tudor, when she married Louis XII in 1514.[23] They have an evident appropriateness to one who was newly a bride and a queen; their traditional application to the Virgin, especially at her Coronation, implies that the Virgin should be the model for earthly queens.

Precisely how Dunbar's poem was "published" is not known, but it clearly formed one item in the celebration of the royal wedding. It resembles the ceremonial gateway that greeted James and Margaret, as they entered Edinburgh. On it were depicted the four cardinal virtues, Justice holding a naked sword and a pair of balances, with Nero lying beneath her feet; Force, armed and under her feet Holofernes; "Temperance, holdyng in hyr hand a Bitt of an Horse, and under hyr feete was Epicurus; Prudence, holdyng in hyr haunde a Syerge [candle] and under Sardenapalus" (Leland 1774: 4.289-90). Similarly allegorical gateways met many other kings in the fifteenth and sixteenth centuries. *The Thrissill and the Rois*, like these gateways, conveys an ambivalent message: behind the compliments is a warning, behind the greeting, an admonition. One of Dunbar's objects is to remind his audience of certain traditional topics, to remind them above all of those virtues to which kings and queens should aspire.

NOTES

1  All citations are from Kinsley 1979.
2  See Kinsley 1979: 333; MacQueen 1967: 151; Fox 1981: 244. See also Ross 1981: 246: "a motto connected with the armorial bearings of Scottish kings"; Mackenzie 1932: 218; and Smith who first suggests treating the words "as a portion of a heraldic motto" (1902: 276).
3  Walther 1963-7, No. 20668; cf. also No. 20672, which differs only in beginning *"Parcere subjectis"*.
4  See further Lehmann 1964: 6-7, and Préaux 1947. I am indebted to Dr S. Mapstone for drawing my attention to the passage in Ireland; see Craigie 1923: 1.57.
5  This work is correctly cited in the Scottish Text Society edition of Dunbar (Small 1884-93: 3.275), but in such a summary way that it seems to have misled later editors who have not consulted the French original.
6  See further Lyall 1976 and Mapstone 1986.
7  See Barrow 1965: 419-20, MacDougall 1982: 201-2, and Macfarlane 1985: 113-4.
8  See "De Clementia" I.v.6 and II.ii.3 fol. in *Seneca's Moral Essays*, ed. and trans. Basore 1928, 1.372, and 1.436 ff., especially 1.438. On Seneca's influence, see Burnley 1979.
9  Tony Hunt 1983 makes a similar point, and discusses the *parcere prostratis* theme. I became aware of his excellent article only after completing my paper.
10  This story is mentioned by Ross (1981: 247), but it has been traced no earlier

than 1829 in Dickson and Walker 1981, an excellent article to which I am much indebted.

11  See Malloch 1978; Gayre 1984 is highly inaccurate. Malloch is sceptical about the existence of an Order at this time, pointing out that a chivalric order does not consist merely in decorative insignia, "but is a corporate body, governed by statutes, with insignia merely denoting membership of this body or fraternity" (p. 37). It is striking that the patriotic author of *The Complaynt of Scotland* (c. 1550) refers to the three Orders of the Golden Fleece, Garter, and Cockle (see Stewart 1979: 117), but makes no mention of any Scottish Order.

12  I am indebted to professors Jean Jacques Blanchot and André Leguai, who drew my attention to this comment by Steyert, annotator of La Mure (see La Mure 1860-8: 2.48-9, n.2). André Favyn published *Le Theatre d'honneur*, 1620; see p. 770.

13  For details of the coinage, see Stewart 1955; rev. edn. 1967. Barker (1979: 234) asserts that James III formally declared that the thistle was to be the official badge and emblem of Scotland, being a native Scottish plant of which the self-protective qualities most aptly illustrated the Royal motto, "*In Defens*", but I can find no evidence to support this assertion. See also Stewart 1964-6: 267, and Burnett 1983.

14  This account is printed in Thomas Hearne's additions to J. Leland's *Collectanea*, 2nd edn., 1774, 4.265-300; see p. 295. (Two manuscripts survive, one a seventeenth century copy; the original is College of Arms MS I.M.13, fols. 76-115.)

15  On Galbraith, see Apted and Hannabuss 1978: 40-1. The contract is dated 17 December 1502 Public Record Office E/39/81. See Macfarlane 1960: 5.

16  For other symbolic properties of the Thistle, see also D'Ancona 1977: 375-7.

17  Bernard Stewart of Aubigny, who is the subject of two poems by Dunbar, bore as his device a rampant lion, red, on a field of silver, sprinkled with many buckles, and the motto *Distantia iungit*; see Giovio (ed. Doglio 1978: 105) who interprets the device as alluding to his role in allying the kings of France and Scotland.

18  According to Burnett (1978: 15), this is the first appearance of the motto. Both mottoes are found, associated with the figure of the Scottish king, in a Burgundian heraldic work, "L'Armorial de la Toison d'Or et de l'Europe", now in the Bibliotheque de l'Arsenal, Paris. Although the work as a whole is dated not later than 1466, the figure of the king of Scotland is apparently "at least a century later than any of the others, and has a renaissance grace contrasting with the gothic character of the rest" (see Pinches and Wood 1971: 11). The figure is reproduced in part on the cover of Grant 1984, and in full in Plate III of Innes of Learney 1956. For other early uses of the motto, see Burnett 1978: 15 ff.

19  This is discussed in Simpson 1955-6: 451-5.

20  Misrahi and Knudson 1965: 111; see also discussion in Germain 1895: 247-8.

21  See le Comte de Quatrebarbes 1844-6: 3.123; also Unterkircher trans. Wilkins 1975 for reproductions of the Vienna manuscript.

22  Communication from Claire Aptel, Conservateur au Musée Historique Lorrain.

23  See Baskervill 1934, in particular page 6. The verses were often quoted in poems written in honour of the Virgin; the York play of the Assumption of the Virgin (Beadle 1982: no. XLV) contains musical settings of texts such as *Veni de Libano sponsa* and *Veni electa mea*.

REFERENCES

Anglo, Sydney (1969). *Spectacle, Pageantry and Early Tudor Policy.* Oxford: Clarendon Press.
Apted, M.R. and S. Hannabuss (1978). *Painters in Scotland 1301-1700, A Biographical Dictionary.* Edinburgh: Scottish Record Society, n.s. 7.
Balderston, Katharine C. (1951). *Thraliana.* 2nd edn. Oxford: Clarendon Press.
Barker, Brian (1979). *The Symbols of Sovereignty.* Newton Abbot: Westbridge Books.
Barrow, G.W.S. (1965). *Robert Bruce.* London: Eyre & Spottiswoode.
Baskervill, C.R. (1934). *Pierre Gringore's Pageants for the Entry of Mary Tudor into Paris.* Chicago: University of Chicago Press.
Basore, John W., ed. and trans. (1928). *Seneca's Moral Essays.* Vol. 1. London: William Heinemann.
Beadle, Richard, ed. (1982). *The York Plays.* London: Arnold.
Burnett, Charles (1977-8). The Development of the Royal Arms to 1603. *Journal of the Heraldry Society of Scotland* 1, 9-19.
—— (1983). The Thistle as a Symbol. In *The Thistles of Scotland*; no editor named (Glasgow: Glasgow Museums and Art Galleries), pp. 8-13.
Burnley, J.D. (1979). *Chaucer's Language and the Philosophers' Tradition.* Cambridge: Boydell & Brewer.
Chibnall, Marjorie, ed. and trans. (1973). *The Ecclesiastical History of Ordericus Vitalis.* Oxford: Clarendon Press.
Cody, E.G. and W. Murison, ed., and James Dalrymple, trans. (1888-95). *The Historie of Scotland.* Edinburgh: Scottish Text Society.
D'Ancona, Mirella Levi (1977). *The Garden of the Renaissance: Botanical Symbolism in Italian Painting.* Florence: Olschki.
Dickson, J.H. and Agnes Walker (1981). What is the Scottish Thistle? *Journal of the Glasgow Natural History Society* 20, 1-21.
Doglio, Maria Luisa, ed. (1978). Paolo Giovio, *Dialogo Dell' Imprese Militari e Amorose.* Rome: Bulzoni.
Favyn, André (1620). *Le Théâtre d'honneur.*
le Feron, Jehan (1555). *Le Simbol Armorial des Armoiries de France & d'Escoce & de Lorraine.* Paris.
Fox, Denton, ed. (1981). *The Poems of Robert Henryson.* Oxford: Clarendon Press.
Gayre, Robert (1984). The Antiquity of the Scottish Order. *The Double Tressure* 6, 6-12.
Germain, Léon (1884). Le Chardon Lorrain sous les Ducs René II et Antoine. *Mem. Acad. Stanislas*, 207-36.
—— (1895). Le Chardon, Embleme du Duc René II et la Branche de Chataignier, Embleme de la Duchesse Philippe de Gueldres. *Journal de la Societé d'Archèologie Lorraine*, 247-8.
Grant, Alexander (1984). *Independence and Nationhood: Scotland 1306-1469.* London: Edward Arnold.
Hunt, Tony (1983). The Lion and Yvain. In *The Legend of Arthur in the Middle Ages*, ed. P.B. Grant and others (Cambridge: D.S. Brewer), pp. 86-90.
Innes of Learney, Sir Thomas (1956). *Scots Heraldry.* 2nd edn. Edinburgh: Oliver & Boyd.
Kinsley, James, ed. (1979). *The Poems of William Dunbar.* Oxford: Clarendon Press.
Laing, D. (1859). *Registrum Cartarum Ecclesie Sancti Egidii de Edinburgh.* Edinburgh: Bannatyne Club.
—— (1873-4). *Poetical Works of Alexander Craig.* Glasgow: Hunterian Society.

Lehmann, Paul (1927, 2nd edn. 1964). *Pseudo-Antike Literatur des Mittelalters*. Darmstadt: Wissenschaftliche Buchgesellschaft.

Leland, J., with additions by Thomas Hearne (1774). *De Rebus Britannicis Collectanea*. London.

Lyall, R.J. (1976). Politics and Poetry in Fifteenth-Century Scotland. *Scottish Literary Journal* 3, 5-29.

MacDougall, N.A. (1982). *James III*. Edinburgh: John Donald.

Macfarlane, L. (1960). The Book of Hours of James IV and Margaret Tudor. *Innes Review* 11, 3-21.

Macfarlane, L.J. (1985). *William Elphinstone and the Kingdom of Scotland 1431-1514*. Aberdeen: Aberdeen University Press.

Mackenzie, W. Mackay, ed. (1932). *The Poems of William Dunbar*. London: Faber.

MacQueen, John (1967). *Robert Henryson*. Oxford: Clarendon Press.

Malloch, R.J. (1977-8). The Order of the Thistle. *Journal of the Heraldry Society of Scotland* 1, 37-45.

Mapstone, Sally (1986). The Wisdom of Princes: Advice to Princes Literature in Late Medieval Scotland. Unpublished doctoral thesis, Oxford.

Misrahi, Jean and Charles A. Knudson, ed. (1965). *Jehan de Saintré*. Geneva: Droz.

La Mure, J.M. (1860-97). *Histoire des ducs de Bourbon et des comtes de Fores*. Paris: Potier.

Peacham, Henry (1612). *Minerva Britanna*.

Pinches, Rosemary and Anthony Wood (1971). *A European Armorial: an Armorial of Knights of the Golden Fleece and Fifteenth Century Europe*. London: Heraldry Today.

Préaux, Jean G. (1947). Thierry de Saint-Trond, auteur du poeme pseudo-ovidien *De Mirabilibus Mundi*. *Latomus* 6, 353-66.

Quatrebarbes, Théodore le Comte de, ed. (1844-6). *Oeuvres Complètes du Roi René d'Anjou*. Angers: Cosnier et Lachèse.

Ritchie, W. Tod, ed. (1928-34). *The Bannatyne Manuscript*. Edinburgh: Scottish Text Society.

Ross, Ian (1981). *William Dunbar*. Leiden: E.J. Brill.

Simpson, Grant G. (1955-6). A Great Signet of James IV. *Proceedings of the Society of Antiquaries of Scotland* 89, 451-5.

Small, John, ed. (1884-93). *The Poems of William Dunbar*. Edinburgh: Scottish Text Society.

Smith, G. Gregory (1902). *Specimens of Middle Scots*. Edinburgh: William Blackwood & Sons.

Stewart, A.M., ed. (1979). *The Complaynt of Scotland*. Edinburgh: Scottish Text Society.

Stewart, Ian H. (1964-6). Some Scottish Ceremonial Coins. *Proceedings of the Society of Antiquaries of Scotland* 98, 254-75.

——— (1967). *The Scottish Coinage*. Revised edn. London: Spink and Son.

Sylvester, R.S., ed. (1959). George Cavendish's *The Life and Death of Cardinal Wolsey*. London: Early English Texts Society, OS No. 243.

Unterkircher, F. ed., and S. Wilkins trans. (1975). *Le Livre du Cueur d'Amours Espris*. London: Thames and Hudson.

Vale, Malcolm (1981). *War and Chivalry*. London: Duckworth.

Walther, Hans (1963-7). *Proverbia Sententiaeque Latinitatis Medii Aevi*. Göttingen: Vandenhoeck & Ruprecht.

Watenphul, H. and H. Krefeld (1958). *Die Gedichte des Archipoeta*. Heidelberg: Winter.

White, T.H. (1954). *The Book of Beasts*. London: Cape.

Wright, Thomas, ed. (1863). Neckam, *De Naturis Rerum*. London: Rolls Series 34.

# THE LORD OF MISRULE IN LATE MEDIEVAL AND RENAISSANCE ENGLAND

Sandra Billington

The ritualised disorder called misrule and led by a lord of misrule is best known in relation to a festive or carnival period,[1] but in late medieval and renaissance England the seasonally elected lord of misrule was only one of three kinds of leader called by this title. In the light of the historical record, the seasonal appearances begin to look like the official state occasions of a whole ideology based on the principle of misrule which could manifest itself in other forms at any time of the year.

The three kinds of misrule lord which appear in the evidence are a leader of outlaws, a leader of peasant rebellion and a leader of seasonal festivity. All but the last are to do with disorder in the fabric of the officially-run society and either the diverse claims and accusations were totally random or, as is more likely, there was a logic as to why the Lord of Misrule title and the images associated with it could apply to heterogeneous examples. The most credible logic is that the condition of misrule was held to be inevitable because the condition of rule was a force in the universe. The boundaries of rule could not be determined without the existence of misrule, therefore misrule defined rule and the two were interdependent. In the sixteenth century a relationship of opposition can be determined between official courtly codes and the codes of courtly misrule entertainments, and the Middle Ages, too, was a period when the concept of interdependent contrarieties flourished. As Peter Elbow writes in *Oppositions in Chaucer* (1975: 15):

> In the medieval period more than in most other periods, thinkers took it for granted that conflicting and even contradictory ideas might both be true. It was a time when, presented with an opposition, one might be instinctively more interested in showing how both sides were true than by how one of them was false.

Therefore the reconciliation of opposites or *concordia discors* was a familiar concept. Elbow is speaking about literary dialectic but William Langland, in *Piers Plowman* C: Passus XXI, argues the relevance of *concordia discors* to human experience. The eventual salvation of Adam and Eve is presented in terms of opposition:

> For hadde thei wist of no wo . wele hadde thei nat knowe;
> For wot no wight what wele is . that neuere wo suffrede, ...

> Ho couthe kyndeliche . with colour discriue,
> Yf alle the world were whit ...
> Yf no nyght ne were . no man, as ich leyue,
> Sholde wite witerly . what day were to mane ...
> For-thi god of hus goodnesse . the furst man Adam,
> He sette hym in solace furst . and in souerayne murthe;
> And sutthe suffrede hym to synege . sorwe to fele,
> To wite ther-thorw what wele was.[2]                  211-31

This argument is more than literary. It posits the belief that the experience of good or happiness cannot be understood without experience of evil. In the case of Adam and Eve their eventual salvation is promised through their experience of evil by which, in future, they may recognise goodness. Langland goes on to draw a parallel between them and the destiny of folk in the troubled society of the 1380s:

> So shal hit fare by this folke . here synne
> Shal lere hem what loue is . and lisse with-outen ende.     236-7

When one then turns to Langland's own society which he was indirectly writing about one finds that disorder was endemic. The background to a complex use of mock king and misrule lord titles was one where the forces of disorder or misrule were in more effective control than was rule. The impression of near mayhem is confirmed by John Bellamy in the opening chapter of *Crime and Public Order in the Middle Ages* (1973: 1):

> In the England of the later middle ages the preservation of public order was very often the biggest problem the king had to face. It was not just a police matter. At heart were the crucial issues of royal authority and the structure of the state.

Bellamy refers to wilful flouting of authority rather than the more justifiable peasant rebellions and he finds the problem extensive. No historian has been able to document the entire period successfully but from localised study of different areas at different periods "not one investigator has been able to indicate even a few years of effective policing in the period 1290-1485" (Bellamy 1973: 1). The point at which the law broke down was the top. Justices of the Peace and Sheriffs were dependent on lordly patrons who more frequently than not applied the law according to their own vested interests. It was not until the gentry broke free of patronage in the mid sixteenth century that crime decreased. This state of affairs helps explain why the boundary between criminal and legal acts was so confused. Interpretation of events differed. Outláws' acts could be seen by the perpetrators, as one might expect, but also by some impartial observers, as acts of justice. What is surprising is that this form of justice could be seen to be in opposition to the king's justice. It appears that organised outlaws behaved according to a mirror image of the king's power, forming themselves into brotherhoods with a mock king as leader.

I would like to begin with the statement by E.L.G. Stones (1957: 135) that "there were people who could not only persuade themselves that they were innocent victims of the law ... but could go on to represent crimes ... as acts of a rival system of justice". The strongest evidence comes from the mid fourteenth century when gangs of outlaws dominated the midlands during Edward's periodic absences from the country. The constable of Rockingham Castle, Sir Robert de Vere, turned his curatorship into protection for outlaws and Rockingham Castle became a safe house for fugitives from three counties (Stones 1957: 124; Bellamy 1973: 74). In one of those counties, Leicestershire, the Folville family was earning its own notoriety from the activities of six of its seven sons. All but the eldest turned to outlawry in 1326 after having murdered one of the king's men, an "unpopular neighbour, Roger Bellers, a baron of the exchequer" (Bellamy 1973: 74). The leader, Eustace de Folville, evaded capture for over twenty years and is believed to have eventually died peacefully in his bed in 1347. The Folville gang joined forces with the Coterel-led band when they embarked on large crimes such as the kidnapping in 1332 of Sir Richard Willoughby, Justice of the King's bench, for ransom, and a few weeks before the Willoughby affair Robert de Vere had threatened another of the King's travelling judiciaries, William la Zouche of Harringworth. This series of attacks on the authority of the king was countered at Westminster and in trailbaston commissions and the challenge was taken particularly seriously because the law-breakers were adopting royal expressions. The trailbaston commission of 1332 reported that there were criminals who had been writing letters "as if in a royal style (*quasi sub stilo regio*)" (Stones 1957: 134). The one extant example comes from a Yorkshire case of 1336. The parson of Huntington, Richard de Snaweshill, thought fit to bring a legal action after receiving a letter which ran:

> Lionel, king of the rout of raveners, to our false and disloyal Richard de Snaweshill, greeting without love. We issue to you as punishment, in so far as you have betrayed us and our laws that you, on reading this letter, do entirely remove the man you maintain in the vicarage at Burton Anneys and you give the abbot of Notre Dame de Bouthum his liberty and election to the said vicarage. ... If you do not do this we give our oath, first to the king of heaven, then to the king of England and to our crown that you will receive the same fate as the Bishop of Excestre en Cheep [Bishop Stapledon, murdered 1326]. And show this letter to your sovereign and tell him he permits false boundaries and false fellowships and let him suffer justice to be done to the aforesaid abbot or on our oath he will have £1,000 of damage done by us and ours. And if you ignore our demand we will order the Viscount of the North to bring great suffering to you. ... Issued from our Castle of the North Wind,

within the Green Tower in the first year of our reign.[3]

In this letter, Lionel writes as though he were rightful administrator of Yorkshire and as though de Snaweshill had insinuated a treacherous alliance with a foreign king by carrying out Edward's appointment. Lionel's vision of himself and his allies is based on a kingly fellowship, as found in Arthurian romance. The outlaws' kingdom both apes and opposes the organisation of Edward's and although the title "rout of raveners" has a festive ring to it, it also has a satiric bite since there was real violence behind Lionel's threats.

It becomes important here to consider the legend of Robin Hood since of the many hypotheses about its origin the one which carries most weight is that it developed out of accumulated stories about outlaws.[4] The first reference comes from William Langland when, in *Piers Plowman* B: Passus VIII.11, he has Sloth say that he knows the "rymes of robyn hode". By the 1490s, Robin Hood had become one of the most popular names for the summer festive king. Difficult as it may seem to equate Lionel, the Folvilles, the Coterels and Robert de Vere with the sympathetic legends handed down from the sixteenth century, it seems that Eustace de Folville in particular could have made a contribution. To begin with, it is as difficult in retrospect as it was at the time to judge the legality or illegality of apparent criminal actions. According to Bellamy (1973: 82):

> To have feuded, used violence, to have poached or pillaged, was not at this time held to debar any man from local or even national office. ... There were a considerable number of "seeming crooks and bandits", guilty of homicides and housebreaking, who were elected to Parliament in the early fourteenth century.

Eustace was pardoned in 1333 for services rendered in the Scottish war; then in 1346, taking further advantage of the king's absence, he resorted once more to violence and yet despite this he died a hero. Henry Knighton considered his murder of Bellers in 1326 a courageous act and saw fit to recall it as a posthumous tribute to Eustace in 1347 among his records of momentous events.[5] Even more surprising than his testimonial is a tribute paid by Langland (again in *Piers Plowman*). It is this recollection of the outlaw near the end of the century which suggests that Eustace and his brothers were slipping into legend. In a vision of the future Langland describes the new society reorganised by Grace. Among tilers, tillers, and other men of craft Langland adds men who were taught by Grace:

> ... to ryde and recouere . that unrightfully was wonne;
> He wissed hem to wynne it agheyne . thorw wightnesse of hande,
> And fecchen it fro fals men . with Foluyles lawes.     B XIX. 239-41

The ethics expressed can be compared with present-day expectations of Robin Hood and there is no doubt that even during their lifetimes the Folvilles and their like had many supporters. They felt justified in what they did to the extent that some of them expressed their inversion of the dominant order in terms of inversion, as mock kings with serious intent. While such men played on the meaning of kingship the problem they raised for the king was the crucial one of his own position.

If outlaws could create an opposition to the king by direct imitation, peasant rebellions more frequently borrowed all the festive customs associated with periods of festive misrule. Demands for wages could be expressed in terms of a "quête", and in both contexts the ale-house was a frequent meeting place and a livery might be worn.[6] The selection of a mock king was a ceremony of some importance in both (Pettitt 1984: 8). Organised rebellion as well as organised outlawry seems to have required a mock king for leader. The 1381 uprising was frequently remembered as Jack Straw's and not Wat Tyler's by Tudor chroniclers (see Brie 1906) and Jack Cade had three titles. Mortimer was the one behind which Yorkist sympathisers rallied and so can be clearly seen as the name of an opposing, alternative king; Captain was the name he was commonly called (Paston, ed. Davis 1971-6: 2.60, 313-5), and it is said that his propaganda name, John Amend-Alle, was the one he preferred (Lyle 1950: 18). This last name was remembered by other men who had a vested interest in justifying an uprising, two years after Cade's revolt. In 1452 a band of robbers operating in Norfolk went through the greenwood ritual of electing a leader. No political grievance can be found for this gang whose activities seem to have been purely criminal. However, they followed the recognised custom and their leader adopted for himself Cade's "favourite" name. It was reported that:

> Rogere Cherche ... was at a gaderyng ... of xv persones in a feleshep vnder a wode in the town of Possewyke ... which feleshep, as it is seid ... was procured and gaderyd be the seid Rogere Cherche and be his councelores, the same Rogere seyng ... he had remembred a gode name for here capteyn, that shuld be John A-mend Alle. (Paston, ed. Davis 1971-6: 1.62-3)

As my final example I would like to look at the rebellion which took place in Norwich in 1443 on either the 24th or 25th of January. This was the culmination of forty years' dispute over land and involved citizens instead of barons or peasants. However, this third estate also followed the pattern of electing an ostensible leader in the form of a mock king.[7] In the charges brought against them the display was interpreted as a deliberate challenge to Henry VI's authority, similar to the concern in 1332. Instead of being accused of writing letters in a royal style, they were charged with presenting an iconographic threat.

> [John Gladman rode through the city] as a King with a crown and sceptre and
> sword carried before him by 3 men unknown ... and others to the number of
> 24 persons [rode] there in like manner before John Gladman with a crown
> upon their arms and with bows and arrows as valets of the crown of the Lord
> King; and they ordered 100 other persons now unknown with swords bows
> and arrows as well on foot as on horseback then and there to follow John
> Gladman. (Trans. from Latin, Hudson and Tingay 1906-10: 1.340)

The rebels held out for about a week before the Duke of Norfolk and the
Earl of Oxford entered the city. In 1448, after the city was restored to the
king's good graces, the mayor and aldermen brought a counter-charge
against the clerk at the previous trial. Despite the fact that Shrove Tuesday
that year fell on March 5th, it was said that John Gladman:

> on fastyngong tuesday made a disporte wt his neighbours having his hors
> trapped with tynessyle and otherwyse dysgysyn things crowned as King of
> Kristmasse in token that all merthe shuld end with ye twelve monethes of ye
> yer, afore hym eche moneth disgysd after ye seson yerof. (Hudson and Tingay
> 1906-10: 1.345)

Without trying to judge the rights and wrongs of the conflict, one can see
here two quite distinct readings of what was claimed to be the same
procession. The fact that it mattered enough to the defendants to
reconstruct this part of the events, instead of simply denying it as they did ·
much of the rest, is interesting; and their reconstruction shows they were
aware of variations that could be made to the idea of misrule display. It may
seem to be forcing the evidence to suggest that everyone who took part was
aware of anything beyond the immediate quarrel, yet the fact that men
were wearing insignia — either a crown or a sign of the month — indicates
that the participants would have understood the metaphor behind their
appearance. Bearing in mind that *general* disorder was endemic to
medieval society, the fact that much of the *organised* disorder we know
about was expressed through a misrule lord or mock king and his retinue
shows that a good many people were aware of ideological oppositions.

Festive misrule was in its turn influenced by the exploits of outlaws —
the Robin Hood legend[8] — and also by memorable rebellions. The most
striking example of an uprising that became incorporated into a festive
custom comes from the records of the Inns of Court. In 1381 the lawyers'
Temple was destroyed by Wat Tyler and his followers, yet some time after
that a lord of misrule called Jack Straw was elected (probably by the
younger lawyers) at Christmas. Record was made of it when the title was
abolished in 1519 (Walker 1897: 1.189):

> For Christmas ...
> Item that Jack Straw and all his adherents be from hensforth uttrely banyshed

and no more to be vsed in Lincolnes Inne, uppon peyne to forfeyt for euery
tyme fiue poundes.

The custom of electing less dangerous Christmas kings was retained in the
same order: one was "King ouer Christmas Day" and the other the "Kyng
of Cokneys" for Innocents' Day. The reason for abolishing Jack Straw was
the damage done in his name and there seems to be here a remarkable
example of the name of "a figure from seasonal folk revelry" (Pettitt 1984:
8) having been borrowed by a rebel leader and then reabsorbed by an
institution constitutionally opposed to misrule, as leader of its own local
indulgence in mayhem. It would be fascinating to pursue the reasons why
misrule customs were adopted by the institution set up to make laws, were
there more evidence available. The possibility is that there was some
philosophical acknowledgement of the counter-force to law and the
adoption of misrule lords could be an example of *concordia discors* in
practice and a way of acknowledging those opposite forces in controlled
circumstances.[9] But if the times of the year set aside throughout society for
the pageantry of misrule were the official, sanctioned or licensed seasons
for venting the forces of misrule, in the Inns of Court and houses of the
great these seasonal indulgences were dependent on outside factors.
Frequently, unsanctioned eruptions prevented the annual election.[10]

The principle I am arguing for behind all manifestations makes the
seasonal custom intrinsically subversive and its popularity among the mass
of society is easy to understand. What is more problematic is the
enthusiasm with which Tudor kings embraced such a dangerous symbol,
but a likely explanation is that the custom became a celebration of the early
Tudors' largely peaceful reigns. John Stowe's recollection in *A Survey of
London* (Stowe, ed. Kingsford 1971: 37) accentuates high spirits:

> There was in the feast of Christmas in the King's house, wheresoever he was
> lodged, a Lord of Misrule or Master of Merry Disports; and the like had ye in
> the house of every nobleman of honour or good worship, were he spiritual or
> temporal. Among the which, the Mayor of London and either of the Sheriffs
> had their several Lords of Misrule, ever contending, without quarrel or
> offence, who should make the rarest pastime to delight their beholders. These
> same Lords beginning their rule on Allhollons eve, continued the same til the
> morrow after the feast of the Purification.[11] ... In all which space there were
> fine and subtle disguisings, masks and mummeries.

During the first peaceful reign of the fifteenth century, Henry VII's, "the
household accounts ... make mention of a Lord or Abbot of Misrule for
nearly every Christmas" (Chambers 1903: 1.403). Misrule lords provided
entertainments at the court of Henry VIII until the 1530s, and the custom
was revived by Edward VI and continued until his death in 1553 (Anglo

1969). Elizabeth seems to have avoided the practice but by her time a renaissance form of the custom was flourishing in the Inns of Court and Universities. Its decline was then assured in the first half of the seventeenth century with the onset of civil strife. In 1652 Sir Thomas Urquhart attacked presbyterian disregard for kingship by comparison with the then defunct custom (Urquhart 1774: 146)

> Verily, I think they make use of kings in their consistorian state ... as the French on Epiphany-day use their *Roy de la Febue*, or king of the bean; ... or as about Christmas we used to do the King of Misrule, whom we invest with that title to no other end, but to countenance the Bacchanalian riots and preposterous disorders of the family where he is installed.

At first the lord of misrule at court played the role, as Stow said, of Master of Ceremonies. The more interesting developments, showing an ingenious reinterpretation of the principle of opposition to kingship, began with George Ferrers' election in 1551/2 and 1552/3 at the court of Edward VI. One finds an idealisation of the misrule world both in these entertainments, and at the Inner Temple following Robert Dudley's election as Lord of Misrule in 1561. The mirror image of the king's world interpreted by or through these men became a complementary opposition. Instead of an engaged opposition to the king expressed through imitation, the imitative display was developed into an artistic fiction. Any conflict between misrule and rule was removed and there was complete *concordia discors* in which the imagined world reflected the dominant world and depended on it for its existence.

These entertainments seem to express the dominant poetic desires of the sixteenth century, which S.K. Heniger shows adopted pythagorean science as a structure for their artistic endeavour. Behind Sidney's definition of poet as "maker" is an assertion of god-like powers of creation. "In this theory of poetry, the poem is an analogous universe created by the poet" (Heniger 1974: 293). What is more it was not tainted by any fall of Adam and therefore was a more perfect cosmos than God's. "In his poem the poet ... generates a universe which rivals Nature's for variety and which surpasses it in excellence" (Heniger 1974: 290). As Sidney himself wrote, "with the force of a divine breath he [the poet] bringeth things foorth surpassing her [Nature's] doings" (Heniger 1974: 305). Sidney's philosophy for his poetics was Plato's "in his most strongly Pythagorean mood" (Heniger 1974: 290). One other pythagorean encouragement poets found in their quest for a perfect world was the pre-Copernican cosmic system in which immutable worlds existed beyond the earth's atmosphere. To quote Heniger again (1974: 125), the "possibility of other worlds held out hope to the perennial band of those who seek Utopias". The notion that there was a more ideal existence on the moon led to flights of fancy from poets who wrote as worshippers of Diana culling much of their information from the ancient world.[11] There is for example the following passage which Heniger (1974: 125) quotes from a sixteenth-century translation of Plutarch:

> The pythagoreans affirme, that the Moone appeareth terrestriall, for that she is inhabited round about, like as the earth wherin we are, and peopled as it were with the greatest living creatures, and the fairest plants; and those creatures within her, be fifteene times stronger and more puissant than those with us, and the same yeeld forth no excrements, and the day there, is in that proportion so much longer.

The belief that life on another planet was more perfect changed any *mundus inversus* based on *alterae terrae* from a reductive to an improving concept. And I think some of these pythagorean qualities can be found in Ferrers' imaginative instructions regarding his second appearance as lord of misrule at Edward's court (Anglo 1969: 309-10):

> First as towching my Introduction where the last yeare my devise was to cum oute of the mone / this yeare I Imagin to cum oute of a place caulled *vastum vacuum*. I. the great waste / asmoche to saie as a place voyde or emptie withoute the worlde where is neither fier ayre water nor earth and that I haue bene remayning there sins the Last yeare. ... I wolde yf it were possyble haue all myne apparell blewe the first daie that I present my self to the kinges Maiestie. ... Again how I shall cum into the courte whether vnder a Canopie as the last yeare, or in a chare trivmphall, or vppon some straunge beast that I reserve to you / But the serpents with sevin heddes cauled hidra is the chief beast of myne armes. / and the wholie holly bushe is the devise of my crest / my worde is *semper ferians*. I. alwaies feasting or keping holie daie.

This description is an intriguing combination of mythology, carnival (the holly bush was the emblem of the Guild of Butchers) and scientific fantasy. On first impression any mention of a *vastum vacuum* might seem to suggest chaos but, on further reading, as it had in it no mutable elements it is clear that Ferrers' model was the immutable heavens and he asked for an appropriate dress of sky blue. It seems that Ferrers leavened the concept of misrule through a fusion with that of Utopia and that he refined the role of the misrule lord into a display based on the wonderful. His relationship to Edward was that of a king visiting on equal terms, taking over Edward's functions and communicating with him by means of ambassadors.

At the Inner Temple the tradition was for the Constable Marshall to be elected Lord of Misrule, and in 1561 an elaborate, idealised world was created when Robert Dudley was invited to the position of Constable Marshall. Whether he himself performed all the tasks of the Christmas Lord or only the more dignified ones is still debatable but the inventions of the 1561 proceedings reached an artistic peak. The idealised world was based on Arthurian and mythological legend with ideas taken from the coat of arms[12] and the chivalric codes of the Knights Templar. Gerard Legh, in *The Accedence of Armorie* (1562), described his approach to their celebration as though he were a Gulliver arriving at an ancient but unknown world near the heart of his own city (fol. 199):

> After I had travelled through the East part of th'unknown world, to vnderstand of deedes of armes, & so arriuing in the faire riuer of Thames, I laded within half a league fro the city of London, which was (as I coniecture) in December last. And drawing neare the citie, sodenly the shot of double canons in so great a number & so terrible that it darkened the whole aire, wherwith although I was in my natiue countrie: yet stood amazed not knowing what it ment. Thus as I abode in dispaire either to return or continue my former purpose, I chaunced to see comming towardes me an honest Citizen, clothed in long garments, keping the high way, seming to walk for his recreation, which prognosticated rather peace than perill. Of whome I demaundeth the cause of this great shot, who frendly answered, It is quoth he warning shot to th'officers of the constable Marshall of the Inner Temple, to prepare for dinner.

Dinner marked the beginning of the evening entertainments controlled by the misrule lord. William Dugdale, in retrospect, wrote that each morning after breakfast: "his lordship's power is in suspense, until his personal appearance at night; and then his power is most potent" (1666: 42). This is reminiscent of the lines in Webster's play, *The Duchess of Malfi*, when the Duchess's secret husband, Antonio, wishes to stay overnight and the Duchess accuses him of being "a lord of Mis-rule". He replies, "Indeed, my rule is only in the night" (III.ii.7-8). Both comments could be taken to mean that disorder is best carried out at night under cover of darkness. However, riot is no respecter of dawn, as rural records show, whereas Antonio says his rule in *only* in the night. Also, the words "rule" and "power" refer to a system of disorder rather than anything actually disordered and the stronger possibility in view of the other evidence is that at court misrule as a principle became allied to the nocturnal hours, possibly because that was the time of the moon's influence.

Like the fantasy world of Ferrers, this *mundus inversus* also had a sense of decorum. Among other formalities, one of the first things the Constable Marshall did on election was to rename the assembly man by man (Dugdale 1666: 41):

> Sir Francis Flatter of Fowlehurst in the county of Buckingham.
> Sir Randell Rackabite of Rascall Hall in the county of Rakehell.
> Sir Morgan Mumchance of Much Monkery in the county of Mad Mopery.

These are mock titles. The misrule lord renamed his "meynee" in much the same way as the records of medieval misrule customs show (Pettitt 1984: 9), but the dishonourable titles are abstracted away from any allusions to actual social conflict. Sir Randell is not Randell Ravener or, more appropriately for that period, Sir Randell Rackrent. The system which embraced the custom fictionalised anything which might have threatened that system. When, in the 1590s, lawyers of the Middle Temple re-engaged with the real world and the misrule lord broke open "chambers in the nyght, levying money as the Lord of Misrule's rent" (Hopwood 1903: 26), the lawyers involved were discommoned. Sixteenth-century lords elected outside the court environment also seem to have largely lost the dangerous, engaged meaning of misrule. The increase in their festive popularity does itself indicate a more secure governmental system.

In conclusion it would seem that the use of misrule lord titles was more than a useful screen for rebels and that they were not just adopted because of a superficial likeness between festive and real riot, but that instead they were used by rebels and outlaws as well as by festive lords because the title was absolutely appropriate to all three. The leaders were, in all cases, lords of the permanent antithesis to rule. Festive lords were chosen for celebratory reasons but the proof that the forces of misrule were a permanent feature of the cosmos could come from any riotous activity happening at any time of the year, and it would seem that prior to the sixteenth century the engaged meaning in the adoption of misrule lord titles coloured the proceedings even when festivity rather than rebellion was intended.

NOTES

1   For discussion of the correspondences between festivity and revolt, see Ladurie 1979, Berce 1976, and Davis 1975, and for discussion of the saturnalian concept of festival, see Bakhtin, trans. Iswolsky, 1978, and Barber 1959.
2   Skeat's nineteenth century edition allows for quotation from either the B or C text depending on which reads the more clearly. The quotations given here are composite texts.
3   Trans. Billington from the Anglo-Norman French given in Stones 1957: 135. The translation "North Wind" for "Bise" is suggested by Stones, n. 3.
4   See Wiles 1981 and Holt 1982 for a discussion of Robin Hood as a real person, and Hilton 1958 for a more likely argument.
5   Knighton, ed. Lumby 1889-95: 2.46. Bowers 1961 notes that "Sir Roger was protected by a retinue of fifty odd armed men which suggests that the ambush involved an almost equal number on the other side; and that accordingly the fray approached the fighting of small private armies."
6   See Pettitt 1984, Simms 1978, and Hobsbawm 1969.
7   The court addressed itself primarily to the mayor and commons of Norwich; see Hudson and Tingay 1906-10: 1.340.
8   At the beginning of the sixteenth century, French pastourelle influenced the Robin Hood May game. The fifteenth century references all connect with the outlaw tradition of the bold exploits; see Wiles 1981: chapter 5.
9   The method of reasoning is similar to what Stephen Greenblatt identifies as

"the containment of a subversive force by the authority that has created that force in the first place". See "Invisible Bullets", Dollimore and Sinfield 1985: 29.

10 See a sixteenth century Candlemas carol from Balliol College, MS 354, in which Christmas bids farewell and says (Greene 1977: 85, stanza 5):
"Anoder yere I trust I shall
Make mery in this hall,
Yf rest and pease in Ynglond may fall;
Now haue gud day!"

11 In this account in Stowe, the lord's election took place at Allhallows (31 October) and his period of office lasted until after Candlemas (2 February). Therefore his reign was allowed to begin the night that dark forces were thought to be abroad; it was allowed to last during the darkest quarter of the year and was brought to an end after a festival of light. Although the misrule lords in court or country only dominated events for one short season, they were frequently elected for a full year, possibly in acknowledgement that the forces of disorder existed, if in abeyance, through the rest of the year. In the universities they were given the paradoxical task of keeping order and were also assigned any administrative duties which connected one season with another. In St John's College, Cambridge, an inventory of costumes was drawn up in 1548 and reads that they were "p[re]servd & kept from yere to yere of him which shalbe Lord in Christmas" and passed by him to his "next Lord successor" (Billington 1978: 2), and it appears from a collection of churchwardens' accounts for Croscombe between 1474 and 1526 that the summer king was the man responsible for money gathered throughout the year and brought to the church at the annual March audit (see Hobhouse 1890).

12 See, e.g., Michael Drayton's, "Endimion and Phoebe" which includes the lines: "And as the sunne unto the day gives light, / So is she onely mistress of the night" (ed. Buxton 1953: 32), and Sir Walter Raleigh's "Praisd be Diana's fair and harmless light". The cult of Diana was, of course, encouraged as a compliment to Elizabeth.

13 The flying horse, Pegasus, is a motif of the Coat of Arms. Dudley was dubbed "The mightie Pallaphilos prince of Sophie, high constable Marshall of the knights Temples, Patrons of the honourable order of Pegasus" (Legh 1562: fol. 124v; see Axton 1970).

REFERENCES

Anglo, Sidney (1969). *Spectacle and Pageantry and Early Tudor Policy*. Oxford: Clarendon Press.
Axton, Marie (1970). Robert Dudley and the Inner Temple Revels. *The Historical Journal* 13, 365-78.
Bakhtin, Mikhail, trans. Hélène Iswolsky (1968). *Rabelais and his World*. Cambridge, Mass.: Massachusetts Institute of Technology.
Barber, C.L. (1959). *Shakespeare's Festive Comedy*. New Jersey: Princeton University Press.
Bellamy, John G. (1973). *Crime and Public Order in the Middle Ages*. London: Routledge & Kegan Paul.
Berce, Yves-Marie (1976). *Fête et Révolte: Des mentalities populaires du XVIe au XVIIe siècle*. Paris: Machette.
Billington, Sandra (1978). Sixteenth-Century Drama in St John's College, Cambridge. *Review of English Studies* n.s. 29, 1-10.
Bowers, R.H. (1961). "Foleuyles Lawes" ("Piers Plowman", C XXII.247). *Notes*

*and Queries* 206, 327-8.

Brie, Friedrich W.D. (1906). Wat Tyler and Jack Straw. *The English Historical Review* 21, 106-11.

Buxton, John, ed. (1953). *Poems of Michael Drayton*. London: Routledge & Kegan Paul.

Chambers, E.K. (1903). *The Medieval Stage*. Oxford: Clarendon Press.

Davis, Natalie Zemon (1975). *Society and Culture in Early Modern France*. London: Duckworth.

Davis, Norman, ed. (1971-6). John Paston, *The Paston Letters*. Oxford: Clarendon Press.

Dobson, R.B. (1983). *The Peasants' Revolt of 1381*. 2nd edn. London: Macmillan.

Dollimore, Jonathan and Alan Sinfield (1985). *Political Shakespeare*. Manchester: Manchester University Press.

Dugdale, Sir William (1666). *Originales Iuridiciales*. London.

Elbow, Peter (1975). *Oppositions in Chaucer*. Connecticut: Wesleyan University Press.

Greene, R.L., ed. (1977). *The Early English Carols*. Oxford: Clarendon Press.

Heniger, Jr., S.K. (1974). *Touches of Sweet Harmony*. California: Huntington Library Press.

Hilton, R.H. (1958). The Origins of Robin Hood. *Past and Present* 13, 30-44.

Hobhouse, E., ed. (1890). *Churchwardens' Accounts of Croscombe, Pilton, Yatton, Tintinhull, Morebath and St. Michael's Bath*. Somerset: Somerset Record Society.

Hobsbawm, E.J. and G. Rude (1969). *Captain Swing*. Harmondsworth: Penguin.

Holt, J.C. (1982). *Robin Hood*. London: Thames & Hudson.

Hopwood, C.H., ed. (1903). *A Calendar of the Middle Temple Records*. London.

Hudson, W. and U.J.C. Tingay, eds. (1906-10). *Selected Records of the City of Norwich*. Norwich.

Kempe, A.J., ed. (1835). *The Loseley Manuscripts*. London.

Ladurie, Emmanuel Le Roy, trans. Mary Feeney (1979). *Carnival in Romans*. Harmondsworth: Penguin.

Legh, Gerard (1562). *The Accedens of Armory*. London: R. Tottil.

Lumby, J.R., ed. (1889-95). *Chronicon Henrici Knighton*. London.

Lyle, Helen M. (1950). *The Rebellion of Jack Cade 1450*. London: George Philip & Son, Historical Association Pamphlet G 16.

Pettitt, Thomas (1984). Here Comes I, Jack Straw. *Folklore* 95, 3-20.

Raleigh, Sir Walter (1593). *The Phoenix Nest*. London.

Simms, Ned (1978). Ned Ludd's Mummers Play. *Folklore* 89, 166-78.

Skeat, W.W., ed. (1886). William Langland, *The Vision of Piers the Plowman in three parallel texts together with Richard the Redeles*. Oxford: Clarendon Press.

Stones, E.L.G. (1957). The Folvilles of Ashby-Folville, Leicestershire, and their associates in crime 1326-1347. *Transactions of the Royal Historical Society* 7, 117-36.

Urquhart, Sir Thomas (1652). *Tracts of the Learned and Celebrated Antiquarian* (1774). London.

Walker, J.D., ed. (1897). *The Black Books of Lincoln's Inn*, vol. 1. London.

Wiles, David (1981). *The Early Plays of Robin Hood*. Ipswich: D.S. Brewer.

Wright, T., ed. (1858). *Political Poems and Songs*. London.

# THE REPRESENTATIONS OF POWER IN SHAKESPEARE'S SECOND TETRALOGY

John Drakakis

Almost nowhere in Shakespeare's plays is the transfer of political power from one king to another effected smoothly. Stories of the death of kings, as Richard II, deprived of the material supports of his regal power, comes to recognise, furnish a catalogue of disasters; he recalls:

> How some have been depos'd, some slain in war,
> Some haunted by the ghosts they have deposed,
> Some poisoned by their wives, some sleeping kill'd,
> All murthered —                    *Richard II*, III.ii.157-60

It has, of course, not been uncommon among certain literary historians to disregard these political facts concerning the transfer of regal power, in favour of a nostalgic vision of "order" rooted, so it is asserted, in the reign of Elizabeth I. Nowhere is that nostalgia more clearly revealed than in the final sentence of E.M.W. Tillyard's *The Elizabethan World Picture* (1943) in which he sets what he calls "the Elizabethan habit of mind". (characterised, it is asserted, by the judicious, not to say selective, documentation of statements about "order") against the modern propensity for chaos and fragmentation. Tillyard laments (1943: 102):

> And, if we reflect on that habit, we may see that (in queerness though not in viciousness) it resembles certain trends of thought in central Europe, the ignoring of which by our scientifically minded intellectuals has helped not a little to bring the world into its present conflicts and distresses.

We may recognise in this critical strategy a familiar appeal to a fictionalised past, a variation on the theme that "fings ain't what they used to be", an appeal that confuses fact and fiction, and which proceeds from there to transform certain carefully selected products of a determinate history into a series of absolute truths applicable at all times. In this way poems such as Sir John Davies's *Orchestra*, Spenser's *Hymn of Heavenly Beauty*, Ulysses's speech from *Troilus and Cressida*, supported by Hooker's *The Laws of Ecclesiastical Polity* and *The Homily on Obedience*, can be accorded a homiletic value in the war against, it would seem, "our scientifically minded intellectuals". Tillyard's essentialist project is nothing less than the reduction of a range of literary, ecclesiastical, and political discourses to a series of propositions which can then be said to disclose "the Elizabethan habit of mind" (1943: 101).

King Richard, however, confronted not with "scientifically minded intellectuals" but with a tangible threat to his political authority, recalls not an idyllic, trouble-free past — that is left, in part, in the play to the aging John of Gaunt — but a process in which two opposing narratives jostle for supremacy. The seemingly inviolable legitimate ruler, inscribed within the symbolic order of kingship, is made to confront his own questionable behaviour, as well as the consequences of the political violation of his authority, thus bringing the facts of a secular political history into direct conflict with a theologically-sanctioned *prescriptive* "reality" whose ideological function is to interpellate and position individual subjectivities. The result, in this case, is a separation of the person of the king from the office of kingship, a violation of the monarch's self-presence which results in the momentary disclosure of the workings of the ideology as it concentrates its own discursive resources upon the smoothing over of contradiction exposed by such a challenge. In this way the ruling ideology can be shown to sustain its domination by "winning out" against any attempt to transform existing social relations. It does this by sustaining what Michel Pêcheux describes as "contact" and "dialogue" with a range of adversarial positions, thus slowing down, or suppressing, any prospect of radical transformation (Pêcheux 1982: 100). In a purely formal sense, this is what generates the dramatic "narrative", but it is, nonetheless, a narrative which is deeply implicated in political process. The movement that I wish to sketch out in Shakespeare's Second Tetralogy is one which begins with a kingly violation of power, authority and responsibility, which renders problematical the representational function of the figure of the king. In the narrative which this generates, "person" is separated from "office", but this, in effect, temporary demystification of the symbolic order is the necessary pre-condition for the reconstitution of the figure of the king as representative of divine authority and efficient source of meaning and order.

In his book *The King's Two Bodies: a Study in Medieval Political Theology* (1957: 41), Ernst Kantorowicz draws attention to *Richard II* as a tragedy which depends "not only upon the concept of a Christ-like martyr king, but also on that most unpleasant idea of a violent separation of the King's Two Bodies." What Kantorowicz points to here is the way in which the dominant ideology effaces the contradiction between the immortality associated with the *corpus mysticum* and the fact of human mortality which poses a threat to its mystifying power. When that spiritual continuity is undermined by the removal of the king by force, even though the disruption is shown to be within the ranks of the ruling class itself, then a tactical adjustment becomes necessary in order to sustain a faltering ideology.

Indeed, from the very outset of *Richard II* the discourse of absolute monarchy, which is distributed among a wide range of characters with differing allegiances, is given an ironic gloss as the cause of the conflict between Bolingbroke and Mowbray is very carefully overlaid with those symbols within which power realises itself. Bolingbroke can wish his sovereign longevity: "Many years of happy days befall/ My gracious sovereign, my most loving liege!", while his adversary, Mowbray, can extend this courtesy into the realm of spirituality: "Each day still better other's happiness/ Until the heavens, envying earth's good hap,/ Add an immortal title to your crown!" (I.i.20-4).

At issue is the political murder of the Duke of Gloucester, an action for which the king himself is thought to have been responsible. Thus, beneath the heavily symbolic discourse of kingship, there lies a king's action which is the negation of human justice, and for which his maligned subjects can achieve no redress. John of Gaunt resists firmly the Duchess of Gloucester's incitement to revenge with an appeal to the doctrine of divine right:

> God's is the quarrel — for God's substitute,
> His deputy anointed in His sight,
> Hath caus'd his death; the which if wrongfully,
> Let heaven revenge, for I may never lift
> An angry arm against His minister.                    I.ii.37-41

In objective terms Gaunt's appeal raises the question in this context of the precise origin and nature of monarchical authority, an issue which had received consistent attention from extreme protestant ecclesiastics and theoreticians since the reign of Mary Tudor.

This objective conflict has, however, been obscured by the tendency of many critics of the play to personalise it as an expression of Richard's "character". Thus, the Arden editor, Peter Ure, locates a humanist essence at the centre of the drama and insists that Richard's "alternating moods go to make up the man rather than to expose the relativity of a doctrine" (Ure 1956: lxviii), although in something of a contradictory vein he then proceeds to suggest that the conflict is between the "new man" Bolingbroke, and the "medieval" Richard with the result that "some sense that an old order is giving place to a new is present to most of its readers" (lxxiii). Similarly, Alvin Kernan can argue that, in historical terms, the dramatic conflict involves "the passage from the middle ages to the Renaissance" (Barroll *et al.* 1975: 270), while at the same time insisting that Richard's problem is that he "takes the great myth of order for absolute fact, mistakes metaphor for science" (272). What much criticism of the play has signally overlooked is that Richard's *identity*, which Gaunt acknowledged without question, and the identities of Richard's own subjects, are derived from within the very symbolic discourses which express their mutual relations. Like Gaunt, Richard has no choice in the matter; he cannot *choose* "science" before "metaphor" since to do so would be to negate his own identity. Indeed, the ceremony of formal combat with which the play opens, references to the institution of monarchy as an immortal corporation, the designation of Richard as "God's substitute", appeals to "heaven", oaths uttered "by my sceptre's awe" (I.i.118) and "by my seat's right royal majesty" (II.i.120), the insistence, even in adversity, that "The breath of worldly men cannot depose/ The deputy elected by the Lord" (III.ii.56-7), the explicitly ecclesiastical positioning of the king as intermediary by prelates such as the Bishop of Carlisle — "I speak to subjects, and a subject speaks,/ Stirr'd up by God thus boldly for his king" (IV.i.132-3) — and Richard's own apt self-dramatisation as Christ delivered by "Pilates" to "my sour cross" (IV.i.240-1), are all constituent elements in the complex integrated discourse of absolute monarchy within which Richard is able to articulate his identity both as temporal authority and as speculary intermediary for the higher authority of God. That in the play he is presented as the origin of misrule renders his own self-dramatisation as "Christ" deeply ironical in that it exposes the gulf between monarchical responsibility and machiavellian political practice. To reconstitute this as a purely temporal conflict — the "medieval" Richard versus the "new man" Bolingbroke — is wholly to misrecognise what is at stake here. What is at issue is a disturbance *within ideology*, in which residual, dominant, and emergent elements contest for positions of supremacy. In fact the entire Tetralogy celebrates "kingship" through each play's exercising of a range of aesthetic preferences from *within* the available discourses all of which are unanimous in their demonising of "rebellion".

The problem posed by Richard's role as self-divided king is ultimately a problem of meaning. Here, in practical terms, the dominant discourse is shown to be "an instrument and effect of power", but it is also, as Foucault points out, "a hindrance, a stumbling block, a point of resistance and a starting point for an opposing strategy" (Foucault 1981: 101). When the fact of absolute power is visibly disengaged from the order within which it is inscribed then tensions invariably arise. As the protestant Bishop Ponet has pointed out in his *A Short Treatise of Political Power* (1556), power which transgresses the boundaries of those discourses which give it meaning can be justifiably negated; thus Edward II and Richard II can be classified as tyrants because in the case of the former explicitly, and the latter implicitly, "Without lawe he killed his subjectes, spoiled them of their goodes, and wasted the treasure of the Realme" (Ponet 1556: 99). It fell, of course, to Richard Hooker to articulate that "lawe" in the 1590s just as, at the level of state propaganda, the Homilies ensured that subjects remained firmly positioned within its symbolic structures.

For Richard, absolute power serves the demands of an anarchic energy, thus separating him from monarchic obligation and responsibility — in the final play in the Tetralogy the "perfect king" Henry V re-unites these elements of the structure — and it is this fragmentation of discourse which enables us to glimpse the contradictory textualisations which play across the phenomenological surface of the king's body. Indeed, what Kantorowicz regards as a duality — "Two Bodies", the one phenomenological, subject to change, and mortal, the other fictive — turns out to be one single entity capable of contradictory textualisations, two modes of signification which, because they pull in opposite directions, threaten to continually decentre the subject. These mutually contradictory textualisations of the king's body alternately privilege a hierarchical structure through which power acquires its representations and sovereignty its authority, while at the same time designating it as the repository of a series of class-specific libidinal energies which achieve their representation as universal human feelings. In this way objective relations of power, i.e. those which it is in the political interest of the dominant class to preserve, are lived spontaneously as the acceptance and acknowledgement of an externally-validated authority *and* as personal control of those energies upon which absolutism depends for its sustenance. For example, the ceremonial expressions of passion from Bolingbroke and Mowbray in the opening scenes of *Richard II*, and their equally ceremonial restraint by the figure of the king, do not, as is commonly supposed, indicate either Richard's weakness or his obsession with his role; rather, they are the ideological signifiers of his political strength. What renders Richard's position ironical is that the public articulation of this "test" obfuscates a private, politically pragmatic, "test" which, when put into operation, systematically empties these signifiers of Richard's authority of meaning: political murder, prodigal behaviour, administrative imprudence, the seizure of land, and the disruption of inheritance. In other words, Richard breaks the very laws which ensure both his authority and the subjection of his subjects, although the play remains equivocal about the nature of the king's own subjection to human law itself.

It would be a mistake, however, to suppose that the issue is simply one of the disturbance of the elements of the symbolic order; that is obviously the case here and in other plays such as *Hamlet, King Lear*, and *Macbeth*. The issue is also one of the imperilling of identity. Up to the moment of his death John of Gaunt speaks for a continuity and a subjection which is manifestly ideological; as a subject he "works by himself" as Althusser would say (Althusser 1971: 181). Richard's sequestration of Bolingbroke's inheritance renders both that *subjection*, and the "subjectivity" through whose ideological mechanisms it operates, highly problematical, as the now perplexed "subject" York points out:

> Take Herford's rights away, and take from time
> His charters, and his customary rights;
> Let not to-morrow then ensue to-day:
> Be not thyself. For how art thou a king
> But by fair sequence and succession?                    II.i.195-9

This process is emphasised even more sharply at the moment when Richard resigns the supreme symbol of his authority, his crown — and with it his identity in an act of self-cancellation — to an adversary who, with the aid of military force, eases his way into the space in the symbolic order which his victim has vacated. The moment is worth pausing over. When asked to abdicate by Bolingbroke Richard demurs — "Ay, no; no, ay; for I must nothing be." (IV.i.201) — but once begun the process is irreversible, ultimately confusing victim and aggressor and eliminating all social distinction:

> Nay, if I turn mine eyes upon myself,
> I find myself a traitor with the rest.
> For I have given here my soul's consent
> T'undeck the pompous body of a king;
> Made glory base, and sovereignty a slave;
> Proud majesty a subject, state a peasant.            IV.i.247-52

The relinquishing of position and power, which the play represents (with possibly an eye on the censor) as a choice for the protagonist, contrives to negate Richard's own subjectivity as the regal pronoun "We" of the opening scenes of the play contracts to the solitary and precarious "I", before dropping out of signifying practice altogether: "I must nothing be."

Emptied of their internal coherence as a currency of exchange within the symbolic economies of power, individual representations become just so many roles which the actor inhabits and which he performs desperately before the irreverent personification, Death, "Scoffing his state and grinning at his pomp" (III.ii.163). This separation of content from form culminates in the handing over of a crown which is, indeed, "hollow". But by the end of the play the sense of theatrical role merely as the opportunity for the actor's improvisatory skills is carried to extremes, as the now perversely speculary figure of Richard replays the process whereby the symbolic representation of his own body textualised as an immortal corporation has been systematically de-realised:

> Thus play I in one person many people,
> And none contented. Sometimes am I king,
> Then treasons make me wish myself a beggar,
> And so I am. Then crushing penury
> Persuades me I was better when a king;

> Then am I king'd again, and by and by
> Think that I am unking'd by Bolingbroke,
> And straight am nothing. But whate'er I be,
> Nor I, nor any man that but man is,
> With nothing shall be pleas'd till he be eas'd
> With being nothing.                                    V.v.30-41

It is dramatically significant that the play should end as it had begun with a secret murder of a member of the ruling class, just as it is ironical that Richard's final gesture of striking down two of his murderers summons the libidinal energy which is both the product *and* support of political power in the play.

*Richard II* is full of examples of the de-realisation of identity. In addition to the case of Richard, Bolingbroke's own identity is a shifting phenomenon as evidenced in his attempt to legitimise what is technically a treasonable act by appealing to a change of name (II.iii.112-3): "As I was banish'd, I was banish'd Herford;/ But as I come, I come for Lancaster." Later he accuses the "caterpillars of the commonwealth", Bushy and Greene, of seeking to erase him from the social order altogether:

> Myself — a prince by fortune of my birth,
> Near to the king in blood, and near in love,
> Till you did make him misinterpret me —
> ........ you have fed upon my signories,
> Dispark'd my parks and fell'd my forest woods,
> From my own windows torn my household coat,
> Rac'd out my imprese, leaving me no sign,
> Save men's opinions and my living blood,
> To show the world I am a gentleman.                   III.i.16-27

York, caught between two warring factions of the ruling class and charged with the responsibility for maintaining order, knows "not what to do" (II.ii.100), and seeks to avoid having to make an impossible choice by politically emasculating himself (II.iii.157-8): "be it known unto you,/ I do remain as neuter." Later in the play when he acts upon the knowledge of his son Aumerle's treasonable plot against the new king, Henry, he is accused of splitting the unity of his family by setting "the word itself against the word!" (V.iii.120), a process which in its public and domestic manifestations is subsumed into the general gloss which the imprisoned Richard provides for it (V.v.12-4): "The better sort,/ As thoughts of things divine, are intermix'd/ With scruples, and do set the word itself/ Against the word." Of course, the play can offer no neutral position free from political signification so that the de-realisation of identity is always already inscribed within ideology insofar as its processes of signification remain available for habitation from within by those who would appropriate power to themselves. Thus Bolingbroke can say "In God's name, I'll ascend the regal throne" while the Bishop of Carlisle can, with equal conviction, assert "Marry, God forbid!" (IV.i.113-4), a see-saw effect which Richard appropriates for his own purposes a little later in the same scene with his image of: "two buckets, filling one another,/ The emptier ever dancing in the air,/ The other down, unseen, and full of water."(IV.i.185-7)

In *Richard II*, and also in the two *Henry IV* plays, the internalised ideological discourses of power produce clear psychic as well as political effects. Usurpation is closely linked with rebellion, where the latter term can find — as it had already done in protestant doctrines of resistance — attenuated ecclesiastical legitimation in the plot spawned by the Bishop of Carlisle and the Abbot of Westminster (IV.i.320 ff.), and, in *1 Henry IV*, political and dynastic legitimation in the plots of the Northern Percies, the Scots and the Welsh. All indicate, however, that the providentialist framework within which claim and counter-claim is made is under severe pressure to contain the contradictions which these conflicts produce. Indeed, although in *Richard II* the conflict is depicted in tragic terms, it is not resolved in the sense that "human experience" is, as Raymond Williams puts it (1966: 52), held up to the order "for ratification and containment". Richard is made to reap the bitter reward of his misrule, certainly, but the play eschews an easy moralism since what is at issue leads directly to the contradiction that lies at the heart of the entire Tetralogy: usurpation culminates in the rule of the "perfect king", but this is not without its difficulties since the result is the decentring of the figure of the king and the consequent generation of a burden of guilt which Henry IV himself carries throughout the two succeeding plays and which is not transmuted into kingly "responsibility" until the final play in the Tetralogy. Thus *Richard II* demonstrates with an almost Brechtian clarity the conditions within which a tragic hero is produced, conditions which are not contingent upon the simultaneous upholding and violation of a discursively produced ethical code. With an all but brutal realism, the new king, Henry IV, articulates this contradiction with his observations that "They love not poison that do poison need" and "Lords, I protest my soul is full of woe/ That blood should sprinkle me to make me grow" (V.vi.38, 45-6). It may be argued, of course, that these are local skirmishes which take place within an over-arching apocalyptic vision culminating in the reign of Elizabeth as a "second coming"; although if this were to be so then the gap between real history and the ideology which masks its operations could be demonstrated to be very wide indeed. Elizabeth's own comment on the play — "I am Richard II. Know ye not that?" — and the reception of Sir John Hayward's controversial *First Part of The Raigne of Henry IV* in 1599 make it clear that the contemporary perceptions owed less to the propagandist formulations that so impressed Tillyard, and more to the dangerous capacity of theatrical performance to refract the historically specific tensions and conflicts within Elizabethan society itself.

By the end of *Richard II* the new king, like his predecessor, is caught between "thoughts of things divine" which are "intermix'd with scruples", a decentring which indicates the gulf between a secular determination and a Christian providentialism. The "scruples" *undo* the "thoughts of things divine". At a personal level, security in the possession of absolute power expressed in terms of a reconstituted monarchy is undermined by the residual troubling psychic effects of a discourse erected upon political murder and coercion. This is what happens when, as Fulke Greville noted in his *A Treatise on Monarchy* (c. 1600), "powre turns nature into art" (Greville 1965: 84) in accordance with the political syntax of a secular script which problematises altogether the argument from providential design.

*The Mirror For Magistrates*, "wherein", the title page of the 1571 edition announced, "may be seene by examples passed in this realme, with howe greueous plagues, vyces are punished in great princes and magistrates, and how frayle and vnstable worldly prosperity is founde" (Campbell 1960: 15), had characterised Richard as a glutton and a lecher, a Lord of Misrule, in fact:

> What pleasure pryckt, that thought I to be just.
> I set my minde, to feede, to spoyle, to iust,
> Three meales a day could skarce content my mawe,
> And all to augment my lecherous minde that muste
> To Venus pleasures alway be in awe
> (Greville, ed. Wilkes 1965: 113)

Holinshed is a little less specific in his description of him as "prodigall, ambitious, and much given to the pleasure of the bodie" (Ure 1956: 192). Shakespeare's play displaces these allegations largely on to Richard's favourites, and the drama is concentrated upon the king's body as the site where conflicting political meanings are contested; hence the fragmentation of Richard's "character", and the necessity for the maintenance of a tragic rather than a comic mood. To adopt too objective a stance in relation to the conflict would be, surely, to risk the full weight of the repressive apparatus of the Elizabethan state falling upon the theatre company.

In the *Henry IV* plays, there is a complete change of mood as similar political ingredients to those contained in *Richard II* are made to undergo a radical re-textualisation. In these two plays, "misrule" and "rebellion" are shown to be *not the consequences of* tyrannical power, but rather the residual manifestations of Henry's own feelings of guilt, feelings which ideology prescribes should be shown as "natural", but which the pragmatics of absolute power require to be contained and publicly re-interpreted. In this connection, Stephen Greenblatt has recently observed that in both the

*Henry IV* plays, the production of ideal images of power "involves as its positive condition the constant production of its own radical subversion and the powerful containment of that subversion" (Dollimore and Sinfield 1985: 20). This is precisely what Pêcheux means when he refers to the ruling ideology "winning out" against the possibilities of radical transformation.

Repetition is a crucial device in the structure of any ideology insofar as it contributes to the imposition of limits upon what is thinkable. Such devices form part of the ensemble of what Fredric Jameson has called "strategies of containment" (Jameson 1981: 53), which, he goes on to argue, "seek to endow their object of representation with formal unity" (54). But that process functions antagonistically, so to speak, sustaining the ruling ideology against any threat to its displacement. To this extent the Elizabethan theatre may be said to imitate, in the words of Pierre Macherey, "the everyday language which is the language of ideology" (Macherey 1978: 59). Juridically speaking, its freedom was "licensed" indicating that such potential for representing the contradictions in society which it had was severely circumscribed; indeed, this was often contextualised within the framework of "carnival". This now familiar identification of what are often referred to as the "popular" elements of Elizabethan drama does, in certain of its domesticated forms of analysis, lead directly to a reinforcement of the view that the social function of the theatre was to reinforce a normative ideology. Such is the view of C.L. Barber, who argues that the "release" afforded by carnival and festivity leads to "clarification" (Barber 1959: 8), while failing to grasp the political implications of his own position: that this represents a reinforcement of existing power-relations displaced on to the axis of a universal opposition between "the heart and the world" (221).

These arguments have direct relevance to the *Henry IV* plays because, like all of the plays in the Second Tetralogy, they are concerned to negotiate a politically sensitive issue. The rupture in the dominant ideology caused by the usurpation of Richard's power can only be partially explained from within its own boundaries, and as such serves to demystify those institutions through which the ruling class maintains its political interests and position. The consequence, though in this case limited, is the implicit rejection, albeit temporary, of a ritualised normative ethic within whose boundaries meaning is conceived as repetition. The identification of meanings as elements in a dialectic process of political struggle depends upon *difference* insofar as they refract a conflict of interests which is itself structured in accordance with the distribution of power. If, as Vološinov has argued, the linguistic sign is the arena for "the clash of live social accents" (Vološinov 1973: 23), then it becomes possible to view those elements of the *Henry IV* plays which we have become accustomed to labelling "carnivalesque" as *ideologically* constructed "others" enabling the dominant "accent" to sustain its authority through the processes of marginalisation and aesthetic closure. In this situation, repetition is no longer adequate as a coercive device, since the past cannot be used as a "mirror" in which the present sees itself unproblematically reflected. It is replaced by conflict for the possession of the sign itself, where what once appeared to be a stable discourse becomes the site of competing claims with political power and domination as the stake.

This is to depart significantly from Tillyard's reading of the plays as exemplifications of "the principle of history repeating itself" just as it is to depart from C.L. Barber's more "carnivalesque" account of the dramatic action. Tillyard's position, which carries a strong ideological charge itself, requires us to see the plays in terms of a "morality" structure in which Hal chooses between "Sloth or Vanity, to which he is drawn by his bad companions, and Chivalry, to which he is drawn by his father and his brothers" (Tillyard 1944: 265), while Barber emphasises the ironies "which bring down the meanings which fly high in winged words" (Barber 1959: 194). But, from the outset, these plays re-distribute roles and positions as the crimes of usurpation and regicide are gradually displaced on to an axis whereby the past is reconstituted rather than repeated. Thus, far from occupying an omniscient position in relation to the dramatic action, Hal is implicated as a subject within a range of disparate discourses, so much so that it is perhaps misleading to speak as Stephen Greenblatt does, of his "improvisational" dexterity (Dollimore and Sinfield 1985: 33-4). Hal is very much bound by a series of subject positions, at least one of which, the identity of the monarch as "man", is facilitated by the tragic fragmentation of the dead Richard as royal subject. But Hal is also, at one level, an effect of his father's crime, the "heir apparent" whose profligacy recalls that of Richard, while at the same time he embodies that anarchic impulse which itself fuels "rebellion".

But as "heir apparent" Hal is already constituted as a royal subject within the discourse of absolutist power, even though events have already rendered the question of dynastic succession problematical. As a site of contradiction, Hal is a "truant" to that "Chivalry" which is the expression of ruling class interest; hence Henry's lament that this son is not the more singular Hotspur (*1 Henry IV*, I.i.80-2): "A son who is the theme of honour's tongue,/ Amongst a grove the very straightest plant,/ Who is sweet Fortune's minion and her pride." Later in the play Henry will draw explicit comparisons between Richard and Hal, Hotspur and himself:

> For all the world
> As thou art to this hour was Richard then
> When I from France set foot at Ravenspurgh,
> And even as I was then is Percy now.
> Now by my sceptre, and my soul to boot,

> He hath more worthy interest to the state
> Than thou the shadow of succession.                    III.ii.93-9

The concern here is with the *fear* of repetition, although it is ironical that Henry's oath, "Now by my sceptre", echoes the ceremonial oaths of his murdered predecessor. Henry is manifestly not wrong in valuing those institutions and practices which support his authority and give it meaning, and it is clear from Hal's soliloquy at the end of I.ii that his son is of like mind as he too begins to articulate the symbolic discourses of absolutism — "Yet herein will I imitate the sun" and "like bright metal on a sullen ground" (I.ii.192, 207) — slowly easing himself into its structures, and into a subjectivity inscribed within them.

For Henry IV, this colonising of discourse is habitual as he systematically reconstitutes the past through a process of subtle negation. In defining his role as that of "Christ", the sacrificial body who is God's representative on earth, Richard identified Bolingbroke as Judas, and Pilate: "So Judas did to Christ" (*Richard II*, IV.i.170), and "yet you Pilates/ Have here deliver'd me to my sour cross,/ And water cannot wash away your sin." (IV.i.240-2). These identifications are selective, since, from the perspective of John of Gaunt, Richard is satanic in his destruction of "This other Eden, demi-paradise" with its reputation "For Christian service and true chivalry" (II.i.42, 54). In the discourse of Henry IV both aspects of the biblical narrative are amalgamated, as he relinquishes the damning identifications with Judas and Pilate for that of the crusading soldier of Christ: "Therefore, friends,/ As far as to the sepulchre of Christ —/ Whose soldier now, under whose blessed cross/ We are impressed and engag'd to fight —" (*1 Henry IV*, I.i.18-21). His reason is the Judas-like guilt which he feels and which prompts him to reconstitute Richard dead as Christ, thus making his victim the displaced object of his pilgrimage. In this way Henry strategically effaces the contradiction in his own position through an appeal to a discreetly re-unified Christian narrative. As the elements in an important ideological state apparatus, the religious archetypes invoked by Henry exert a powerful talismanic effect, but more than once they are undone and then reconstituted in the *Henry IV* plays as secular accounts threaten to displace, or at the very least render ironical, these Christian sentiments. The result is that the initial disruption in *narrative* through which the dramatic action operates is prevented from achieving the status of a truly ruptural unity. In cases such as this, irony is appropriated as a weapon whereby the ruling ideology can sustain itself through the production of its own "critical" perspective.

A good example of this process occurs in the relation between Hal and Hotspur in *I Henry IV*, where Hotspur's expressions of "honour" as part of the discourse of "true chivalry" are made to seem ludicrously extravagant in their uncompromising absolutist import; his interest in chivalrous exploits is conditional (I.iii.204-5): "So he that doth redeem her thence might wear/ Without corrival all her dignities." His uncle, the politician Worcester, despairs that his nephew inhabits a fantasy "world of figures here" (I.iii.207), and so he does. But later in the play Hal confides to his father that "Percy is but my factor, good my lord" (III.ii.147), and in the final act of the play both participate in Hotspur's "world of figures", where the stakes are not some imaginary exploit but real power (V.iv.64-6): "Two stars keep not their motion in one sphere,/ Nor can one England brook a double reign/ Of Harry Percy and the Prince of Wales." Thus, though "honour" can be regarded critically, can suffer a severe debunking at the hands of Falstaff, it emerges strengthened at the end as a constituent element of the public discourse of absolutism, and, through its distribution across two roles, what begins as a de-mystification of institutions and practices, turns out to be an intensification of a mystified political expediency. In this way the *Henry IV* plays oscillate between a "realistic" political discourse in which power relations are presented nakedly as those of the dominant class fraction, and ideologically as a fully ritualised religious discourse. Throughout, the one constantly challenges the other, thus allowing us to glimpse the process whereby the material history of political struggle is received into the symbolic discourses of the dominant ideology. In their reconstitution of the apparatus of authority depicted in fragments in *Richard II*, the *Henry IV* plays inadvertently expose those discursive practices through which it receives its legitimation. The reconstitution which takes place, and which seeks to mask itself as a return to an innocent language, is therefore both political and aesthetic, involving the application of an artistry of power whereby the interests of the dominant class are carefully mediated through a connected series of political, juridical, and religious discourses, all of which the new regime systematically appropriates. Here propaganda is shown to be the support at an intentional level of those less easily accessible structures of political power within whose boundaries subject positions are always already inscribed. Thus, the earlier, politically expedient, aesthetic strategy of decentring Richard now requires to be reversed if the body of the new king, Henry IV, is to be successfully inscribed in the new order, and if rival dynastic claims from within the ruling class fraction are to be resisted. Thus, in structural terms, and while at the same time preserving an appropriate sense of guilt for the events of the past, the *Henry IV* plays construct an imaginary centre by banishing all threats to the king's absolute power to the margins. Domestic unrest forces the new king to forgo the distraction of a foreign pilgrimage — in *Henry V* this strategy of busying "giddy minds/ With foreign quarrels, that action hence borne out/ May waste the memory of the former days" (*2 Henry IV*, IV.v.213-5) fuels a comprehensively political absolutism — but even this, fought out on the battlegrounds of

Scotland and Wales, is geographically located as "stronds afar remote" (*1 Henry IV*, I.i.4). On the borders of civilisation unspeakable acts are committed on the "body" of the king as represented by his vassals, but the "beastly shameless transformation,/ By those Welshwomen done, as may not be/ Without much shame retold or spoken of" (I.i.44-6) upon the body of Mortimer turns out to be nothing less than marriage, an act of fraternisation perpetrated by one who was "proclaim'd,/ By Richard that dead is, the next of blood" (I.iii.143-4) upon the daughter of "that great magician, damn'd Glendower" (I.iii.82).

In addition to the momentary absolutist re-textualisation of marriage as an act of treachery, Mortimer's action and the fabulous "characterisation" of Glendower serve as a means of sharpening the distinctions between order and chaos, while at the same time underlining the contest for meanings which is in progress. Glendower's own personal history is unceremoniously questioned by an incredulous Hotspur, thus casting serious doubt upon the appropriation of a metaphysical explanation of power for the cause of rebellion. In this way the metaphysical explanation of absolutist power is raised in a context which *reverses* the egalitarian appeals in which Richard had sought refuge from political weakness, and which, in drawing attention to its palpable distortion, serves to foreclose a much more radical questioning of its authenticated usage. Moreover, the fact that Mortimer's wife "can speak no English, I no Welsh" (III.i.187) provides a domestic linguistic analogue for the Babel of discourses in the rebel camp from which in general terms it was, as Francis Bacon observed, the function of "grammar" to rescue man (Bacon, ed. Kitchin 1965: 138), the means whereby man may "re-integrate himself in those benedictions, from which by his fault he hath been deprived". The subtle displacement of "original sin" from Richard on to the rebels does much to invalidate their claims. This is the culmination of a gradual process whereby the rebels' denigration of Henry as "this ingrate and canker'd Bolingbroke" (I.iii.135), set against Richard, "that sweet lovely rose" (I.iii.173), is shown ultimately to occupy a position "beyond grammar" so to speak, toiling in the consequences of the original sin — what Bacon called "fault" and "deprivation" — of which they themselves can be said to be the efficient cause. In this extraordinarily delicate way legitimate counter-claims to the throne are invalidated *without* calling into serious question either the discourse of legitimacy *or* the militaristic ethic required to secure and maintain power.

Of course, the *Henry IV* plays are by no means uncritical of ritualised violence, although the ultimate result of that critique is its ratification. The Falstaffian critique of "honour" and Falstaff's own involvement with the mechanics of war in *1 Henry IV* sound a dissentient note which is not effectively neutralised until *Henry V*, and only then by re-directing military energies towards an external enemy in what is inferred to be a "holy" war. For Falstaff, and for those stage representations of social groups who are wholly excluded from the machinery of power, a strategy of containment is required which is different from that used in relation to a fragmenting aristocracy. For fractions within the dynastic group, subversive practice such as treason is, paradoxically, as the case of Hotspur clearly demonstrates — as indeed does that of the nobles and ecclesiastics who supported Bolingbroke's treason but who now revert to a position of loyalty to the dead Richard — defined within the ruling ideology as an excess of those objectively generated subjective feelings which as a "structure of feeling" sustains the dynastic order itself. Thus, in *Henry V* the traitors Scroop, Grey and Cambridge, can participate with some enthusiasm in the speculary practices of coercion of which they are the victims; Grey speaks for all three when he says:

> Never did faithful subject more rejoice
> At the discovery of most dangerous treason
> Than I do this hour joy o'er myself,
> Prevented from a damned enterprise.
> My fault, but not my body, pardon, sovereign.    II.ii.161-5

The gradual instalment of this process throughout the Tetralogy is undertaken with some care. Worcester meets his end with a tight-lipped appeal to the demands of personal safety at the end of *1 Henry IV*: "What I have done my safety urg'd me to;/ And I embrace this fortune patiently" (V.v.11-2). By *2 Henry IV* the machiavellians, Mowbray and the Archbishop of York, can appeal to the very values of "honour" and "faith" problematised by their rebellion: "Is this proceeding just and honourable?" and "Will you thus break your faith?" (IV.ii.110, 112). At the same time, at the end of *1 Henry IV* Henry can authorise a duplicity — the wearing of his arms by other men — which constitutes a literal representation of the corporationist doctrine of monarchy whereby the king is conceived as being nowhere and everywhere, a protective device which takes us back to the *failure* of his predecessor. Most audacious of all is Prince John's unctuous appeal in *2 Henry IV* to the indeterminacies of hermeneutic process as he swears to his adversaries that "by the honour of my blood,/ My father's purposes have been mistook,/ And some about him have too lavishly/ Wrested his meaning and authority" (IV.ii.55-8), and then proceeds to engineer a misinterpretation which culminates in the rebels' defeat while at the same time glossing his duplicity with the chilling claim that "God, and not we, hath safely fought today" (IV.ii.121). Prince John's displacement of responsibility on to "God" will be reiterated in a less problematic context in *Henry V*, when after Agincourt Henry ritualises his victory:

> O God, thy arm was here;
> And not to us, but to thy arm alone,
> Ascribe we all! IV.viii.108-10

By this time the discourse of "subjection", and of the royal subject, problematised by the usurpation of Richard's crown, has been fully restored.

Each element in this intricate web of signification points inwards towards the issue of representation. Richard's discovery from the empirical evidence furnished by brute reality that the king's name is *not* "twenty thousand names" (*Richard II*, III.ii.85) effectively drives a wedge between the essential "reality" of kingship and those theatrical, ceremonial, exterior shows which represent it. Throughout the Second Tetralogy, representation becomes a problem to which each individual play returns; indeed, in *Henry V* the entire theatrical representation is something for which an apology is required, as the pre-condition for a new justification of monarchy, one which can recuperate for a dominant ideology those subversive strands foregrounded by the exposure of regal inadequacy and consequent usurpation.

Nowhere in the *Henry IV* plays is this issue of representation brought into sharper focus than in those scenes involving Falstaff and his companions. Leaving aside the question of what Falstaff was originally intended to represent, as the Rabelaisian embodiment of carnival excess he is that "other" against which authority defines itself, a voice which under normal conditions is repressed in official ideology, but which continues to erupt through its smooth surfaces. As "holiday" and "licence" his subversive energy can be domesticated, but, in that case, why does the ethos which he represents provoke so firm a disclaimer from Hal at the very outset, and why is it necessary to marginalise this force to the point that by the end of *2 Henry IV* it is repressed altogether? The sentimental answer to this question is, of course, a familiar one, asserting the attractiveness and wit of Falstaff: "much more than a prolongation of the traditional lord of misrule; he stands for a perpetual and accepted human principle" (Tillyard 1944: 289); "the power of individual life to continue despite the collapse of social roles" (Barber 1959: 212). What is less commonly observed is that he embodies in displaced form certain characteristics of the popular conception of the usurped Richard which the text of the earlier play handles with some caution. As the embodiment of venal excess Falstaff is the dramatic means whereby Richard's failure, initially mediated as "tragedy", can be brought within the bounds of an authorising laughter. To laugh *at* Falstaff is to laugh away anarchic energies which in political terms make deposition an unwelcome necessity, and, by reducing deposition itself to a theatricalised parody, to raise in a new context the problem of representation with which the Second Tetralogy began.

These issues are concentrated for us in II.iv of *1 Henry IV*, the scene in which Falstaff is brought to book for his cowardly behaviour at the Gadshill robbery, and in which he is, as the parodic representation of Hal's father, deposed. The deposition "play extempore" is proposed for purposes of diversion from the anarchic liberties which Falstaff takes with the process of linguistic representation itself. This diversion begins, not by pointing back into "history", but rather towards the future, to Hal's forthcoming encounter with his father. What then follows in fact points *both* ways, back to deposition, now re-contextualised as a comedy of venality, and forward to a new order where "faults" are banished to the margins of political behaviour. In a deconstructive turn, which temporarily diminishes authority as it theatricalises it, Falstaff proposes another distortion — "This chair shall be my state, this dagger my sceptre, and this cushion my crown." (II.iv.373-4) — one which is not lost on Hal, who promptly re-constructs the symbolic language which Falstaff's gesture threatens to subvert — "Thy state is taken for a joint-stool, thy golden sceptre for a leaden dagger, and thy precious rich crown for a pitiful bald crown." (II.iv.375-7). Because of his monstrous failure to imitate a regal discourse, Falstaff is "deposed"; even his imitation of Hal — a transfer of venal excess from monarchy itself into the realm of a pre-political area of experience, "youth" — collapses into an egocentric justification of the behaviour of "Jack Falstaff", in a veritable orgy of misrepresentation; but this is speedily suppressed by the intervention of another, *authorised* drama with the entry of the Sheriff as the representative of "law".

Whereas in *Richard II* authority was shown to have undermined itself within the figure of the king as opposed systems of signification leading directly to tragedy, already in *1 Henry IV*, and to an increasing extent in the later plays in the Tetralogy, the subversive element in that division is progressively isolated before being re-constituted and filtered back into the dominant ideology which it had threatened. Richard's essential "humanism" — what he claims, defensively, makes him a man like other men — translated into comic terms becomes Falstaff's "All the world". It is this humanism, threatening to disrupt the idealist conception of corporate monarchy, that the play *Henry V* and its eponymous hero are charged with re-integrating in a new discourse which is an amplification of the old. The coercion of subversive elements, their marginalisation as "other", or their integration in the service of authority, are represented as necessary monarchic *self-repression* — an internalisation of the objectively constituted system of differences within whose play subjectivity is inscribed — thus enabling political power to re-inscribe its own practices with a re-furbished theological discourse which unites "the means that heaven yields" with the necessary earthly force required to sustain a hierarchy of subjection. Thus, Richard's separation of a human essence from the signifying framework of "respect,/ Tradition, form, and ceremonious duty" (*Richard II*, III.ii.172-3), whereby kingship sustains its meanings and its power, re-appears in *Henry V* not repeated but re-worked as part of a more pragmatic definition in which it is not "the balm, the sceptre and the ball,/ The sword, the mace, the crown imperial,/ The intertissued robe of gold and pearl,/ The farced title running 'fore the king,/ The throne he sits on, nor the tide of pomp/ That beats upon the high shore of this world" (IV.i.266-71) but rather the responsibility for maintaining order which epitomises the figure of the king: "but in gross brain little wots/ What watch the king keeps to maintain the peace,/ Whose hours the peasant best advantages." (IV.i.288-90). Henry's soliloquy, significantly delivered before Agincourt, neatly sidesteps the objective question which it poses of what it is that constitutes a king. The objective question is answered subjectively in terms of what the king is not; he is not a careless "peasant", rather he is weighed down with a responsibility whose origins remain shrouded in mystification.

In this effective re-ordering of the elements of the dominant discourse, Hal accepts the burdens of theatricalisation which the king must bear, the public "ceremony", but what his soliloquy before Agincourt moves towards is the assertion that outward theatricalisation is a true representation of an authority whose own inner life is hidden from public view. To propose, tragically, that authority can violate itself, or comically, as Falstaff does, that it is a monstrous theatricalisation of the ego, is to recall a process of decentring which always leads to deposition, usurpation, banishment, and, ultimately, chaos. Hal's correction of a contrary narrative twice in the same scene in *1 Henry IV*, and his revision of the contradictions which had destroyed Richard immediately before his victory at Agincourt, returns the process of authorising discourse to its familiar place in the hierarchy of power relations, by insisting that the king is also a "subject", while at the same time justifying his exemption from "subjection". At such moments, and there are many of them in these plays, possibilities are opened up only to be closed down as aesthetics is shown to be working hand-in-hand with ideology.

The changing signification of the Falstaffian "body" from genial festivity to monstrous excess is contiguous to the conflict which rages in *1* and *2 Henry IV* over the textualisation/possession of the body politic itself. The gradual prizing away of Falstaff from the ethos of festive licence, and his re-inscription within a more explicitly insurrectionist discourse in *2 Henry IV*, fixes offending anarchy as the "other" of civil order, although that process can never quite eradicate the traces of what it seeks to exclude. Power and meaning are brought firmly into focus from the very outset of *2 Henry IV* and "Rumour" multiplying narratives and problematising signification altogether. But whereas *1 Henry IV* began with insecure monarchy objectifying guilt as insurrection, *2 Henry IV* begins with insurrectionist strategy itself, and in a manner which underscores the importance of the possession of the means of signification. Morton's account of the Archbishop of York's appropriation of "religion" for the practice of insurrection reveals a truly machiavellian strategy to re-unite "body" and "mind", thus inadvertently de-mystifying those tactics through which political hegemony secures itself:

> But now the Bishop
> Turns insurrection to religion;
> Suppos'd sincere and holy in his thoughts,
> He's followed both with body and with mind,
> And doth enlarge his rising with the blood
> Of fair King Richard, scrap'd from Pomfret stones;
> Derives from heaven his quarrel and his cause.      I.i.200-6

Morton's faintly scandalous sexual metaphor, in addition to exposing "religion" as an ideological state apparatus, also hints that York's legitimisation of political riot is Falstaffian excess but in a different register.

It is a problem that hangs over the entire Tetralogy, and in *2 Henry IV* it is projected psychologically onto Hal as he encounters at a purely subjective level the fleshly craving that constantly challenges political and personal restraint. Hal tells Poins that his desire for "small beer" and such "humble considerations" as make him "out of love with my greatness" (II.ii.11-2) are wearying, and he goes on to tell his companion that "the rest of thy low countries have made a shift to eat up thy holland" (II.ii.21-2). Falstaff, for his part, privileges "flesh" above "Grace", and meets Doll Tearsheet's appeal to Hal to adjudicate the allegation that the Boar's Head Tavern is a brothel with: "His Grace says that which his flesh rebels against." (II.iv.348).

This persistent concern, articulated here from radically opposed perspectives, becomes a pathological fear, in the mind of the dying King Henry, of what will happen when his son succeeds (IV.iv.58-61): "The blood weeps from my heart when I do shape/ In forms imaginary th'unguided days/ And rotten times that you shall look upon/ When I am sleeping with my ancestors." So paranoid is his possessiveness that, on finding his crown removed, he immediately constructs a grotesque "imaginary", characterised by the principle of riotous excess: "Pluck down my officers; break my decrees;/ For now a time is come to mock at form —/ Harry the fifth is crown'd! Up vanity!/ Down, royal state!" (IV.v.117-20). This fear, articulated as shrilly as anything in the Homily on Obedience, catches the dying king in contradiction since his own power has its origin in the very principle of desire, which he would now characterise as "other". But this is merely the beginning of what will be a series of more startling contradictions as he then proceeds to traverse a range of subject roles in an attempt to explain his own strategy. Here he is simultaneously architect of power and victim, the one role sliding imperceptibly into the other as he reclaims for himself Richard's role as a Christ figure (IV.v.189-90): "For all the soil of the achievement goes/ With me into the earth." We glimpse in this process of reclamation the material strategies whereby the dying king has secured and sustained power, as Henry, in a rare moment of candour, lays bare his "art" of monarchy:

> And all my friends, which thou must make thy friends,
> Have but their stings and teeth newly ta'en out;
> By whose fell working I was first advanc'd,
> And by whose power I well might lodge a fear
> To be again displac'd; which to avoid,
> I cut them off, and had a purpose now
> To lead out many to the Holy Land,
> Lest rest and lying still might make them look
> Too near unto my state. Therefore, my Harry,
> Be it thy course to busy giddy minds
> With foreign quarrels, that action hence borne out
> May waste the memory of the former days.     IV.v.204-15

Others, the claim is, "advanc'd" Henry, and their political elimination is, therefore, justified. But what he also proposes is a re-constitution of the past, not as repetition, but on a new terrain of pragmatic politics, underpinned by the very same theological discourse whose ritualised order he tacitly admits to having violated. Hal accepts that "right" comes with "possession" (IV.v.222), and then, in an outrageous piece of duplicity, Henry praises God for making it possible for him to die *not* in the Holy Land — that imaginary realm of resolution in the Tetralogy — but in "the lodging where I first did swoon", the Jerusalem Chamber (IV.v.233-4).

Within a scene of Henry's death, his fantasy of excess is dispelled as the Lord Chief Justice is installed in his rightful position, Doll Tearsheet and Mistress Quickly are hauled off to be whipped for being whores, and Falstaff's own fantasies of satisfied riotous desire are dashed. And all this under the imprimatur of God (V.v.57-8): "For God doth know, so shall the world perceive,/ That I have turn'd away my former self." Thus, firmly of the world, the new king represses in himself that excess which had destroyed Richard, but the process is one of repression and displacement. That, it would appear, can only be represented in *Henry V* by what is, in effect, a refusal of representation, requiring the complicity of an audience. Thus a dramatic analogue of Richard Hooker's notion of the subject's acquiescence in subjection is constructed, as the responsibility for the veracity of the symbolic order is deftly shifted from the axis of coercion on to that of compliance. It is that process of complicity, and of what Sinfield and Dollimore have called "subordination or supportive alignment"

(Sinfield and Dollimore 1985: 217), that *Henry V* addresses.

In his edition of *Henry V* Gary Taylor argues that the play aspires to a unity of, among other things, "politics and joy", and that the dramatic process is one of a dialectical advancement towards that objective; but he also suggests that "no sooner is a unity established, than we are made aware of what that unity excludes, until that too can be contained" (1982: 71). Just so, up to a point, although what Taylor applauds as the play's full-mouthed "epic" inclusiveness is very much the product of an ideological manoeuvre which neutralises contradiction. To this extent the dramatist's consummate art overlays that of the politician, though neither can fully erase the traces of their own production. The ubiquitous Prologue in *Henry V*, who, in denying authority effectively re-asserts it, invites his audience to succumb to the power of artistic suggestion: "And let us, ciphers to this great accompt,/ On your imaginary forces work" (Prologue, ll. 17-8), but then returns it to an active role of construction: "For 'tis your thoughts that now must deck our kings" (Prologue, l. 28). This illusion of freedom, which we encounter in the formulations in Hooker's *Laws*, leads us back to that tension between the real relations of power and their idealised representations which is an abiding concern of the Second Tetralogy, and which might be framed in the form of the question: "How can subjects be made to work by themselves?".

In one sense *Henry V* is a drawing together of disparate strands in a project which effectively re-inscribes the absolute monarch at the centre of power but the corollary of that is the re-constitution of the subject who works by himself in conditions which are changing. England may no longer be that "other Eden, demi-paradise" whose passing Henry's dying grandfather, John of Gaunt, had lamented, but in the final play of the Tetralogy that paradise is located from the very outset in the king's body itself, as the Archbishop of Canterbury makes clear:

> Consideration like an angel came,
> And whipp'd th' offending Adam out of him,
> Leaving his body as a Paradise,
> T' envelop and contain celestial spirits.                    I.i.28-31

This re-textualisation is the culmination of a journey through the post-lapsarian vision of Richard's fragmentary body politic, through the material bodily "other" of the Eastcheap scenes of *1* and *2 Henry IV*, to a new corporationist definition of the absolute ruler as the repository of all social accents, the absolute subject who *contains* all social contradiction. Not entirely without irony, such absolutism is shown to secure itself through the theological sanctioning of possession, that idealised representation of the material currency of power. Hence the claim made against France, which is the expression of that power, but which also serves to displace, for the last time, internal social tension on to an external adversary. The politics of this process, formulated by Henry IV on his deathbed, is a politics of displacement; the "offending Adam" in Richard is transferred simultaneously onto the grossly comic figure of Falstaff, and onto his political analogues, the rebels; it is re-admitted in the form of repression at the end of *2 Henry IV*, and it re-emerges in *Henry V* as the successfully resisted violations of a "foreign" body. Thus, in an obsessively repetitive trope, the dominant ideology constructs its "other", drives it to the margins of its own discourses, as the necessary precondition for subduction through coercion. The sub-text of this process is, of course, fear, since the unity achieved produces its own contradictions in the form of freebooting vagabonds such as Pistol, who can be coerced, but never recuperated. For the hitherto marginalised Welsh, and the more problematical Irish, their subversive potential can be re-cycled and domesticated through a genially comic laughter, while for the French, they can be separated from their diseases, bequeathed to the likes of Doll Tearsheet who, Pistol believes, has died "i' the spital/ Of malady of France" (V.i.85-6), and drawn into the web of dynastic relations that guarantees ordered transfer of land and power. Thus Henry becomes "Rex Angliae, et Haeres Franciae" (V.ii.360) through dynastic marriage, re-uniting, to adapt Terence Hawkes's phrase, "the king" with "kingship", the man with the institution (Hawkes 1975: 75). What begins as a fracturing within the dominant power elite is gradually repaired so that it can be finally represented as an imperial, territorial imperative sanctioned by God. The Chorus, in his final appearance, following the divinely sanctioned unity through marriage of England and France, sums up the imperialist project of the "star of England" thus (Epilogue, ll. 6-8): "Fortune made his sword,/ By which the world's best garden he achiev'd,/ And of it left his son imperial lord."

But the question is not merely one of the exertion of physical control. Through the Tetralogy self-control and the control of others are presented as two sides of the same coin as far as the figure of the king is concerned. But the disguised Henry's conversation with Williams and Bates on the eve of Agincourt ranges across the entire question of the relationship between obedience, subjection and responsibility in what is clearly an attempt to reconcile the contradictions which are contained in them. Hal's formulation that "Every subject's duty is the king's; but every subject's soul is his own" (IV.i.182-4) draws ready assent, but it does little to assuage Williams's scepticism that at the end of the day the private subject has no redress against a monarch. That scepticism is, in fact, never countered; rather, it gets caught up in an ethos of success which makes an answer unnecessary. Williams suffers for it, but is bought off, though not without allowing us a brief glimpse of the absolutist control over the subjects' freedom (IV.viii.51-2): "Your majesty came not like yourself: you appeared to me but as a common man." It is, of course, precisely the gulf between "duty" and practice that the king is faced with negotiating, since it is the obstacle to the re-establishment of corporationist doctrine, and the play negotiates this problem via a circuitous route.

It is in the marriage between Henry and Katherine that the figure of the monarch as immortal corporation is reconstituted. Queen Isabel provides the focus for it in her congratulatory speech:

> So be there 'twixt your kingdom such a spousal
> That never may ill office, or fell jealousy,
> Which troubles oft the bed of blessed marriage,
> Thrust in between the paction of these kingdoms,
> To make divorce of their incorporate league.   V.ii.380-4

Marriage in the play is the supreme act of incorporation in that it gives universal credence to the actions of a ruling elite, and in this case guarantees its political hegemony. The king's participation in those institutional practices which underpin his power serves also to lend credibility to the concept of regal responsibility, an issue which Hal had wrestled with privately before Agincourt. There the king was presented as bearing the burden of upholding human institutions: "Upon the king! let us our lives, our souls,/ Our debts, our careful wives,/ Our children, and our sins lay on the king!" (IV.i.236-8); in other words he is the origin and guarantor of that "humanity", of the lives which "private men enjoy" (IV.i.243). Such is the self-presentation of the figure of the king. But, paradoxically, as Williams reminds us, and Henry himself later confirms, he is also a member of a ruling elite, preserving, but at the same time mediating, its political power. Thus, in his courtship of Katherine he has a freedom which refuses confinement "within the weak list of a country's fashion" since he is one of those "makers of manners" who authenticate civilised behaviour (V.ii.285-7). The play has it both ways, representing the figure of the monarch as one burdened by subjection to those institutions through which his political position and power are given civilised expression, while at the same time insisting upon a monarchic liberty which, in its revisionist form, effectively disdains subjection.

As part of his argument for human complicity in the rule of law, Richard Hooker emphasised the need to "regiment" man's corrupt nature (Hooker, ed. Morris 1965: 191). For Francis Bacon the ordering discipline of "grammar" was the means whereby a lost perfection could be re-possessed (Bacon, ed. Kitchin 1965: 138). Regimentation and repossession are clearly operative terms in *Henry V*. Henry's marriage to Katherine, which, interestingly, involves her learning (and subverting meanings in) English, concentrates wonderfully those political and libidinal energies essential to absolutist rule, which the entire Second Tetralogy has wrestled to contain and civilise. Here it is appropriate, I think, to speak, not of "politics and joy" but rather of a "politics *of* joy", and of an artistry of political power inscribed in the discourses and institutions through which they achieve their representations. Shakespeare's circumscribed choice of a controversial period of history, in which monarchy was both problematised and asserted, and which was held by some to refract current struggles within the ruling class fraction, serves both to provide us with a public re-affirmation *and* a critique, with an open prescription for order *and* with a spontaneous experience of lived ideology replete with its contradictions and strategies for containing them .

## REFERENCES

Althusser, Louis (1971). *Lenin and Philosophy*. London: New Left Books.
Bacon, Francis, ed. G.W. Kitchin (1965). *The Advancement of Learning*. London: Dent.
Barber, C.L. (1959). *Shakespeare's Festive Comedy*. Princeton N.J.: Princeton University Press.
Barroll, J. Leeds *et al.* (1975). *The Revels History of Drama in English. Vol.3, 1576-1613*. London: Methuen.
Campbell, Lily B. (1960). *The Mirror For Magistrates*. Cambridge: Cambridge University Press.
Dollimore, Jonathan (1984). *Radical Tragedy: Religion, Ideology and Power in the Drama of Shakespeare and his Contemporaries*. Brighton: Harvester Press.
Dollimore, Jonathan and Alan Sinfield, eds. (1985). *Political Shakespeare*. Manchester: Manchester University Press.
Foucault, Michel (1981). *A History of Sexuality*. Harmondsworth: Penguin Books.
Gramsci, Antonio (1971). *Selections From Prison Notebooks*. London: Lawrence and Wishart.
Greville, Fulke, ed. G.A. Wilkes (1965). *The Remains being Poems of Monarchy and Religion*. Oxford: Oxford University Press.
Hawkes, Terence (1973). *Shakespeare's Talking Animals*. London: Edward Arnold.
Hooker, Richard, ed. C. Morris (1965). *The Laws of Ecclesiastical Polity*. London: Dent.
Jameson, Fredric (1981). *The Political Unconscious: Narrative as a Socially Symbolic Act*. London: Methuen.
Kantorowicz, Ernst (1957). *The King's Two Bodies: A Study in Medieval Political Theology*. Princeton, N.J.: Princeton University Press.
Macherey, Pierre (1978). *A Theory of Literary Production*. London: Routledge.
Pêcheux, Michel (1982). *Language, Semantics and Ideology: Stating the Obvious*. London: Macmillan.
Ponet, John (1556). *A Short Treatise of Political Power*.
Sanders, Wilbur (1968). *The Dramatist and The Received Idea*. Cambridge: Cambridge University Press.
Shakespeare, William, ed. A.R. Humphreys (1960). *1 Henry IV* London: Methuen.
———, ed. A.R. Humphreys (1966). *2 Henry IV*. London: Methuen.
———, ed. J.H. Walter (1960). *Henry V*. London: Methuen.
———, ed. Gary Taylor (1982). *Henry V*. Oxford: Clarendon Press.

————, ed. Peter Ure (1956). *Richard II*. London: Methuen.
Tillyard, E.M.W. (1943). *The Elizabethan World Picture*. London: Chatto and Windus.
———— (1944). *Shakespeare's History Plays*. London: Chatto and Windus.
Vološinov, V.N. (1973). *Marxism and the Philosophy of Language*. New York and London: Seminar Press.
Williams, Raymond (1966). *Modern Tragedy*. London: Chatto and Windus.

# THE AB CYCLE AND KINGSHIP IN UGARITIC THOUGHT

## N. Wyatt

This short article arises out of my reflections on the arguments developed in two papers offered the Traditional Cosmology Society in 1985 (Wyatt 1986b, 1987). The gist of the second of these, given to the Kingship conference,[1] was that a number of "fall" narratives in the Old Testament, including the "horizontal fall" described in *Genesis* 2.3 (see Wyatt 1981), are to be interpreted against the background of coronation rituals in the ancient Near East, and that their "perversion" from the norm implies a critique of the norm, amounting to an ambivalent conception of kingship. The same thinking was also noticed in various Ugaritic texts. I alluded to discussion elsewhere (Wyatt 1986a) in which I suggested that such elements betray a surprising realism in mythology, which is concerned not simply with treating of an ideal world, but with coming to terms with the real one.

The question arises as to the nature of Ba'al's kingship in the Ugaritic AB cycle of myths. This "cycle" is the understanding arrived at in a half-century of Ugaritic studies of the significance of six of the most important tablets from Ugarit (now assigned the sigla *KTU* 1.1-6 — further fragments, numbered *KTU* 1.7-11, 13, 82, 83 are probably to be related to the cycle at least in terms of alternative recensions of various episodes in the main tradition). These deal respectively with the enthronement of Yam (Sea) and his subsequent death at the hands of Ba'al (the storm god) — tablets 1 and 2; the conflicts of 'Anat, consort of Ba'al, and the building of his palace, followed by his enthronement — tablets 3 and 4; the challenge issued to Ba'al by Mot (Death), Ba'al's death and resurrection, and inconclusive final conflict with Mot — tablets 5 and 6.[2] A general presentation of the overall theological picture of the cycle has been given recently by Gibson (1984). But one of the strange features of the cycle is that Ba'al is no sooner crowned than he is deposed and killed, and while he can be said in a sense to emerge triumphant by virtue of his resurrection and subsequent victory ("on points!") over Mot,[3] this is not due to his own prowess, and the cycle may be said to end on a provisional note: while Mot is subdued — by the sun-goddess Šapš rather than by Ba'al himself — he is not killed, so that Ba'al's kingship is not absolute. It is provisional not because it is only microcosmic (Peterson and Woodward 1977) but because its establishment is fragile and liable to interruption. This must not be understood to mean that the seasonal interpretation is to be assumed (e.g. de Moor 1971; see rebuttal in Grabbe 1976): there is no justification for seeing a cyclical, repetitive structure in the mythology. Indeed, while it would be wrong to speak of a strictly "linear" view of time in the context, we can certainly speak of a beginning, a middle, and an end to the cycle. (This term having become conventional, it would be pedantic to reject it: it has the same force as an Arthurian or any other literary tradition, and need have no implication of circularity.) There is a definite progress through the narrative, clear in spite of considerable gaps from time to time in the record. But through the linearity there is a disturbing process of constant reversal, which I have indicated elsewhere in drawing attention to the chiastic structure of the cycle as a whole (Wyatt 1987). It is worth examining this further here, because it has further implications:

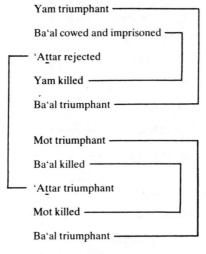

Figure 1

This diagram helps us to discern the way in which the plot develops through a series of mirror images, each main block of material centring round the figure of 'Attar, whose progress from rejection to triumph frames the establishment of Ba'al's palace and offers a parody of it. But I feel that it would be wrong to dismiss 'Attar as a figure of fun. He may indeed be a substitute king, but not a poor substitute. The construction of Ba'al's palace appears from its place in the narrative to have an ambivalence of its own: no sooner is Ba'al established within it than he is challenged and killed, as Yam had been previously. Its very composition seems to bear the seeds of its destruction. So the framing of it by the episode involving 'Attar indicates another reversal:

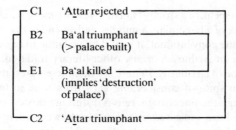

Figure 2

The sigla applied to each stage here correspond to those in Figure 3, which shows that the oppositions contained in Ba'al's relationship to 'A̱ttar are equivalent to those contained in his relationship to Yam and Mot:

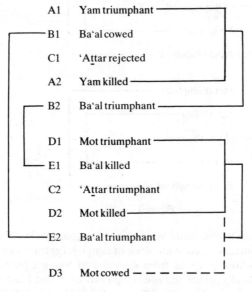

Figure 3

We may express these relationships as a series of equations:

$$A1:A2 = -(B1:B2) - Yam, Ba'al;$$
$$D1:D2 = -(E1:E2) - Mot, Ba'al;$$
$$C1:C2 = B1:B2 = E1:E2 - 'A̱ttar, Ba'al;$$

in these terms, 'A̱ttar is seen to parallel Ba'al in opposition to Yam and Mot: that is, he complements Ba'al, as we might expect of a substitute king, who by his coronation perpetuates Ba'al's rule and continues to keep at bay the chaotic forces represented by Yam and Mot.

But it is also the case that

$$B2:E1 = -(C1:C2)$$

that is, the relationships in Figure 2. While 'Attar sides with Ba'al, as it were, in the series of equations above, on another level represented in this last equation, he is in opposition to Ba'al, and thus is aligned with Yam and Mot over against him. I think this points to two important features concerning 'Attar. Firstly, his role in the AB cycle is clearly pivotal. In discussion of my paper (Wyatt 1986b) it was suggested that I had overestimated his importance. On the contrary: I feel that previous discussion of the mythology has consistently underestimated his importance, if he is not simply ignored. But our diagrams and equations show that he is the one deity in the myth who participates in two worlds: those of Yam and Mot on the one hand ("chaos") and of Ba'al on the other ("cosmos"). He is thus, as I have proposed elsewhere, both a "boundary figure" (Wyatt 1986b) in that he hovers between two realms, and a cognate figure with Yam and Mot who indeed are ultimately to be seen as hypostases of him (Wyatt 1973-4). This complexity of role in the god who stands in as Ba'al's substitute appears to represent a critique of the kind of kingship represented by Ba'al.

This gives rise to an intriguing possibility which appears not to have been recognised hitherto. In a refreshing reappraisal of the Keret story from Ugarit (*KTU* 1.14-6) it has recently been suggested (Parker 1977) that it was intended in its final form to be a severe critique of traditional conceptions of kingship. But it is no coincidence that, as the colophons indicate, both the Keret story and the AB cycle (together with the Aqhat story, *KTU* 1.17-9) have survived through the agency of one man, a priest of high office called Ilumilku (*KTU* 1.4 viii edge, 1.6 vi 54-8, 1.14 vi edge, 1.17 vi edge). It is possible that he was merely a scribe, but in view of his other titles this seems unlikely, and the term *spr* may not illegitimately be rendered "author", providing we recognise that his work was largely redactional, shaping traditional forms into new narrative. But the attitude to the monarchy that is exhibited both in the Keret story and, if my argument so far is convincing, in the AB cycle, is surely too revolutionary to be the product of a nebulous collective authorship or "tradition" (which is simply a catch-all for anonymity of authorship, given that individual minds lie behind every reshaping of a traditional form). Indeed its very subtlety of expression points in both instances to a singular shrewdness of mind and skill in expressing the message in disguised form: coating the unpalatable pill with the sugar of accepted theological or narrative form. Ilumilku's

redactional and compositional work is thus fused with a quite striking
orginality of thought. This also has implications for our understanding of
the Aqhat story, but that is a matter for further study.

A final diagram will draw our attention to one more detail in the AB
cycle, as yet unexplained.

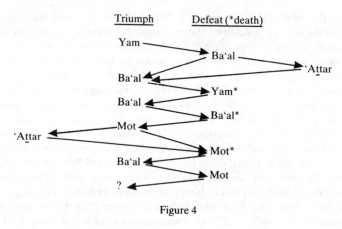

Figure 4

In Figure 3 I added a rider in the form of D3, showing that at the end of the
cycle Mot is not killed, as he had been at D2, but is held under control by the
power of the sun-goddess, who appears to confront him in the netherworld
(*KTU* 1.6 vi 43-53). This gives to the cycle an open-ended conclusion (if
that is not a contradiction in terms): it finishes on a note of anticipation, and
casts further doubt on the idea that the whole cycle ends cosily with Ba'al
firmly established on the throne. We now see that in addition to all the
internal oppositions there is a constant dialectic throughout the cycle,
which does not simply end in a satisfactory resolution at the end, but invites
expectation of more development. It ends on a dynamic note. There is no
warrant for assuming, *à la* seasonal pattern, that this anticipation implies a
reversion to the beginning, so that the whole thing begins over again.
Rather does it show the impermanence of any resolution: the dialectic
points into an unresolved, undefined future — an eloquent suggestion that
all the old cliché formulae offer no final answer to man's predicament. This
can be sought only in a receptive attitude. It may seem overbold to describe
this as a "historical awareness", but in contrast to the supposition that the
Ugaritic mind was circumscribed by a closed system of myth-and-ritual
circularity, there is no more adequate way to characterise it. (Contrast the
highly schematic and artificial system of Gaster 1950, with my comments on
historical awareness in Wyatt 1979.)

Figure 4 also suggests more to 'Attar's role, for while he appears out on the fringe, a symbol of his boundary nature, he is also the only one of the chief protagonists in the cycle who is not killed at some stage during the proceedings. If this appears to ignore the role of other important characters in the AB cycle (viz. El, Ašerah, and 'Anat) my fuller treatment elsewhere (Wyatt 1986a, 1986b) considers their importance; here we have been concerned primarily with issues relating to kingship. In not dying, and in participating in both "worlds" (those of Ba'al on the one hand, and of Yam and Mot on the other), 'Aṭṭar shows himself to be a more full-blooded figure than his peers: they are almost caricatures, allegories of certain narrow issues in human experience. 'Aṭṭar embodies the fuller nature of man, in whom these various oppositions and distinct qualities take on three-dimensional form. He is therefore the appropriate divine embodiment of kingship.

NOTES

1   The Traditional Cosmology Society's Kingship conference was held in Edinburgh on 4-6 August 1985.
2   For recent translations, see Jirku 1962, Aistleitner 1964, Caquot *et al.* 1974, Gordon 1978, Gibson 1978, Coogan 1978, Del Olmo Lete 1981. The last mentioned has the most up-to-date discussion of the broad literary issues involved. See Clifford 1984 for a critique of the recent consensus on the unity of the AB cycle. *KTU* = Dietrich *et al.* 1976.
3   On the overall structure of the cycle, see Petersen and Woodward 1977 and Wyatt 1986a.

REFERENCES

Aistleitner, J. (1964). *Die mythologischen und kultischen Texte aus Ras Schamra.* Budapest: Akadémiai Kiadó.
Caquot, A., M. Sznycer and A. Herdner (1974). *Textes Ougaritiques* i. Paris: Editions du Cerf.
Clifford, R.J. (1984). Cosmogonies in the Ugaritic Texts and in the Bible. *Orientalia* 53, 183-201.
Dietrich, M., O. Loretz and J. Sanmartín (1976). *Die keilalphabetischen Texte aus Ugarit.* Alter Orient und Altes Testament 24. Neukirchen: Kevelaer, Butzen und Bercker.
Gaster, T.H. (1950). *Thespis.* New York: Schuman.
Gibson, J.C.L. (1978). *Canaanite Myths and Legends.* Edinburgh: T. and T. Clark.
——— (1984). The Theology of the Ugaritic Baal Cycle. *Orientalia* 53, 202-19.
Gordon, C.H. (1977). Poetic Legends and Myths from Ugarit. *Berytus* 25, 5-133.
Grabbe, L.L. (1976). The Seasonal Pattern and the Ba'al cycle. *Ugarit-Forschungen* 8, 57-63.
Jirku, A. (1962). *Kanaanäische Mythen und Epen aus Ras Schamra-Ugarit.* Gütersloh: Gütersloher Verlagshaus.
De Moor, J.C. (1971). *The Seasonal Pattern.* Alter Orient und Altes Testament 16. Neukirchen: Kevelaer, Butzen und Bercker.
Del Olmo Lete, G. (1981). *Mitos y Leyendas de Canaan.* Madrid: Ediciones Cristiandad.

Parker, S.B. (1977). The Historical Composition of *KRT* and the Cult of El. *Zeitschrift für die Alttestamentliche Wissenschaft* 89, 161-75.

Petersen, D.L. and M. Woodward (1977). Northwest Semitic Religion: a study in relational structures. *Ugarit-Forschungen* 9, 233-48.

Wyatt, N. (1973-4). 'Attar and the Devil. *Transactions of the Glasgow University Oriental Society* 25, 85-97.

——— (1979). Some Observations on the Idea of History among the West Semitic Peoples. *Ugarit-Forschungen* 11, 825-32.

——— (1981). Interpreting the Creation and Fall Story in Genesis 2-3. *Zeitschrift für die Alttestamentliche Wissenschaft* 93, 10-21.

——— (1986a). Cosmic Entropy in Ugaritic Religious Thought. *Ugarit-Forschungen* 17, 383-6.

——— (1986b). Who Killed the Dragon? *Aula Orientalis* 4, in press.

——— (1987). The Hollow Crown: ambivalent elements in West Semitic royal ideology. *Ugarit-Forschungen* 18, in press.

# SOVEREIGNTY, BOILING CAULDRONS, AND CHARIOT-RACING IN PINDAR'S *OLYMPIAN* 1

Gregory Nagy

Pindar's *Olympian* 1 was commissioned by the tyrant Hieron of Syracuse on the occasion of a pan-Hellenic victory, in a single-horse competition at the Olympics of 476 BC, and the preoccupation of Pindar's composition with the theme of chariot-racing shows clearly that the tyrant is looking forward to winning a future Olympic victory in the more prestigious four-horse chariot competition (Köhnken 1974: 205).

In *Olympian* 1, the voice of the poet explicitly rejects the myth that told of the dismemberment of Pelops and how he was cannibalised at a feast of the gods. In its place, there is an explicit substitution of a myth that told of the young hero's abduction by the god Poseidon, who eventually repaid Pelops by helping him win a chariot-race with Oinomaos. The telling of the second myth, however, is launched in *Olympian* 1 with a partial retelling of the first: Pelops was abducted "after" Klotho the *Moira* "Fate" took him out of the "purifying cauldron" (line 26). Instead of assuming that Pindar is literally substituting one myth for another, I argue in a recent article (Nagy 1986) that the "substitution" as represented in *Olympian* 1 is in fact a poetic expression of a pre-existing fusion of two myths, where the earlier myth is officially subordinated to but acknowledged by the later myth. Furthermore, I argue that the relative earliness and lateness of these two myths has to do not with any innovation by Pindar himself but rather with the historical sequence of the accretion of traditional myths officially associated with the complex institution of the Olympics. In other words, my claim is that both myths are traditional and in fact signal that they are traditional. As for the subordination of the myth that told of the dismemberment of Pelops to the myth that told of the abduction of Pelops by Poseidon and the hero's victory in the chariot-race, I argue that this pattern corresponds to the subordination of the oldest athletic event of the Olympics, the single-course foot-race, to the most prestigious athletic event of the Olympics in Pindar's time, the four-horse chariot-race. In this sense, Pindar's *Olympian* 1 may be said to reflect the actual aetiology of the Olympics in the early fifth century.

Winning in the four-horse chariot-race at the Olympics was a mark of sovereignty, much sought after in the archaic and early Classical periods of Greece by any aristocratic family that aspired to supreme power in a given city-state. A prominent example is the patriliny of Miltiades, the Philaidai, characterised as the steady producer of four-horse teams that win at chariot-races (Herodotus 6.35.1); the eponymous ancestor, Philaios, was son of Ajax, grandson of Aiakos (besides Herodotus, cf. Pherecydes FGH 3 F 2 [Jacoby 1923: 59]). Another example is the patriliny of the Alkmaionidai of Athens, the lineage of the celebrated Kleisthenes, Reformer of Athens, maternal grandson of the elder Kleisthenes, tyrant of Sikyon (Herodotus 5.66-8). One of the ancestors in this lineage of the Alkmaionidai, whose actual name was Alkmaion, was the very first Athenian to win the chariot-race at the Olympics (Isocrates 16.25).

Such rich and powerful families, one of whose primary means of demonstrating prestige was victory at the pan-Hellenic Games, could readily be perceived as a potential threat to the polis — as potential achievers of tyrannical power. A notable example is a figure called Kylon, an Olympic victor himself (probably 640 BC), who nearly succeeded in becoming tyrant of Athens in a coup d'état attempted at a time when the Olympics were in progress (possibly 632 BC; cf. Herodotus 5.71, Thucydides 1.126; Plutarch *Solon* 12.1-3). It was the Alkmaionidai who were held responsible for the guilt of murdering some of the perpetrators, perhaps including Kylon, as they sought asylum after the failed attempt (same sources, with varying details). The Alkmaionidai, as stemming from Megakles, who was held primarily responsible for the murders, were officially exiled (*Solon* 12.3). It was the son of this Megakles, Alkmaion, who was the first Athenian to win the chariot-race at the Olympics (again, Isocrates 16.25). The son of Alkmaion, another Megakles, was the one who married the daughter of the tyrant of Sikyon, Kleisthenes (Herodotus 6.130.2). For this reason (cf. Herodotus 6.131.1) and for many others (e.g. Herodotus 1.59-61), the Alkmaionidai throughout their history were perceived as potential tyrants.

In this era, when important families were generating public personalities that could and did overreach the institutions of the polis, enter the figure of Pindar, master of choral lyric poetry, protégé of powerful families of tyrants or quasi-tyrants, such as the referent of Pindar's *Olympian* 1, Hieron of Syracuse, whom Pindar addresses as *basileus* "king" (e.g. *Olympian* 1.23) as well as *turannos* "tyrant" (in a non-pejorative sense: *Pythian* 3.85). As a telling example of quasi-tyrants, I cite the pointed reference in Pindar *Pythian* 7.1-8 to the family of Megakles of Athens, of the *geneā* "lineage" of the Alkmaionidai.

Besides victory in the four-horse chariot-race, another prominent symbol of sovereignty in the context of the Olympics was the cauldron that boiled the sacrificial meat to be eaten at the victors' feast. We may note the portent recounted in Herodotus 1.59.1 about Hippokrates, father of the tyrant Peisistratos of Athens, as the envoys of the Greek city-states were approaching the altar of Zeus on the occasion of the Olympics. When Hippokrates, who was one of these envoys, approached the altar, the water inside the sacrificial cauldrons started to boil before the application of fire. This portent seems to have conveyed the idea that the very presence of Hippokrates, as the future father of Peisistratos, was the equivalent of the Olympic victor's fire that was required to start the sacrifices at the altar of Zeus (see Burkert 1983: 100).

The purpose of this my presentation is to stress that these two Olympic symbols of sovereignty, victory in the chariot-race and the cauldron that boils the sacrificial meat for the victory-feast, are combined in Pindar's *Olympian* 1 as a foundation, as it were, for the political authority of the tyrant Hieron. With this purpose in mind, I propose to restate, in brief, some of the points that I have argued in the article already mentioned.

The chronologically oldest athletic event in the Olympics was the *stadion*, a single-course foot-race in the stadium (the recording of victors in this race starts with 776 BC; see Burkert 1983: 95-8). This event was as a rule inaugurated with the sacrifice of a black ram at the *Pelopion* "precinct of Pelops",[1] to be followed by the corresponding sacrifice of a bull (Burkert 1983: 98, n. 25) at the altar of Zeus. The single-course foot-race which was to follow the sacrifices had the *Pelopion* as its original starting point and the altar of Zeus as the finishing line (Burkert 1983: 97). Thus the inaugural set of sacrifices to Pelops and to Zeus before the foot-race unites the hero and god in a "polar tension" (Burkert 1983: 97), while the foot-race itself "presupposes the bloody act of killing" (Burkert 1983: 98).

This foot-race, then, framed by the set of sacrifices at the precinct of Pelops and at the altar of Zeus, is the ritual core of the Olympics. And we can see the deeper significance of this ritual core as a diachronic feature of initiation by following through on Burkert's discovery (1983: 100) that the very festival of the Olympics was from the earliest times onward correlated with a myth that told how the hero Pelops was killed, dismembered, and served up by his father Tantalos as sacrificial meat boiled inside a tripod cauldron, to be eaten by the gods — only to be reassembled and brought back to life inside the same sacrificial cauldron by the agency of these same gods.[2] Burkert concludes (1983: 100): "The cannibalistic myth of Pelops that so shocked Pindar clearly refers to the Olympic festival."

I propose two qualifications. First, Pindar's "shock" is a poetic convention that allows the subordination of one myth, the dismemberment and reintegration of Pelops, to another myth. Second, the myth of Pelops' dismemberment and reintegration need not be viewed as an *aition* for the Olympic festival as a whole. True, it suits admirably the oldest aspect of the festival, the foot-race of the *stadion* as framed by the sacrifices at the precinct of Pelops and at the altar of Zeus. But we must keep in mind that the Olympics kept evolving with later accretions of further and further athletic events, and that the ritual features of these events would have required a corresponding evolution in aetiology, with later accretions of myths.

I draw attention to the athletic event of the chariot-race at the Olympics, supposedly introduced there in the year 680 (Pausanias 5.8.7; Burkert 1983: 95). Corresponding to the athletic event of the chariot-race is an *aition*, the myth of the life-and-death chariot-race of Pelops with Oinomaos. The death of Oinomaos, resulting from the race, led to the very foundation of the Olympics by Pelops. As an *aition* for the foundation of the Olympics from the standpoint of the chariot-race, the myth of the death of Oinomaos would at first seem to be at odds with the myth of the death of Pelops, an *aition* from the standpoint of the foot-race. But in fact the two layers of myths are integrated into a sequence, just like the two layers of athletic events. Pelops had his chariot-race with Oinomaos *after* he had been restored to life.

Pindar's emphasis on the myth of the chariot-race over the myth of the dismemberment and reintegration of Pelops is in keeping with the pan-Hellenic prestige of the chariot-race as the central event of the Olympics in Pindar's time: I cite the testimonia of the Kypselos chest of about 570 BC (Burkert 1983: 95; cf. Pausanias 5.17.7) and the pedimental sculptures on the east side of the temple of Zeus at Olympia (Burkert 1983: 95). In fact, I prefer to think that the mythological rearrangements in *Olympian* 1 reflect the official contemporary aetiology of the Olympics.

The most remarkable of these rearrangements in *Olympian* 1 is a narrative substitution, whereby the story about the dismemberment of Pelops is ostentatiously replaced by a story that starts with his abduction by Poseidon, which leads into the story about the chariot race of Pelops. The story that tells about the dismemberment of Pelops by Tantalos and about the eating of his flesh by the gods is being ostentatiously rejected as a "false" substitute for the "true" story that told about the abduction and rape of Pelops by Poseidon (Pindar *Olympian* 1.28-9, 30-42, 46-53). And yet, the "true" story turns out to be aetiologically equivalent to the rejected "false" story. In the "true" story as well, Pelops undergoes a process of symbolised "death" and "rebirth", since his being abducted and sexually forced by Poseidon is a scenario of initiation into adulthood.[3]

In compensation for his abduction, Pelops receives from Poseidon the gift of a magnificent chariot-team (Pindar *Olympian* 1.86-7). With this chariot-team, the young hero wins his chariot-race against Oinomaos and the hand of Hippodameia, thereby inaugurating a kingship that serves as foundation for the royal Peloponnesian dynasties of Argos, Sparta, and Messene.[4] To repeat, this theme of sovereignty is pertinent to Hieron in *Olympian* 1: after having won in the single-horse competition of 476 BC, the tyrant is looking forward to winning a future Olympic victory in the chariot competition. But the chariot-race of Pelops, and his political authority over the Peloponnesus, would not have been possible had he not emerged from the boiling waters of the reintegrating cauldron. If Hieron one day wins the chariot-race, in the logic of Pindar's poetry, he too can be presumed to be similarly reborn.

## NOTES

1  See Pausanias 5.13.1-2, and the comments in Burkert 1983: 98.
2  See the survey of testimonia in Burkert 1983: 99, n. 32.
3  For further details, see Nagy 1986: 83-5.
4  In this context, I refer to an important article by R.B. Koehl (1986) where we see Minoan analogues to the myth of the abduction of Pelops by Poseidon. In Athenaeus 601 f., there is a report of a Cretan version of the myth of Ganymede where it is King Minos himself, not Zeus, who abducts Ganymede.

## REFERENCES

Burkert, Walter, trans. Peter Bing (1983). *Homo Necans: The Anthropology of Ancient Greek Sacrificial Ritual and Myth*. Berkeley, Los Angeles and London: University of California Press.
Jacoby, Felix (1923). *Die Fragmente der Griechischen Historiker*, Part 1. Berlin: Weidmannsche Buchhandlung.
Koehl, Robert B. (1986). The Chieftain Cup and a Minoan Rite of Passage. *Journal of Hellenic Studies* 106, 99-110.
Köhnken, A. (1974). Pindar as Innovator: Poseidon Hippios and the Relevance of the Pelops Story in *Olympian 1*. *Classical Quarterly* 24, 199-206.
Nagy, Gregory (1986). Pindar's *Olympian* 1 and the Aetiology of the Olympic Games. *Transactions of the American Philological Association* 116, 71-88.

# WHITES AND REDS: THE ROMAN CIRCUS AND ALTERNATE SUCCESSION

Emily Lyle

In this exploratory study of kingship in the context of duality, I am looking at suggestions arising from comparison of features in different types of society, and indications within a particular culture. For comparison I am mainly taking Shang China as set against Indo-European societies, and for internal indications I am examining the foundation legend and circus tradition of Rome.

The task of comparison has been simplified by the recent advance in the understanding of the relationship between certain small-scale societies and the civilisations stemming from such societies which comes from a grasp of the dualistic structure present in both. The subject is discussed fully in Maybury-Lewis and Almagor (in press) and is articulated briefly in Maybury-Lewis 1985: 19.

> Dual organization is ... a kind of world view that links the social order with the cosmic order. It is a theory of equilibrium which, if put into practice, attempts to maintain social peace by modelling it on cosmic harmony. In relatively small societies, that are not subject to the central authority of a state, the effect of dual organization is to guarantee justice, since it constrains the social system within the parameters of cosmic equilibrium. This delicate balance is threatened by state formation, unless the rulers themselves subscribe to the theory and put some form of it into practice. This, I suggest, is what happened in ancient China, ancient Egypt and the Inca empire. The absolutism of their rulers has to be seen in context. These ancient empires were organized along dualistic lines and ruled by divine kings, who linked human society with the cosmos while mediating in their persons the contending forces that could wreak havoc on earth.

Maybury-Lewis's analysis of the process of "passage from dual organization in a tribal society to an empire ordered on dualistic principles" (1985: 19) throws a good deal of light on the question of why, when one comes at the societies through the study of dualism, each of the two different types appears to be capable of assisting in the interpretation of the other. It is only in the case of Mesopotamia, Maybury-Lewis argues, that the adaptation to a pristine civilisation was accompanied by the introduction of secular values that radically altered the picture in a way that would make comparison with a small-scale society less directly relevant. I shall be suggesting that, in the matter of alternate succession, the historical and archaeological evidence from Shang China and the indications from the myth and practice of Indo-European tribes are mutually reinforcing.

The institution of sacred kingship was common to tribes and states. Its existence did not compel a society to transform itself into a state, but it did pave the way to statehood in the case of the pristine old world civilisations. Other factors are, of course, involved in the creation of a state society (Claessen and Skalnik 1978: 624-5), but sacred kingship has an important part to play, as Robert Netting points out (1972: 233):

> I would claim that on the road to statehood, society must first seek the spiritual kingdom, that essentially religious modes of focusing power are often primary in overcoming the critical structural weaknesses of stateless societies. ... The overwhelming need is not to expand existing political mechanisms (they are in certain respects radically inelastic) but literally to transcend them. The new grouping must be united, not by kinship or territory alone, but by belief, by the infinite extensibility of common symbols, shared cosmology, and the overarching unity of fears and hopes made visible in ritual. A leader who can mobilize these sentiments, who can lend concrete form to an amorphous moral community, is thereby freed from complete identification with his village or section or age group or lineage. The cultural devices for actualizing such a status are as varied as human imagination ...

I want to look at a particular cultural device for actualising the status of king in the archaic old world. It is a quite specific one with a) a cosmology resting on three axes of polarity, and b) alternate succession.

In previous papers I have defined three axes of polarity in old world cosmology (see especially Lyle 1984b). Now that these dualities have been set out, it is possible to move on to the study of alternation, which can usefully be thought of as duality in action. The proposed system is not a static but a mobile one, active in time, and the three axes of polarity give rise to, or at least permit, the rather intricate pattern of double or cross alternation that I shall describe.

Since I find that alternation is of central importance in Indo-European and other old world cosmologies, I am pleased to see that Rodney Needham has recently concluded that it should be given the status of a basic concept (1983). Bruce Lincoln, too, has devoted much of his study on *Myth, Cosmos, and Society: Indo-European Themes of Creation and Destruction* (1986) to exploring alternation, referring, e.g., to "two processes alternating in a never-ending cycle" (35) and noting "that within the common IE system of cosmological speculation there is no movement without a counter-movement" (127). His discussion may be related to earlier studies (Lyle 1984c; 1985; 1986) where I have treated what I have defined as the C axis of polarity (light/darkness or life/death). Lincoln does not deal with alternate succession and, as will be seen, this lies along a different axis of polarity (B, wetness/dryness), although the life/death polarity is also relevant to a total view of the alternations involved.

The notion of alternate succession to the kingship is relatively unfamiliar outside anthropological circles and the procedure may therefore seem an unlikely one, but the system can be studied in the modern period working fluently in the Abron kingdom of Gyaman in West Africa. In this kingdom, there are two maximal segments, known respectively as *Yakase* and *Zanzan*. "Every sovereign of Yakase origin must be succeeded by a sovereign of Zanzan origin [and vice versa]. ... In the sixteen royal successions since the Abron arrived in their present territory, i.e. from the end of the seventeenth century to the present time, there has only been one infraction of this rule." (Terray 1977: 280) North-East Africa provides a number of cases of another institution relevant to this discussion, that of alternating generation sets. I will take two examples where the alternate generations are identified by colour since I will be referring to colour in the Indo-European context. Among the Turkana, there are two groupings or alternations. Every male child at birth automatically becomes a member of that of his grandfather, and is therefore in the opposite one from his father. The members of the alternations are called the Stones, who are especially associated with black ornaments, and the Leopards, who are especially associated with white ornaments (Gulliver 1958). Among the Karimojong, those belonging to one of the two alternate generation sets are referred to as yellow and wear brass ornaments, and those of the other are referred to as red and wear copper ornaments. Dyson-Hudson, in his account of the Karimojong, states that the system gives "a sense of social continuity, of time and traditions continually recreated and relived" (Dyson-Hudson 1963: 399).

After this preamble, which indicates the basic nature of alternation and shows it in operation in society, it will not come as a surprise that a form of alternate succession can be suggested for archaic peoples in China and Europe. I am not implying that the three-axis system I am studying included alternation in quite the same form as in any of these African instances, but both alternate succession and contrasted generations seem to be essential concepts in the system, and these modern examples make it possible to flesh out the ideas by showing them in operation in the contexts of particular societies. We have to drop all the specific associations, carrying over only the concepts themselves and the conviction, derived from the particular instances, that they are effective means of social organisation.

To turn now to Shang China and the Indo-European group of peoples, the first thing to note is that there have been marked advances in understanding structure in both areas within the last fifty years or so. The big advance in China has been archaeological, the finds having been interpreted in the light of anthropological and historical examination. Study of Shang oracle bones of the second millennium BC dug up within the present century has confirmed, with only a few exceptions, the genealogy of the Shang dynasty in *Shih chi* (c. 100 BC) which had been regarded as legendary (Chang 1976; 1980: 3-7, 174-5). What appear to be the tombs of Shang kings have also been discovered in a cemetery at An-yang, with seven placed in a western sector and four in an eastern sector (Chang 1980: 111-9). Kwang-chih Chang has made the suggestion that both kinds of evidence point to a type of succession by which kings in alternate generations belonged to different moieties (Chang 1976; 1978; 1980: 165-89). The matter has been the subject of considerable debate, but I think it may be said that the main features of Chang's case are being accepted. A recent study of *The Socio-Political Systems of the Shang Dynasty* by Lin Chao is critical of Chang's work in detail, particularly as regards kinship, but accepts his main position.

The suggestion that kings in alternate generations belonged to different moieties is made possible because of having information both about succession for seventeen generations and also about the system of *kan* names, which requires some explanation. The ten *t'ien kan* or celestial stems are the names of a ten-day week. The names are still in use today in a calendrical system where they are combined with a set of twelve terms to form a sixty-day cycle, but the ten-day week alone was in use among the Shang. These ten *kan* signs were also employed as the second element of the posthumous names of kings. We need only pay particular attention at the moment to two *kan* signs of outstanding importance — Yi (alternatively spelt I) and Ting. The oracle bone inscriptions refer to the "Yi door" and the "Ting door" and do not refer to any other *kan* signs in relation to doors. This point and their greater frequency set them apart and Chang takes them as the main representatives of the two moieties. In Table 1 (adapted from Chao 1982: 14) I have numbered the seventeen generations of the Shang dynasty and indicated whether a generation is Yi or Ting. Chia is paired with Yi in the *kan* system and so is shown as equivalent to Yi in this context; Hsin is found in association with both Ting and Yi. It will be seen that the succession often passed to a member or members of the same generation, and that the only definite exception to the alternation of Yi and Ting in alternate generations is in generation 8 where the change occurs within the generation. This generation is also anomalous in other ways, as Chao notes (1982: 12-3), and, in indicating alternate generations by X and Y, I have treated generation 8 as if it consisted of two generations.

| Generations | | Names | | Yi or Ting |
| --- | --- | --- | --- | --- |
| (Predynastic) | | Pao-chia | | |
| | | Pao-yi | | |
| | | Pao-ping | | |
| | | Pao-ting | | |
| | | Shih-jen | | |
| | | Shih-kuei | | |
| X | 1 | Ta-yi (T'ang) | | Yi |
| Y | 2 | Ta-ting | | Ting |
| | | P'u-ping | | |
| | | Chung-jen | | |
| X | 3 | Ta-chia | = | Yi |
| Y | 4 | Wo-ting | | Ting |
| | | Ta-keng | | |
| X | 5 | Hsiao-chia | = | Yi |
| | | Yüng-chi | | |
| | | Ta-wu | | |
| Y | 6 | Chung-ting | | Ting |
| | | P'u-jen | | |
| X | 7 | Ch'ien-chia | | |
| | | Tsu-yi | | Yi |
| Y | 8 | Tsu-hsin | = | Ting (or Yi) |
| X | | Ch'iang-chia | = | Yi |
| Y | 9 | Tsu-ting | | Ting |
| | | Nan-keng | | |
| X | 10 | Hu-chia | | |
| | | P'an-keng | | |
| | | Hsiao-hsin | | |
| | | Hsiao-yi | | Yi |
| Y | 11 | Wu-ting | | Ting |
| X | 12 | Tsu-keng | | |
| | | Tsu-chia | = | Yi |
| Y | 13 | Lin-hsin | | |
| | | K'ang-ting | | Ting |
| X | 14 | Wu-yi | | Yi |
| Y | 15 | Wen-wu-ting | | Ting |
| X | 16 | Ti-yi | | Yi |
| Y | 17 | Ti-hsin | = | Ting (or Yi) |

Table 1

The Shang Dynasty

According to my theory of the three axes, the concept of the establishment of the cosmos in three phases or generations was common to China and the West and was early and fundamental (see Lyle 1985), and, by this interpretation, Yi and Ting correspond to the Greek Uranus and Cronus and represent the first two generations. I suggest that they establish the two types of kingship and that all later kings in both traditions are either Uranus/Yi kings or Cronus/Ting kings and that the change from one to the other comes ideally with a change to a new generation. The concept of alternate succession by generation is compatible with a) a total population divided into generation sets, or b) a royal line, as among the Shang, or c) a marriage of the new king to a daughter of the former king, as in the Classical legend of Oenomaus discussed below. From the point of view of this analysis, it does not matter whether the new king comes from inside the total community, or from outside the total community as the type of stranger-king discussed by Sahlins (1981; 1985: 73-103); what is implied is that the king of a new generation is from a different category than the former king.

On the Indo-European side, the advance in understanding structure has come largely through the painstaking and imaginative researches of Georges Dumézil (see Littleton 1982). Dumézil brought out the dual nature of Indo-European kingship and his ideas have been developed most interestingly in relation to Sparta by Sergent (1976) and have been set in a broad comparative framework by Needham (1980; 1985). Dumézil's three functions relate to the colours white, red, and blue/black in that order, and Uranus belongs, in my interpretation, in the first slot (white) and Cronus in the second slot (red). I shall use these colours to distinguish the first-king or X generation (white) and the second-king or Y generation (red).

Dumézil's understanding of the kingship developed over time. Initially recognising two complementary aspects of sovereignty, he placed both in the first function (1948; 1977). Later he particularly developed the concept of the trifunctional king relating to all three functions (1973). Working closely with Dumézil's ideas and material, Dubuisson has expressed the view that all three functions have complementary aspects, which he represents as $A + A'$, $B + B'$, and $C + C'$ (1985: 109-10, 117). I also find that this is so, and argue that the two aspects can be referred to as light and dark (1985: 9-13). Dubuisson also (110-1) has explored very fully the concept of the king as the synthesis of the three functions (*la synthèse des trois fonctions*) and represents this by X(s3f). I find that the king as synthesis also has a complement in his dark twin and, in terms of Dubuisson's notation, I would accordingly say that the total scheme, excluding the female element, can be set out as: $A + A'$, $B + B'$, $C + C'$, $X(s3f) + X(s3f)'$. Since I am using X to identify one of the alternate

154                                                                   *Emily Lyle*

generations and A, B, and C to identify the three axes of polarity, I shall
alter the notation and express the same scheme as: 1a + 1b, 2a + 2b, 3a +
3b, Ka + Kb, which, applied to the total scheme I have used formerly
(which includes places for the goddesses not considered here), can be set
out as in Figure 1.

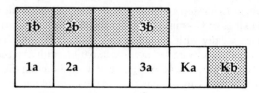

Figure 1

The complementariness in the Ka + Kb formulation is that of the king as
ruling jointly with the king of the dead (Lyle 1985). The other
complementariness relevant to kingship I find to be that of 1b and 2b, the
dark or "old god" aspect of the first two functions (white and red), the king
representing alternately one or other of these two. The Varuna and Mitra
pair that Dumézil found expressive of the two aspects of dual sovereignty, I
would tentatively place as 1b and 2b, one white and one red. Varuna is
associated with ordeal by water, whereas Mitra is associated with ordeal by
fire (Boyce 1975: 34), and this distinction may possibly accord with an
alternation between wetness and dryness in the X and Y generations. In
India, the living king (Ka) is the human counterpart of Indra (Gonda 1966:
53, 132), and it is also possible to distinguish the king of the dead (Kb) — he
is Yama, who has been identified with Remus (Puhvel 1975; Lincoln 1975;
Lyle 1985: 3-4).

    In the Roman tradition, told as human history, the first king is Proca,
the second king is his son Amulius and the third king is Romulus, with his
brother Remus as king of the dead. In Greek tradition, of course, the king
of the gods is Zeus (third king, following in succession from his grandfather,
Uranus, and his father, Cronus) and his brother Hades is king of the dead.
In Scandinavian tradition, I would place Thor as third king and, like
Dumézil (1977: 196-9), I would identify Tyr and Odin as expressing the two
aspects of sovereignty among the old gods, but would prefer to hold open
the question of which is first and which is second king for further discussion
as there is no full succession myth in this case. In the Celtic case, on the
other hand, one can see a sequence of three divine kings quite clearly (Mac
Cana 1983: 58): they are Nuada, Bres, and Lug. I suggest, then, that the
following can be placed as successions of kings in a sequence of X, Y, X
generations.

| X | Proca | Uranus | Nuada |
|---|-------|--------|-------|
| Y | Amulius | Cronus | Bres |
| X | Romulus | Zeus | Lug |

Table 2

Of the triad of kings, the first two establish the alternation and each holds total power in turn. The situation is different, though, in the third generation, and here the story of the hostile twins has to be seen as the narrative equivalent of "the differentiation of light and darkness out of the primordial twilight" as Wyatt calls it, in speaking of the activity of Indra (1986: 65). The story makes it clear that the king of the living (Ka) is the one who is expected to be king in this generation, but tells that the other twin (Kb) somehow establishes a prior claim to kingship and is given the dark part of the now divided kingdom while his brother rules the light part. It is in this third generation that the process of creating the cosmos is completed and the rule of the twin brothers forms a paradigm for human kingship, but it is only in this first generation to experience a world of light and darkness that there is a need to find a king of the dead from the same generation as the king of the living. As I understand it, from this point on each king of the living becomes the next king of the dead, so that the two kings are of alternate generations. In the case of Rome, the reign of Romulus, by one account, ends with his being torn apart and the pieces of his body being buried in the earth (see Lincoln 1986: 42-3), and this is open to interpretation as the transfer of Romulus, through sacrifice, from his royal role in life to that in death.

Rome is marked by a number of traces of a period of reversal within the year, the Saturnalia for example, and these have been set in the context of current anthropological understanding by Sahlins who notes that during periods of reversal in parts of Europe and Polynesia, as well as Africa and the Near East, the reigning monarch might be "replaced by a mock king or superseded god of the people" (1981: 123; 1985: 92). By my reading, in the case of the archaic old world system I am studying, the anti-king does not appear out of nowhere at this time, but is one evidence of a general process of reversal of above and below. Sahlins observes in a Hawaiian context that "men wear loin cloths on their heads" during the period of reversal (1981: 113) and similarly, I suggest, the king of the dead, who is conceived of as normally ruling below the ground, makes a visible appearance above the ground at this time. The period of reversal, thought of from the point of view of the reigning monarch, can be regarded as an interregnum, but in a total view it appears to be one of the two facets of an alternation: there are two kings throughout the year, but they take turns in ruling the two realms above or below the earth. I have found in studying the archaic year calendar

that it is possible to understand its structuring as including a short period of
culturally imposed "darkness" corresponding to night (Lyle 1984c; 1986),
and I see this as the period when the king of the dead rules on earth. It
should be said that I take it, as is commonly done, that the ritual pattern can
be expressed at varying scales, and that the annual cycle and the life cycle
are in correspondence, so that study of the year cycle can illuminate
alternations whether they take place annually or by generation.

I can now present in diagram form my hypothesis about how the
alternation set up in the creation myth is carried on into the historical
process (Figure 2).

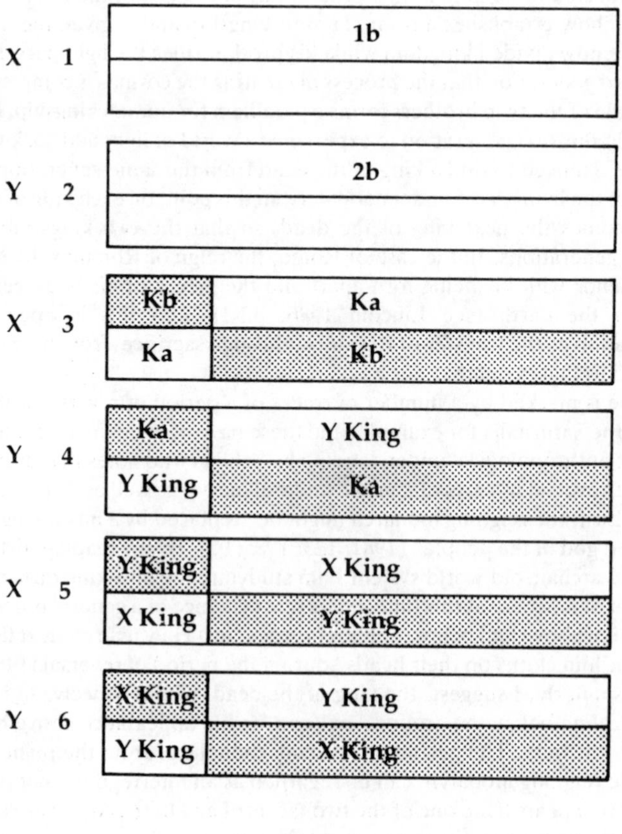

| X | 1 | 1b | |
|---|---|---|---|

| Y | 2 | 2b | |
|---|---|---|---|

| X | 3 | Kb | Ka |
|---|---|----|----|
|   |   | Ka | Kb |

| Y | 4 | Ka     | Y King |
|---|---|--------|--------|
|   |   | Y King | Ka     |

| X | 5 | Y King | X King |
|---|---|--------|--------|
|   |   | X King | Y King |

| Y | 6 | X King | Y King |
|---|---|--------|--------|
|   |   | Y King | X King |

Figure 2

Rome provides in the person of Romulus a particularly good instance of how the divine modulates into the human; a comparable figure in India is the human Manu who has Yama, god of death, as his brother. It is, I suggest, the third generation as shown in Figure 2 that is on the borderline between gods and men so that we find here Zeus and Romulus, Indra and Manu, depending on whether the divine or the human aspect is being stressed. The first two generations of kings are unambiguously gods. Already in the first generation there is a division into above and below,[1] but the below is the place of the female. The sky god, Uranus, is first king, and his son, Cronus, also a sky god, is second king, and each rules in turn the totality of all that exists. In the third generation there is a division into darkness and light so that there are two realms ruled by two kings, who are brothers, e.g. Zeus or Romulus (Ka) and Hades or Remus (Kb), with the alternations of above and below previously noted. In generation 4, there is still a trace of the divine in that the Romulus figure (Ka) becomes the king of the dead although the king of the living can be any human. Thereafter, both kings are human, and the kings of generations 5 and 6 and all additional generations are a matter of history though continuing to enact the pattern of alternations expressed in the myth of origin.

When it comes to the question of the transfer of power from one human generation to the next, Rome remains helpful, through the tradition of chariot-racing in the circus. In this case, the Romans took their charter from an explicitly Greek legend for, although it was said that Romulus introduced chariot-racing into Rome, chariot-racing itself was held to have been instituted by Oenomaus who raced against the suitors who wished to marry his daughter and killed those whom he defeated (see Nagy in this issue). He was eventually defeated and killed by Pelops who married his daughter and became king in his stead.

The charioteers in the Roman circus represented four colours — white, red, green, and blue — and both Dumézil and I have related these to Dumézil's three functions, though differing on the placing of green (Lyle 1984a: 834-5). The four colours were paired in historical times, with dominant blue and green subsuming their partners white and red, but, since Tertullian (*De Spect.* 9) says that initially only white and red were worn by the charioteers, I have suggested that these may have been the dominant colours which formerly subsumed blue and green. It is for this reason that I have referred in the title of this article to "whites and reds" where one would expect, in a historical context, a reference to "blues and greens". My view is that the contending moieties were white-and-blue and red-and-green, and that, while blue and green are more helpful in dealing directly with the circus evidence, white and red are more likely to be useful when trying to place the circus contest in a comparative setting.

The tradition of the Roman circus continued to flourish in Byzantium up to the twelfth century AD, and we owe the following interesting account to John Malalas, a Byzantine writer of the sixth century who drew on earlier sources.

> Now Oenomaus, the king of the country of Pisa, instituted a contest in the European regions in the month of Dystros, that is on 25th March, in honour of the Titan Helios on the ground that he was exalted on the occasion (it is said) of the contest between the earth and the sea, that is between Demeter and Poseidon, the elements subject to Helios. And lots were cast between King Oenomaus and people coming from this or that country, that they should contend with him; and when the lot summoned Oenomaus to contend on behalf of Poseidon, he wore dress consisting of blue clothes, that is the colour of water, and his adversary wore green clothes, that is the colour of the earth. And on the other hand if the lot resulted in Oenomaus wearing the clothes representing Demeter, he wore green clothes and his adversary wore the clothes of Poseidon, that is the colour of water, blue. And the loser was killed. And a vast multitude from every country and city began to watch the annual contest of the king. And those who inhabited the coastal cities and islands, and villages near the sea, and sailors, prayed that the wearers of the blue clothes (Poseidon's, that is) should win, because they augured that, if the one contending on behalf of Poseidon were defeated, there would be a dearth of all kinds of fish, and shipwrecks and violent winds. Whereas those who dwelt inland, and peasants, and all those who had to do with agriculture, prayed for the victory of the one who wore the green clothes, auguring that, if the one contending on behalf of Demeter (on behalf of the earth, that is) should lose, there would be grain-famine, and a shortage of wine and olive-oil and of other fruits. And Oenomaus conquered many adversaries for a long period of years: for he had Apsyrtus to teach him the art of chariot-driving. But Oenomaus was beaten by Pelops the Lydian and killed.[2]

This is a very illuminating passage which aids reflection in this area of investigation. The story of Pelops and Oenomaus is elsewhere told in narrative form. Here it is given a ritual context and the chariot contest is described as a recurrent event happening every spring. The passage brings out the point that "the loser was killed". In the story, it could be a chance matter that Oenomaus is killed as well as being defeated in the race. Not so here; his death is obligatory. The outcome of the chariot-race determines who is to be blessed with good fortune and who is to die. The account also draws attention to the point that the king and the challenger are classified as opposites, and altogether, although it deals with specific characters, it comes remarkably close to a detached structural statement, with the following components:

The king may be either of the land moiety, characterised by the colour green, or of the sea moiety characterised by the colour blue.

The challenger is of the opposite moiety.

If the king wins, the challenger is killed.

If the challenger wins, the king is killed [and the challenger marries his daughter and becomes king].

A win by green augurs good fortune for the land moiety and bad fortune for the sea moiety, and a win by blue augurs good fortune for the sea moiety and bad fortune for the land moiety.

The people of both moieties are present and place their hopes on the appropriate champion.

James Vaughan, in a recent study of ritual regicide (1980), draws particular attention to the point that the killing is intimately bound up with succession, and in this passage we can see it suggested that the succession is not just personal but a matter of rotating moieties, by which the good luck goes now to one, now to the other, so that either land (the dry half) or sea (the wet half) is fortunate in turn. Similarly, in the context of Shang China, Chang notes the likelihood that the alternate generations of kings were associated with different directions, different decorative art, and different ritual practices (Chang 1976: 93-5, 103-13; 1980: 183-8). When a moiety system is involved, the entire community is liable to be directly affected by the change of kingship, one half yielding and the other half gaining the dominant position. This accession to a new role by a section of the community while another section cedes its place is familiar in societies with age class systems. Such societies today are acephalous (Bernardi 1985: xiv, 153, 157) and so cannot be fully compared with a society centred on kingship, but the friction and fighting attendant on the time of transition in these societies (Bernardi 1985: 30, 33, 60, 153) has an affinity with the ritual contest between individual opponents when these are seen as representative of halves of the community. The similarity to age class society becomes more marked when there is the difference of generation between the opponents that is indicated here by the marriage of the challenger to the daughter of the former king.

Terence Turner (1984: 360), in drawing a comparison between Dumézil's three functions and aspects of social systems in Central Brazil, has made the valuable suggestion that formal analysis "may make possible the discovery of structural relations between functional systems of the Indo-European type, which are associated with societies in which the division of labor has developed to a point where distinct social groups can be identified on a permanent basis with particular functions (e.g. *varna*, estates, classes, etc.), and systems of a less differentiated level, in which distinct functions are associated, not with globally distinct sub-groups, but only with status-role categories of various kinds that can potentially be fulfilled by any member of society." I doubt whether kingship in Indo-European and other archaic old world societies can be fully understood simply in terms of class, and think that looking at systems of a less differentiated level may help us to understand it, and that, in the matter of alternation, it is the structuring of societies divided into age classes that is especially helpful. As each wave of young men comes up, there is potential or actual conflict with the set of older men who hold positions of influence and who (in some cases) alone can marry (Bernardi 1985: 29, 60, 149). Eventually, the young men replace the older men, who go into retirement. The young men, now become the dominant group, are in turn under threat from the next wave of young men coming up. It seems as if this pattern is concentrated in the three-axis society in the figure of the king. The thrust behind the change of king is not then a matter of individual ambition, but the expression of the desire of a moiety for its turn. This suggestion has as corollary the idea that the first function "priests" and second function "warriors" are analogically related to, and may derive from, age class alternations associated respectively with white and wetness and red and dryness. The myth of origin suggests that the alternations are in some sense generation sets.

Alternate succession can occur in the form of a king of another moiety succeeding after the natural death of his predecessor, as perhaps in Shang China. However, it may well be that the other form found in the archaic old world, in which the king was subject to ritual challenge, was prior to the form depending on death in the course of nature. In this form, the power of the king is subject to severe limits, reminiscent of the limitations on individual power in the acephalous age class systems discussed by Bernardi.

The limitations imposed by the two alternations noted in this article especially in relation to Rome can be outlined as follows:

a) The king rules jointly with his dead predecessor and at ritually fixed intervals (such as every year) must give up his power to him during a period of reversal. Even when he is in power, it is likely that the moiety of the dead has a living representative that to some extent shares rule with him, although this likelihood has not been discussed here.

b) At ritually fixed intervals, the king must enter into contest with a challenger from the other moiety, and, when he loses, he is killed. This may have its positive side for the king himself, since he may accept his death and see it as having value for the community (Vaughan 1980: 123; Bloch and Parry 1982: 16), but, even if this is the case, he still does not retain power as a living ruler.

The double alternation in the hypothesised three-axis system thus emerges as a mechanism both for continually regenerating the kingship, and for ensuring that individual control of royal power remains circumscribed. It may perhaps be classed with the other means noted by

Luc de Heusch (1981: 24-5; cf. 1985: 98-9) which have the effect of countering the threat of tyranny inherent in the institution of sacred kingship.

## NOTES

1  The polarity above/below is the A axis of the three-axis system.
2  Malalas, Bonn, pp. 173-4. I am very grateful to Dr R.C. McCail for providing this translation. For discussion of the circus and its symbolism, see Cameron 1976 and Lyle 1984a. It will be evident that no attempt is being made here to relate the passage to what actually happened historically in early Rome; this may well be beyond recall (cf. Poucet 1985).

## REFERENCES

Bernardi, Bernardo (1985). *Age Class Systems*. Cambridge: Cambridge University Press.
Bloch, Maurice and Jonathan Parry (1982). *Death and the Regeneration of Life*. Cambridge: Cambridge University Press.
Boyce, Mary (1975). *A History of Zoroastrianism*, Vol. 1 *The Early Period*. Leiden/ Köln: Brill, Handbuch der Orientalistik 1.8.1.2.2A.
Cameron, Alan (1976). *Circus Factions: Blues and Greens at Rome and Byzantium*. Oxford: Clarendon Press.
Chang, Kwang-chih (1976). Some Dualistic Phenomena in Shang Society. In Kwang-chih Chang, *Early Chinese Civilization: Anthropological Perspectives* (Cambridge, Mass. and London: Harvard University Press), pp. 93-114.
——— (1978). *T'ien kan*: a key to the history of the Shang. In *Ancient China: Studies in Early Civilization*, ed. David T. Roy and Tsuen-hsuin Tsien (Hong Kong: Chinese University Press).
——— (1980). *Shang Civilization*. New Haven and London: Yale University Press.
Chao, Lin (1982). *The Socio-Political Systems of the Shang Dynasty*. Nankang, Taipei, Taiwan: Institute of the Three Principles of the People, Academia Sinica, Monograph Series No. 3.
Claessen, Henri J.M. and Peter Skalnik, ed. (1978). *The Early State*. The Hague, Paris and New York: Mouton.
Dubuisson, Daniel (1985). Materiaux pour une typologie des structures trifonctionelles. *L'Homme* 93, 105-21.
Dumézil, Georges (1948). *Mitra-Varuna: essai sur deux représentations indo-européennes de la souveraineté*. 2nd ed. Paris: Gallimard.
——— (1973). *The Destiny of a King*. Chicago and London: Chicago University Press.
——— (1977). *Les dieux souverains des Indo-Europeens*. Paris: Gallimard.
Dyson-Hudson, Neville (1963). The Karimojong Age System. *Ethnology* 2, 353-401.
Gonda, J. (1966). *Ancient Indian Kingship from the Religious Point of View*. Leiden: Brill.
Gulliver, P.H. (1958). The Turkana Age Organization. *American Anthropologist* 60, 900-22.
Heusch, Luc de (1981). *Why Marry Her?: Society and symbolic structures*. Cambridge: Cambridge University Press.
——— (1985). *Sacrifice in Africa: A structuralist approach*. Manchester: Manchester University Press.
Lincoln, Bruce (1975). The Indo-European Myth of Creation. *History of Religions*

162                                                                                 *Emily Lyle*

15,121-45.

—— (1986). *Myth, Cosmos, and Society: Indo-European Themes of Creation and Destruction*. Cambridge, Mass. and London: Harvard University Press.

Littleton, C. Scott (1982). *The New Comparative Mythology: An Anthropological Assessment of the Theories of Georges Dumézil*. 3rd ed. Berkeley, Los Angeles, and London: University of California Press.

Lyle, Emily (1982). Dumézil's Three Functions and Indo-European Cosmic Structure. *History of Religions* 22, 25-44.

—— (1984a). The Circus as Cosmos. *Latomus* 43, 827-41.

—— (1984b). Distinctive Features in Cosmic Structure. *Shadow* 1, 22-8.

—— (1984c). The Dark Days and the Light Month. *Folklore* 95, 221-3.

—— (1985). The Place of the Hostile Twins in a Proposed Theogonic Structure. *Cosmos* 1, 1-14.

—— (1986). Archaic calendar structure approached through the principle of isomorphism. *Semiotica* 61, 243-57.

Mac Cana, Proinsias (1983). *Celtic Mythology*. 2nd ed. Feltham, Middlesex: Newnes.

Malalas, John, ed. Ludovic Dindorf (1831). *Chronographia*. Bonn: Weber, Corpus Scriptorum Historiae Byzantinae.

Maybury-Lewis, David H.P. (1985). On theories of order and justice in the development of civilization. *Symbols: a publication of the Peabody Museum and the Department of Anthropology, Harvard University*, December 1985, pp. 17-21.

Maybury-Lewis, David H.P. and Uri Almagor, ed. (in press). *The Attraction of Opposites: Thought and Society in a Dualistic Mode*. Ann Arbor: University of Michigan Press.

Nagy, Gregory (1986). Sovereignty, Boiling Cauldrons, and Chariot-Racing in Pindar's *Olympian* 1. *Cosmos* 2, 143-147.

Needham, Rodney (1980). Dual Sovereignty. In Rodney Needham, *Reconnaissances* (Toronto and London: University of Toronto Press), pp. 63-105.

—— (1983). Alternation. In Rodney Needham, *Against the "Tranquility" of Axioms* (Berkeley, Los Angeles, and London: University of California Press), pp. 121-54.

—— (1985). Dumézil and the Scope of Comparativism. In Rodney Needham, *Exemplars* (Berkeley, Los Angeles, and London: University of California Press), pp. 178-87.

Netting, Robert McC. (1972). Sacred Power and Centralization: Aspects of Political Adaptation in Africa. In *Population Growth: Anthropological Implications*, ed. Brian Spooner (Cambridge, Mass. and London: MIT Press), pp. 219-44.

Poucet, Jacques (1985). *Les origines de Rome: Tradition et histoire*. Brussels: Facultés universitaires Saint-Louis.

Puhvel, Jaan (1975). *Remus et frater*. *History of Religions* 15, 146-57.

Sahlins, Marshall (1981). The Stranger-King or Dumézil among the Fijians. *Journal of Pacific History* 16, 107-32.

—— (1985). *Islands of History*. Chicago and London: University of Chicago Press.

Sergent, Bernard (1976). La représentation spartiate de la royauté. *Revue de l'histoire des religions* 189, 3-52.

Terray, E. (1977). Event, structure and history: the formation of the Abron kingdom of Gyaman (1700-1780). In *The Evolution of Social Systems*, ed. J. Friedman and M.J. Rowlands (London: Duckworth), pp. 279-301.

Turner, Terence (1984). Dual Opposition, Hierarchy, and Value: Moiety Structure and Symbolic Polarity in Central Brazil and Elsewhere. In *Différences, valeurs, hiérarchie: textes offerts à Louis Dumont*, ed. Jean-Claude Galey (Paris: Ecole des Hautes Etudes en Sciences Sociales), pp. 335-70.

Vaughan, James H. (1980). A Reconsideration of Divine Kingship. In *Explorations in African Systems of Thought*, ed. Ivan Karp and Charles S. Bird (Bloomington: Indiana University Press), pp. 120-42.

Wyatt, N. (1986). Devas and Asuras in Early Indian Religious Thought. *Scottish Journal of Religious Studies* 7, 61-77.

# BALINESE KINGSHIP IN PAGUTAN

Andrew Duff-Cooper

Pagutan is one of six realms (*kerajaan*; Skt. *praja*, cf., e.g., Hooykaas 1964: 52-3) on Lombok, in eastern Indonesia, which are recognised by villagers (cf. Duff-Cooper 1985a).[1] Villagers give different accounts, though not systematically, of the way in which they come to be living on Lombok. One account is that they were invited there in about 1723 by the Raja of Lombok for a limited period, but they stayed on, taking over the island and ruling it until 1894 when the Dutch arrived (cf., e.g., Leendertz 1894). Another account has the Balinese, led by Bhatara Sakti Wau Rauh (cf., e.g., Lekkerkerker 1926: 198), being told by the deity (*déwa*) Siva to go from the realm of Karangasem on Bali to Lombok. The Bhatara won the island bloodlessly for the Balinese through the strength of his holiness; created springs at Suranadi, Narmada, Lingsar, and Meru Mayura in Cakranegara by striking his staff into the ground (cf., e.g., Sneeuwjagt 1926; Bosch 1961: 155-6, 162); and then moved on to Sumbawa, to the east of Lombok, leaving the island in jural charge of sons of the king of Karangasem.

Many Balinese villagers say that the Balinese quarters (*kekliangan*) of Pagutan, as well as the Gria Taman, once a pleasure park (*taman*) of the kings of Pagutan given by one of them to the antecedents of the present Pedanda (cf., e.g., Duff-Cooper 1984c: 485; 1985c: 82 n.3) in the direct male line many generations ago, have been in existence for at least seven generations.[2]

Goris has written (1969: 92) that "Klungkung was — as Gelgel had been earlier [cf., e.g., Robson 1978] — still regarded as the place of residence of the sovereign prince of Bali, a tradition which persists even today". In Pagutan, little emphasis was attached to this fact, although the Déwa Agung of Klungkung (cf. *post*) ranks higher than the king of Pagutan. What counts for the Balinese is that they nearly all came from the eastern Balinese realm of Karangasem and that the area where the Balinese reside in western Lombok, where the proper rites are performed, is ideologically a part of Karangasem. The various parts which constitute the whole are ruled over by members of one descent line.

The king and his officials have long been replaced by a set of administrative offices which run *pari passu* with other aspects of Balinese (and of Islamic Sasak) life. The study of kingship in Pagutan which follows is therefore not based on first-hand field enquiry, although I knew and sometimes spoke with the pretender, so to say, to the kingdom. Rather, it is based on data gleaned in the course of fieldwork from villagers of various

Balinese quarters as well as from Brahmana and Ksatrya (cf. *post*) resident in Pagutan; and on the literature about Balinese kingship in Lombok and in Bali.

Crawfurd suggests (1820: 143) that "the princes of this family [the kingly line of Karangasem], but they alone, of the sovereigns of Bali and Lombok, are of the Wesia or mercantile class; the rest uniformly of the Satria tribe". It may be that since the time that Crawfurd was describing descendants of the Karangasem Wesia have become Ksatrya. More likely, I think, is that Crawfurd's report is inaccurate: the kings of Pagutan have "always" been Ksatrya, according to villagers. Furthermore, of course, if Crawfurd is right, then the kings of Karangasem must also have become Ksatrya; but, for instance, the funeral towers (*badé*) of the kings of Karangasem always had nine rooves; the towers of Wesia only ever have seven rooves (cf. Wirz 1928; Mershon 1971: 210). The local descent group, also, which is resident at the central Pagutan *puri* (Ksatrya compound) considers itself, as others consider it, as Ksatrya. Members of this group take the Ksatrya appellations I Gusti (male) and Ni Gusti Ayu (female). These styles are considered proper by villagers, and their use, either by the Ksatrya in question about themselves or by villagers in referring to or addressing these Ksatrya, causes no comment.

In Klungkung (Bali), the king is termed Déwa Agung; in Badung and Tabanan (Bali), Cokorda; in Buléléng, Jembrana, Bangli, Karangasem, and Gianyar (Bali), Anak Agung. In Pagutan, the king is also called Anak Agung. Villagers acknowledge that Déwa Agung is a status which rates higher (sc. finer and higher) than the others; but the relative standing of the statuses Cokorda and Anak Agung is more problematical. I cannot say with certainty which, if either, ranks higher than the other.

The collective ideas which frame the lives of the Balinese of Pagutan have been described at length elsewhere (cf. n. 1). The Balinese form of life in Pagutan (and I very much suspect elsewhere in Bali and Lombok) is a sacred totality which in a metaphysical (*sarva-surya*) idiom derives from the Balinese high deity, Ida Sang Hyang Vidhi.[3] Vidhi is pervasive in the world, and as Sang Bindu, the point or dot, contains everything in it. Vidhi takes many forms: for example, Siva the god at the centre of eight of the points of the Balinese compass (*nawa sanga*) (cf., e.g., Covarrubias 1972: 296-7); Surya the sun god; *atman*, the "soul" which in one way or another animates everything that is taken to possess regenerative potential (*bayu*) in Balinese ideology; the couple (*pakurenan*) composed of a male and a female in one house, with its own fire to cook on; the gods in the compound temple, and in the other temples to which communities of Balinese of various extension are related. Vidhi is also expressible in the formula (*mantra*) [*a/b*], where two entities *a* and *b* are juxtaposed (/). Perfect bilateral symmetry obtains between *a* and *b*. These entities correlatively are what Leibniz calls "indiscernible": any objective statement which can be made about *a* can also be made about *b*. The closest approximations to this perfect symmetry are to be found at various points, formally termed centres of reference, in the Balinese world. The greater the number of different objective statements which can be made about *a* and *b*, the greater the asymmetry of the relations which obtain between them, relative to a centre of reference; or, in other words, the greater the distance, ideologically and often physically, of one of the two entities from a particular centre of reference, the greater the asymmetry in the relations obtaining between the two. The entity which of two is represented as being higher and closer to the centre of reference is correlatively finer and purer than the other of the two.

These principles of order have been elicited from studies of a number of indigenously defined aspects of the Balinese form of life.[4] It remains to be seen whether these principles of order also inform Balinese kingship.

The king reigned because of his *dharma*, duty, as a Ksatrya. His reign also was constrained by *dharma*, i.e. by what was proper according to local, current convention (*désa kala patra*). Over what, though, did the king reign? Gadd writes (1948: 33) that "it would seem an axiom that there must be a people for a king to rule over ...", but this is not quite true of Balinese kings. It is clear from the brief accounts given by the Geertzes, for example (Geertz and Geertz 1975: 23-7; Geertz 1980: 140), that a Balinese king, both in Bali and in Lombok, did not rule over a clearly defined territory, nor over a specific people coterminous with such a territory. Rather, for contingent reasons, lines or sub-lines of descent or other groups of people were allied with a particular king through what the Geertzes characterise as "highly unstable pyramids of authority; at the apex of each was a king, prince, or lord" (1975: 24).[5] This apex is physically the compound of the king and his local descent group, and the village (*désa*) temples, with jural authority exercised ultimately by the king in the *puri*. This authority was exercised, albeit notionally, however, over an area called *jagat* or *negara* (Ind., *daerah*) and its inhabitants. This area over which the king exercised ultimate authority in jural matters — an area which was well-defined but not within one boundary — was the realm.

A king's duties may be distinguished as those due to the realm as a totality, to the three other estates (*warna*), individually and severally, and to his closest relations and himself as the embodiment, at least, of kingship. This last aspect of a king's duties is common to every Balinese person of whatever status, though it may be modified by the principle of relative age; and it is also personal to the king because (in this case) he is the Ksatrya king in Pagutan.

The king's paramount concern is to secure life for the realm in accordance with *dharma*.[6] That is, the life and actions of people must be such as to be taken by them to be in accord with divine cosmic order and harmony (cf., e.g., Schärer 1963: 74-5). There were three areas of social life where the participation of the king (and to a greater or lesser extent a Pedanda) was taken to be crucial to ensure that life was thus secured: war, the administration of justice, and the performance of rites.

These terms do not mean what they might at first sight appear to mean: *war* refers to the duty of the king to protect the realm not only from other kings' ambitions to expand the area of competence of their gods at the expense of others' gods; but also from demons and such human beings as witches (*léak*), who wish only to cause harm and disorder. In all these situations the king who protects the realm through fearless leadership upholds order and harmony and overcomes beings who create disorder and disharmony. Kings who fail in these duties do best to lead the inhabitants of the realm into a *puputan* (from *\*puput*, finished), a "fight to the end", i.e., mass ritual suicide (cf., e.g., Covarrubias 1972: 34-7). War and the protection of the realm more generally, like much else connected with kingship, has cosmological significance therefore (cf. Downs 1983: 135-8).[7]

The administration of justice is equally to be understood as keeping the actions of empirical individuals in the realm in balance or in harmony, i.e. in accord, so far as is possible, with Sang Dharma; or of re-ordering the realm after its disturbance through such things, as used to be the case, as the birth of opposite-sex twins to Sudra parents (cf., e.g., Van der Kraan 1983: 325) and the marriage of a male and a female forbidden one to the other through the female's higher estate. Before the penalties were relaxed in 1921, the couple was killed. This response to the couple's actions, though, was not so much the execution of a death sentence as the offering of a human sacrifice to the gods, in line with the gravity of the breach of *dharma* (cf. Schärer 1963: 106). This mystical character of the judicial process is emphasised by courts being held in a temple, the *pura penataran*, situated in the king's compound. Thus justice was administered, for acts which affected the whole realm, in temples where "the living unity of the realm was commemorated, celebrated, maintained, and confirmed by religious means" (cf. Goris 1960a: 87; 1960b: 109; 1969: 91). These means included the administration of justice and the subsequent treatment of the parties whose actions were not in accord with *dharma*. Thus Pedandas, until recently, played an important part in the judicial process, and a Pedanda sometimes acted with the king as a judge (cf. Swellengrebel 1960: 64).

The king's duty of ensuring life, finally, refers to his duty to perform rites. The material prosperity of the realm depends in the last instance upon the proper performance of rites, for natural phenomena (as we understand them) such as rain, earthquakes, volcanic eruptions, and such like, are the responses of the gods to humankind's actions, within a particular bounded area (cf., e.g., Hobart 1978: 55). Especially important was the king's duty to carry out the rite of *pekelem* at Segara Anak, the crater lake on Mount

Rinjani, on the full moon (*purnama*) of the fifth Balinese month. This rite, now financed by the provincial (jural) authorities, was instituted by the first king of Lombok, Anak Agung Ngurah, according to tradition (cf. Duff-Cooper 1983: 119-22) and ensures that enough rain comes on time. The rite for making water in the form of rain (*ngujanang*) or in previously dry wells can, however, be performed by anyone who knows the correct procedure and the right *mantra* etc. These can be got from a local medicine man or woman (Balian).

These duties of the king also fall to Visnu. Visnu, the deity who is especially linked to the Ksatrya estate, is the "Man-Lion" who destroys all difficulties and beings like demons. They also fall to Siva, who protects the world and *dharma*; and to Surya (Aditya) armed with a thousand arrows, the Man of energy, protector of the world and the granter of boons (cf. Goudriaan and Hooykaas 1971: 116-7, 73-7, 343-4, 511-2, 155-6). The king's responsibility for the administration of justice (understood as above) is related to Siva (as Surya) being "Producer of the day": like the sun, Pedanda and kings dispel the beings of darkness and slay enemies of *dharma* (cf., e.g., Hocart 1927: 53, 55; Gonda 1959: 172).

A Ksatrya king's relations with the three other estates, though, are not all the same. To Brahmana, and especially to Pedanda and other senior Brahmana, a king shows the deference which is due to the standing of these statuses, ultimately the highest and closest to Vidhi in the material, visible (*sekala*) world. On some occasions the pre-eminence of Brahmana over Ksatrya and of a Pedanda over a king are reversed (cf., e.g., Dumézil 1974: 631). But in Balinese life, this reversal is only ever temporary and occurs infrequently. A king ultimately defers to Pedanda, as do all others. Equally a king and all others should support, through *punia*, statuses such as Pedanda, so that the latter can live, as he or she ought to live, by having nothing to do with making and accumulating money and goods (*artha*).

The four Balinese estates, *warna*, are termed Brahmana, Ksatrya, Wesia, and Sudra, the last usually being called *Anak* Bali (Balinese people) on Lombok. Each estate is related to the other three in various ways; and they are also related as a set (*catur jalma*) to other aspects of the Balinese universe. The order of the estates listed here, which is variously confirmed by Liefrinck, Van Eck, and Korn (cf. Korn 1932: 140; Raglan 1949: 77), accords with the convention that in the middle world (*madyapada*), the world of material human beings (*mertyapada*), what is less high, fine, and pure is addressed or referred to after what is higher, finer, and purer.

*Artha* are the prime concern of Wesia, merchants, and of *Anak* Bali who "should work hard, in the rice fields, repairing roads or buildings belonging to the king and Pedanda and so forth" (Hobart 1979: 114). Wesia should engage in commerce and organise the market, dealing in the produce of the labour of Sudra, to generate wealth for the king and for others. The king was entitled to collect taxes from his subjects. These taxes and the returns from the Wesia's work financed the king's duties to the realm and to Brahmana. A king, like Brahmana, should be generous to the poor, the Sudra among whom had the reciprocal duty to fight, to the death, to protect the realm under the leadership of the king. In this duty, *Anak Bali* are akin to the Muruts, the gods of the commons, the only gods to help the Vedic kingly god Indra slay the serpent Vritra (cf., e.g., Hocart 1970b: 14-5).

Finally, the king should set a good example to everyone else by being constant (like the sun god), and dedicated to ensuring that the customs and manners of the realm were in accordance with *dharma*; a king should always be fair and just in exercising these prerogatives (cf. Hobart 1979: 114).

Although he possesses these (jural) prerogatives for mystical reasons, the material and immaterial constitution of a king does not differ from that of other people. Nor is the character of a king any less influenced by such matters as descent, naming, and day of birth than that of others (cf. Duff-Cooper 1985c: e.g. 82). His physical body and the configuration of qualities (*guna*) which, among other things, determine his character, thoughts, emotions, and predispositions, are composed of the same elements and qualities etc. as those of all others.

Hocart writes (1970a: 296) that "descent, not ability, is the qualification for office". In Balinese life, though, descent and ability run hand in hand: a Ksatrya born to the union of a Ksatrya male and a female of the same estate, themselves the products of such unions through many earlier generations, is most likely to be someone who is most influenced by the quality *rajah*. This quality conduces to courage, determination, and to the other kingly qualities and characteristics which we have mentioned, when influenced by or inclined towards the quality *sattwa*, correlated with Brahmana. Even a king who did not embody such characteristics, though, would be granted the external signs of respect and veneration which are the due of a king (and *a fortiori* of a Pedanda) because of his standing and function.

For instance, if anyone wanted to petition the king, he or she dressed in white, after bathing and using holy water (cf., e.g., Duff-Cooper 1984a: 38-9 n. 13), and sat from early morning to late afternoon outside the gates of the *puri*, enduring the hardships of heat, thirst, and hunger, before being summoned to present the petition. The king had a duty to listen sympathetically to such petitions (cf. Worsley 1972: 45).[8]

These conventions were observed whether the king was primarily influenced by the quality *rajah* (and was thus a good king) or not (and so was not). But in the latter case the king would not be held in great popular affection: people would grumble about having to pay taxes, at having to

contribute goods and labour to rites, and at having to fight. This situation is
far from harmonious. A good king, in whom *rajah* predominates, is held in
great popular affection and is helped in his duties by Sudra who contribute
generously and willingly (*darma alus dana goya*).

A king should ensure that his life is in accord with his status both by
assiduously performing the rites required of him outside the *puri* (such as
*pekelem*) and inside it with his (co-resident) local descent group. By doing
so, the king is *ipso facto* thus far a good king, who reigns (thus far) in
accordance with *dharma*. In this way the aspects of the king we have alluded
to are in accord with the king's *dharma*. Thus the king is more godlike, i.e.,
finer and purer, than he would otherwise be. He can therefore protect the
realm, ensuring its prosperity and harmony, better than he would otherwise
be able to.

A question which arises here is: Who succeeded to the status on the
incumbent's death?[9] In line with the conventions of the inheritance of real
and other property, which ultimately descends through generations in the
male line (*saking purusa*); and in line with the ultimate pre-eminence of the
male over the female in other ways, a son, either born to the deceased king
by one of the latter's wives, or adopted, succeeded a father. Geertz and
Geertz write (1975: 142) that the *oldest* son was "formally" entitled to
succeed. In the absence of other explication of the word, "formally" must
here be understood as simply one example of the pre-eminence in most, but
not all, contexts of a person who is older, either generationally, or in terms
of years or of status, over another who is younger in one or more of these
ways. The principle of relative age is an aspect of the diarchy which
pervades the Balinese form of life (cf. Duff-Cooper 1985a).

The person who succeeded the dead king was not crowned in a
coronation ceremony but was "consecrated" with his wife (c.f., e.g.,
Swellengrebel 1960: 47-50; Geertz 1980: 215),[10] as a couple composed of a
male and a female is consecrated in the rites of marriage (*ngantén` ), during
which the couple is seated high, as though they were king and queen (cf.,
e.g., Rimbaud 1964; Hocart 1927: 99).[11]

The relations which obtain between the status of king and other
statuses in Balinese life can be shown to be transformations of Vidhi from
perfect bilateral symmetry ([a/b]) to a number of degrees of asymmetry.[12]
Thus the relations which obtain between a king and others resident in his
compound are asymmetrical. However, they are no more asymmetrical
than the relations which obtain between a senior male and other males and
females in his compound. Like others, the king is in many regards the same
as his brothers and sisters by reference to the origin-point (*kawitan*) from
which they all derive. This point is composed of the king's (and his brothers'
and sisters') parents. The position of a king, that is, like that of a Pedanda,
is pre-eminent in his compound — but only to the extent that any of his

brothers could also have acceded to the status in question, for a younger brother can accede over an older brother. The king, like a Pedanda, should strive, moreover, to mitigate the asymmetry between himself and his brothers and sisters which derives from his accession to the status. This mitigation is concerned with both the material and the spiritual aspects of Balinese life. Ultimately, though, a king could not be replaced by another without his death, or conflict involving violence, and a Pedanda could not be replaced without discussion at least. Still, the degree of asymmetry which obtains between a king or a Pedanda ($a$) and his local descent group ($b$) is very slight. This degree of asymmetry can be represented as $[a > b]$ where the guillemot stands for the first degree of asymmetry and the brackets for the context, which is over-ridingly important.

The relations which obtain between a king and those outside his compound, to whom he is not closely related through origin-points, are more varied. In his dealings with a Pedanda ($a$), the king ($b$) is the less eminent. But, again, this asymmetry is very slight. Both are a "foot" of the god (cf. *post*), and one stands to the other as right is to left, as the sun is to the moon, and as male is to female. The Pedanda, associated with right, the sun, and male, is purer than the king, associated with left, the moon, and female. This correlates with the fact that, for instance, the right hand is purer than the left hand.

A Brahmana is of the *raga keksatryan*, i.e. allowed to behave like Ksatrya, until he or she becomes "old" (*lingsir*), either through a (first) marriage or by becoming a Pedanda; a Ksatrya may become a Pedanda Resi. Both, we have noted, administer justice as judges. Both Brahmana and Ksatrya can bear the appellations "Bagus" (handsome, fine: male) or "Ayu" (beautiful: female) through birth. In daily life, both are accorded the same conventions which are among the most formal (sc. finest) of Balinese life. The relations which obtain between a Pedanda and a king and between Brahmana and Ksatrya are only slightly asymmetrical, like those which obtain between older and younger brothers. These relations are expressible as $[a > b]$.

The position of Wesia is more ambivalent. Some may of course become kings, though not Pedanda. Wesia also bear appellations — "Gusti" (male), "Gusti Ayu" (female) — similar to those taken by Brahmana and Ksatrya. They are referred to and addressed in middle or, more usually in Pagutan, in high (fine) Balinese. However, Wesia are associated like Sudra with goods and money (*artha*) and with the quality *tamas*, both of which, like the language used to address and to refer to Sudra by "caste" Balinese, are not very fine. In most contexts, though, the asymmetry which obtains between a king (and a Pedanda) ($a$) and a male or female Wesia ($b$) is analogous to that which obtains between Brahmana ($a$) and Ksatrya ($b$), which together comprise the twice-born (*dvija*), and between elder (*a*) and younger (*b*) brothers, i.e. [*a* > *b*].

The relations which obtain between a king (and a Pedanda) (*a*), and between Brahmana, Ksatrya, and Wesia (the *triwangsa*) (*a*) and Sudra (*b*) are more greatly asymmetrical, for the former (*a*) are interchangeable only in a very limited number of contexts with the latter (*b*). The degree of asymmetry is representable as [*a* >> *b*].

All these formulas are replications of Vidhi. Physically and ideationally the pre-eminent entity in each case (*a*) is closer to a particular centre of reference than *b*. The greater the degree of asymmetry, the more the physical and ideological disparity between the standing of *a* and *b* relative to many centres of reference. Material circumstances, it should be emphasised however, are not correlated with this disparity.

The cline of transformations which has been elicited from the present study — [*a/b*], [*a* > *b*], [*a* >> *b*][13] — corresponds to the cline of transformations which is discernible in the "economic" relations which obtain between various aspects of the Balinese nation (*bangsa*). Thus a Pedanda is to a king, Brahmana are to Ksatrya, and Brahmana and Ksatrya are to Wesia to the first degree of asymmetry. This degree is equivalent to that which obtains between a seller and a buyer of goods and/or services from the seller's own village. Between these buyers and sellers and between the constituents of the various dyads just listed, relations of quasi-brotherhood (*semotonan*) obtain. These relations do not obtain between a seller and a buyer from different villages and, *a fortiori*, different realms; yet the degree of asymmetry of these relations — the second — is modified by the seller and the buyer constituting dyads composed of entities which are both Balinese.

Greater asymmetry, the third degree [*a* >>> *b*], obtains between the four Balinese estates (the *catur jalma*) on one hand and Indonesians who are neither Balinese nor Hindu Indians on the other. Indeterminate asymmetry obtains between Balinese, Hindu Indians, and other Indonesians, on one hand, and all others on the other. These degrees of asymmetry (in which the first-mentioned entity in each dyad is pre-eminent) are correlated with the prices conventionally required from a buyer of goods and/or services by a Balinese seller.

A final point should be addressed before we conclude this study. In the literature about Balinese kings, both on Bali and on Lombok, it is widely reported, with varying degrees of emphasis, that the king is a god. Geertz, for example, says (1980: 129) that the king, "like the gods, and as one", ensured the prosperity of the realm. Stutterheim writes (1931: 4) that "the king after his death is absorbed in the god whose incarnation he was during life ..."; while Grader reports (1960: 172) that the king is an incarnation, especially of Visnu; and Goris suggests (1969: 93) that Siva incarnates himself in each ruling prince. More generaly, Raglan has it (1945: 83) that the divine king is a deity. Hocart, finally, asserts (1970a: 83) that the king is a repository of the gods who becomes another god when he conquers another people.

Hocart's assertion is reminiscent of the way in which a Brahmana Pedanda, during his morning worship of the sun (*surya-sevana*) empties himself or herself so that Siva may enter the empty body to make holy water (*tirtha*) of various kinds (cf., e.g., Pudja 1976).

Pedanda are to kings (we have noted) as elder brothers and sisters are to younger brothers or sisters. In certain contexts an elder brother and his younger brother(s) etc. are considered to be so similar, males to males and females to females, that they can be substituted one for another. This substitution is akin to the fact that a Ksatrya who could have been a king can become a Pedanda Resi instead.

Now, Pedanda, according to Goris (1969: 93), also incarnate Siva, as the sun god Surya or Aditya, while Lévi remarks (1926: 10) that a Pedanda "est partout vénéré comme une sorte de divinité terrestre". Other writers, though, do not suggest that Pedanda are gods, nor that they incarnate gods, nor that gods incarnate themselves in Pedanda (cf. *supra*). To the contrary: while Geertz reaffirms (1976: 22) that Pedanda are "holy", but not gods, Hooykaas considered (1976: 242) that a Pedanda is not "a 'holy' man, neither to be sought nor found in Bali ..., but a *learned* man, a pundit ...". That is, a Pedanda is considered to be only akin to a god, or something other; his younger brother, by contrast, is a god or incarnates one or other god. This situation is puzzling given that, of elder and younger, the former is ultimately pre-eminent, but not a god, while the subordinate latter is a god or incarnates a god. That a Ksatrya, let alone a Wesia, could be a god, or an incarnation of a god, while a Brahmana Pedanda, on all but Goris's account, is a material human being, even though holy or learned, leads to the suspicion that the Balinese status of king has not always been represented faithfully in the literature.

The question whether the king is a god is hard to answer for at least two important reasons. First, in English the term *god* is so charged with various meanings that it is barely useful as an analytical tool (cf., e.g., Leenhardt 1979: 27), as opposed merely to its use as an odd-job word. Second, and even more important than the first reason, is that *all* material human beings, once they have been cremated, enter the sphere of the mystical, the domain of the gods. These cremated beings are present at various times in the temples where groups of Balinese of various extension honour them periodically. To affirm that the king is a god, as opposed to a (mere) human being, requires the same kind of distinction as that upon which Raglan relies: "the Brahman moves always within the sacred world, to which others are admitted only on special occasions, such as initiation or sacrifice. ... The same applies in general to the more sacred parts of churches, temples, and palaces ... which ... are the abode of the Deity, or the Divine King." The distinction *sacred/profane* is not distinguishable in Balinese ideology. It therefore follows that the distinction between the king-god, who lives in a sacred world, and mere mortals, who live in a profane world, cannot hold. Nor, of course, is the king invisible and essential (*niskala*), prime attributes of mystical beings, such as gods, in Balinese life.

Because of these reasons, at least, we must consider Balinese kingship under a new aspect (cf., e.g., Needham 1983: 2-3, 22-3). The most general word for king in Balinese is "Rajah". This word not only means king, prince, or lord, but also fate, destiny, fortune, *widhi*. It is also the name for a sign in magic. According to the Balinese, its second meaning is the quality (*guna*) of being active in the world (cf. Warna 1978: 465 s.v. *rajah* I, II). The first meaning of "Rajah" derives from Skt. *raj—*, which has two main senses: direct, rule, be first, be master of, king of; shine, be illustrious, distinguish one's self (Lanman 1884: 229).

There are a number of other words for king. "Déwa Agung" means Great God and "Maha Raja" (another term for the king of Klungkung), Great King. "Déwa", god, is an appellation for one class of Ksatrya. This word also means king in the language of the stage (cf. Friederich 1959: 101). The word derives from IE *\*div*, to shine; this word expresses godhead (Hocart 1927: 18). "Bhatara" similarly means god, protector, and is used to address a king (Hooykaas 1973: 24). "Anak Agung", literally Great Person, is also the appellation of kings. "Cokorda", a style borne by some senior Ksatrya on Lombok though not resident in Pagutan, and "Pedanda" both mean "foot" (Hooykaas 1973: 13). "Sang Prabu" (*prabu*, head) also means king (Warna 1978: 449 s.v.). "Ratu", king, is a term used as an honorific to address and to refer to members of the *triwangsa*, the three senior estates. Finally, "Adi" (Ind., *paling*, most; *utama*, excellent, eminent, chief, main, leading) means prince, when it is used of the holy water sprinkler (*lis*), "a magical tree enchanted by Bhatara Siva" (Hooykaas-van Leeuwen Boomkamp 1961: 5).

This short survey clearly shows that kings and other Balinese such as Brahmana are attributed among other things a god-like character. Deities, though, are also regified, so to say. Balinese texts are replete with allusions to deities as lords or princes, as is demonstrated by just a few examples: Aditya (the sun) is Déwa-raja, king of the gods; Visnu is "devānām sawa-bhūtānām", lord of the gods and of all living things; Dhruwa Rsi is god of gods and lord of the world, Siva, most exalted one (parā-param) (cf. Goudriaan and Hooykaas 1971: 28-9, 73-7, 343-4); Yama is the lord (Raja) of judgement (cf., e.g., Hooykaas 1973). Other appellations are applied to the gods: Surya (Aditya) is protector of the world and man of energy; Siva is also protector of the world (Jagan-nātham) and protector of *dharma*, the Balinese form of life (Goudriaan and Hooykaas 1971: 512, 155-6, 343-4,

511-2).

This reciprocal regification of the gods and deification of the king is expectable. Whatever there is in the microcosm (*bhuvana alit*), there is in the macrocosm (*bhuvana agung*) too. These are the domains of material human beings, such as kings, and of the gods and other mystical beings respectively: the visible and material (*sakala*) and the invisible and essential (*niskala*). But none of this means that the kings are gods, nor that the gods are kings. It suggests that, in their respective domains, which may be enantiomorphs one of the other (cf. Duff-Cooper forthcoming), gods and kings are analogues.

Before we conclude, there appears to be a contradiction which we should address. That is, a king is termed the foot (Cokorda) as is a Pedanda; but the king is also Sang Prabu, the head. In the human body, the head, the top element, is radically opposed to the feet, the bottom element. It would appear therefore that a king, and a Pedanda, stand to the rest of humanity, and especially to the fourth estate and non-Balinese (excluding Hindu Indians) as the head stands to the other elements of the body, and especially to the feet. In one version of the story of how the four estates came into existence in the middle world, Brahmana emerged from Brahma's fontanelle, Ksatrya from his mouth, Wesia from his midriff (sc. navel?), and the Sudra from his feet. However, the king (and his "elder brothers", Pedanda) also stand to the high beings of the essential world, located at, among other places, the top of Mount Rinjani, as the feet stand to the head.

The relation of the feet one to the other relative to a centre of reference (the navel) is shown schematically in the *uku kepeng*, the "doll" made the size of a corpse out of white thread and old Chinese coins (*pipis bolong*) and cremated with the corpse (cf. e.g., Covarrubias 1972: 366). More schematically still, the figure below shows the relation of the right foot (*B*, Brahmana) to the left foot (*K*, Ksatrya) relative to a centre of reference (*C*). Empirically, for example, this figure shows the relation of a Pedanda and a Ksatrya Pedanda Resi (the Pretender to the Pagutan kingdom) when seated talking at the Gria Taman, the compound of Pedanda Gdé Madé Karang, with whom I lived for part of my time in Pagutan. The centre in this case could be understood as Mount Rinjani, to the northeast of Pagutan.

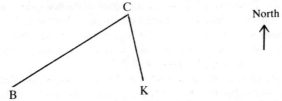

The two feet, Pedanda (*B*) and king (*K*), relative to a centre of reference (*C*).

The figure shows the slight asymmetry which obtains between a Pedanda and a king: the former sits facing east, the latter, west. East is to west as right is to left and as male is to female.

In each of the cases which we have considered — the head to the feet; Brahmana to Ksatrya; Brahmana and Ksatrya to Wesia and Sudra; Brahmana, Ksatrya, and Wesia to Sudra; gods to Pedanda and kings — the pre-eminent entity, which is mentioned first in each case, is represented as being higher than the entity to which it is dyadically opposed. The pre-eminent entity is also closer to the centre of reference in question than its opposite. This holds even for the dyad shown in the figure: although $B$ and $K$ appear not to be equidistant from $C$, physically they are for all intents and purposes. Ideologically, $B$ is closer to the gods at $C$ than $K$. This fact accords with $B$'s ultimate pre-eminence in relations with $K$, and with the slight asymmetry which obtains in the relations between $B$ and $K$. Similarly, the head is higher than the feet, relative to the fontanelle where Siva is located, and should be kept in that order; kings sit higher and more directly face the east or the northeast than all others bar Pedanda, are treated with the utmost deference, and are addressed and referred to in fine Balinese.[14] Gods, equally, are higher than all others, at the top of Mount Rinjani and in temples set higher than the area to which they pertain; gods are addressed and referred to either in the highest, finest Balinese or in Sanskrit.

If, though, kings are best understood as analogues of the gods, can they still be said to be incarnations of gods? They can, in this sense; we have noted that in Balinese metaphysics Vidhi pervades the world. Everything that is in it derives from and replicates the form of Vidhi. The nine gods of the *nawa sanga* which are constantly referred to directly or indirectly both in the worship of the sun god by Pedanda and in the rites associated with kingship (cf., e.g., Lintgentz 1856; Swellengrebel 1960: 62), are one aspect of Vidhi and constitute a set comprising various dualities. These dyadically related gods and human Pedanda and kings are analogues one of another: north is to south as Pedanda is to king; east is to west as Pedanda is to king, and so on. In as much as the relations which obtain between dyadically related entities such as the gods Iswara and Mahadéwa at east and west respectively (cf., e.g., Swellengrebel 1960: 47) replicate Vidhi in transformation, Pedanda and kings, as analogues of the gods, do so also. In this sense, and in as much as certain qualities, rights, and duties are associated both with the gods and with kings and Pedanda, these latter statuses reincarnate (sc. replicate) the gods of the *nawa sanga* and, ultimately, Vidhi (cf., e.g., Hidding 1959: 58)[15]

This replication of the nine gods and Vidhi by kings and Pedanda, however, is discernible in other, often disparate aspects of the Balinese form of life. Basu has it (1959: 169) that "there is nothing sacred about the king himself; if Visnu is in the king, he is in the people also". In our case, it is more accurate to say that the king is sacred to the extent that all aspects, if any, of Balinese life are sacred, constituting a totality which is ultimately Vidhi, expressed as Ida Sang Hyang Sunya, the Void, or as Rwa-Bhinéda, diarchy (cf. Hooykaas 1980: e.g. 16, 133; Needham 1985: e.g., 64-5, 180-5).

Kingship — a particular standing in the material world correlated with rights and duties relative to other complementary rights and duties, and analogous to various gods' standing in the essential world, also correlated with rights and duties — is similarly sacred. That is, to recapitulate: gods stand to Pedanda and the king as heads are to feet; Pedanda and the king stand to other Balinese and non-Balinese people as heads are to feet. Each of these dyads constitutes a unity, i.e. an exhaustive universe of discourse. This unity in duality replicates Vidhi.

This study of Balinese kingship concentrates upon relations. Such an approach helps us to understand the significance of the king and of kingship in Balinese life. That is, we have been able to specify to various degrees the character of the relations which obtain between the king and kingship on one hand and other aspects of the Balinese form of life on the other.

NOTES

1 The data upon which much of this essay is based were collected during the course of about twenty-one months fieldwork in Pagutan, western Lombok, which was funded by the Social Science Research Council of Great Britain and by awards from the Emslie Horniman Anthropological Scholarship Fund. I am indebted to these bodies for their support. Fuller treatment of the topics raised in the present study will be found in the publications by the present writer listed in the References below, and especially in Duff-Cooper 1985a.

2 Very little is known about the internal history of Lombok prior to 1894. See Van der Kraan (1975; 1983) for useful historical accounts of the island. Islamic Sasak claim that they were the original inhabitants of Lombok, as indeed of Pagutan: Teeuw reports (1958: 164) that he was told by one Sasak that Pagutan had been established by Sasak four generations before, and that at that time there were no Balinese living there.

3 In many ways Vidhi is similar to the high god interestingly but very generally discussed by Hidding (1959, esp. pp. 55-9).

4 For a discussion of *aspect* as used in the present study, see Duff-Cooper (forthcoming).

5 This description of the administrative shape of Balinese life may lead some to think that the form of life is hierarchical. Although I have fallen in with this view in a number of places (e.g., 1984d; 1985c), it is now my view that it is not simply hierarchical (1985b: 138): it is more usefully considered as a system of relations which are symbolised in the vertical and horizontal planes. The relations thus symbolised may be symmetrical or of various degrees of asymmetry.

6 For an important discussion of Balinese conceptions of *dharma*, see Hobart (1985: 180-8).

7 Downs writes (1983: 134): "The picture ... obtained of the custom [of head-hunting] as a ritual struggle between two groups representing the two halves of the universe, suggests that it is closely related to the less sanguinary one of

'village wars' or mock combats so widespread in Indonesia. These are, of course, not peculiar to that region, being commonly associated with dual organization in many parts of the world". The Balinese form of life is, of course, diarchic. Such mock battles are held at the temple of Lingsar (Lombok) on the temple festival (*odalan*, from *edal*, emerge, come out) held on the full moon of the sixth Balinese month (cf. Duff-Cooper 1983: 122-3).

8  Here, Worsley writes that "the realm exists not only for the good of the monarch but also for the sustenance of its population. The king was required to furnish the needs of his people and was dutybound to listen to their grievances."

9  A Balinese king was never killed, so far as I am aware, as soon as he showed signs of physical and/or mental incapacity, as was often the case with divine kings.

10  The rite *madiksa* (from *diksa*, rosary) is a purificatory rite when a Brahmana dies and is reborn as a Pedanda similar to the rites held to consecrate a king, to validate the union of a man with a woman, and through which material human beings pass from birth to death and, usually, rebirth.

11  A king, like a Pedanda, had to have at least one wife when he acceded to the status.

12  Cf. Needham (1980: 94) who writes that "it is precisely what one expects of a principle that it should assume a variety of forms, and that these forms should be describable by a number of alternative labels". I have demonstrated that in Balinese thought, at least, symmetry and equality are not synonymous as has sometimes been suggested (cf., e.g., Valeri 1980: 182). Nor is it the case that asymmetry implies hierarchy, as this word is variously understood. Asymmetry may be discernible in societies which possess a non-hierarchical form of classification (cf. Duff-Cooper 1984b).

13  The cline of transformations, it will be noticed, most economically involves the modification of the minimum (ideal) number of features — one (cf., e.g., Needham 1984: 230).

14  Balinese consists of various kinds of language (cf. Kersten 1970: 13-25), which range from Sanskrit, the finest, through the fine (*alus*) forms to the coarse (*kasar*) forms.

15  At the place cited, Hidding writes that "the king is a replica in earthly proportions of the High God".

REFERENCES

Basu, A. (1959). Hindu Doctrine of Divine Kingship. In *The Sacral Kingship*, ed. Widengren, pp. 167-71.
Bosch, F.D.K. (1961). Guru, Trident and Spring. In *Selected Studies in Indonesian Archaeology* (The Hague: Martinus Nijhoff), pp. 153-70.
Covarrubias, Miguel (1972). *Island of Bali*. Kuala Lumpur: Oxford in Asia Paperbacks.
Crawfurd, J. (1820). On the Existence of the Hindu Religion in the Island of Bali. *Asiatick Researches* 13, 128-60.
Downs, R.E. (1983). Head-hunting in Indonesia. In *Structural Anthropology in the Netherlands: A Reader*, ed. with an introduction by P.E. de Josselin de Jong. 2nd edition. (Dordrecht, Holland and Cinnaminson, U.S.A.: Foris Publications), pp. 117-49.
Duff-Cooper, Andrew (1983). A Study of the Collective Ideas of a Community of Balinese on Lombok. Unpublished D.Phil. thesis, University of Oxford.
——— (1984a). An Essay in Balinese Aesthetics. *Occasional Papers No. 7*.

University of Hull: Centre for South-East Asian Studies.

—— (1984b). Review of *Society and Cosmos: Chewong of Peninsular Malaysia* (Singapore: Oxford University Press, 1984) by Signe Howell. *Journal of the Anthropological Society of Oxford* 15, 258-61.

—— (1984c). Principles in the Classification, the Marriages, and some Other Relations among a Community of Balinese on Lombok. *Anthropos* 79, 485-503.

—— (1984d). Hierarchy, Purity, and Equality among a Community of Balinese on Lombok. *Journal of the Anthropological Society of Oxford* 15, 15-29.

—— (1985a). Duality in Aspects of a Balinese Form of Life in Western Lombok. *Cosmos* 1, 15-36.

——(1985b). A Response to Sven Cederroth. *Bijdragen tot de Taal-, Land- en Volkenkunde* 141, 138-9.

—— (1985c). An Account of the Balinese "Person" from Western Lombok. *Bijdragen tot de Taal-, Land- en Volkenkunde* 141, 67-85.

—— (forthcoming). Aspects of the Aesthetics of Rice-growing in a Balinese Form of Life on Lombok. In *Anthropology: Art and Aesthetics*, ed. Jeremy Coote and Anthony Shelton.

Dumézil, Georges (1974). *Mythe et Epopée 1: L'idéologie des trois fonctions dans les épopées des peuples indo-européens*, 2nd edition. Paris: Gallimard.

Friederich, R., ed. E.R. Post (1959). *The Civilization and Culture of Bali*. Calcutta: Susil Gupta (India) Private Ltd.

Gadd, C.J. (1948). *Ideas of Divine Rule in the Ancient East*. London: Oxford University Press.

Geertz, C. (1976). Hooykaas on (The) Geertz(es): A Reply. *Archipel* 12, 219-25.

—— (1980). *Negara: The Theatre State in Nineteenth Century Bali*. Princeton: Princeton University Press.

Geertz, H. and C. Geertz (1975). *Kinship in Bali*. Chicago and London: University of Chicago Press.

Gonda, J. (1959). The Sacred Character of Ancient Indian Kingship. In *The Sacral Kingship*, ed. Widengren, pp. 172-80.

Goris, R. (1960a). The Religious Character of the Village Community. In *Bali: Studies in Life, Thought, and Ritual*, ed. Wertheim, pp. 77-100.

—— (1960b). The Temple System. In *Bali: Studies in Life, Thought and Ritual*, ed. Wertheim, pp. 101-11.

—— (1969). Pura Běsakih through the Centuries. In *Bali: Further Studies in Life, Thought, and Ritual*, ed. Jan van Baal and others (The Hague: Van Hoeve), pp. 89-104.

Goudriaan, T. and C. Hooykaas (1971). *Stuti and Stava (Bauddha, Saiva, Vaisnava) of Balinese Brahman Priests*. Amsterdam: N.V. Noord-Hollandsche Uitgevers Maatschappij.

Grader, C.J. (1960). The State Temples of Měngwi. In *Bali: Studies in Life, Thought and Ritual*, ed. Wertheim, pp. 115-86.

Hidding, K.A.H. (1959). The High God and the King as Symbols of Totality. In *The Sacral Kingship*, ed. Widengren, pp. 54-62.

Hobart, Mark (1978). Padi, Puns and the Attribution of Responsibility. In *Natural Symbols in South East Asia*, ed. G.B. Milner (London: SOAS), pp. 55-87.

—— (1979). A Balinese Village and its Field of Social Relations. Unpublished Ph.D. thesis, University of London (SOAS).

—— (1985). Is God Evil? In *The Anthropology of Evil*, ed. David Parkin (Oxford: Basil Blackwell), pp. 165-93.

Hocart, A.M. (1927). *Kingship*. Oxford: Oxford University Press.

—— (1970a). *Kings and Councillors: An Essay in the Comparative Anatomy of*

*Human Society*, ed. with an introduction by Rodney Needham, with a foreword by E:E. Evans-Pritchard. Chicago and London: University of Chicago Press.

—— (1970b). *The Life-giving Myth, and Other Essays*, 2nd impression ed. with a preface by Rodney Needham. London: Tavistock Publications.

Hooykaas, C. (1964). *Agama Tirtha: Five Studies in Hindu-Balinese Religion*. Amsterdam: N.V. Noord-Hollandsche Uitgevers Maatschappij.

—— (1973). *Kama and Kala: Materials for the Study of Shadow Theatre in Bali*. Amsterdam: N.V. Noord-Hollandsche Uitgevers Maatschappij.

—— (1976). A Short Answer to the Geertzes. *Archipel* 12, 226.

—— (1980). *Drawings of Balinese Sorcery*. Leiden: E.J. Brill.

Hooykaas-van Leeuwen Boomkamp, J. (1961). *Ritual Purification of a Balinese Temple*. Amsterdam: N.V. Noord-Hollandsche Uitgevers Maatschappij.

Kersten, J. (1970). *Tata Bahasa Bali*. Ende, Flores: Arnoldus.

Korn, V.E. (1932). *Het Adatrecht van Bali*. 2nd edition. 's-Gravenhage: Naeff.

Van der Kraan, A. (1975). The Nature of Balinese Rule on Lombok. In *Pre-Colonial State Systems in South-East Asia: The Malay Peninsula, Sumatra, Bali-Lombok, South Celebes*, ed. A. Reid and L. Castles (Kuala Lumpur: Monographs of the Malaysian Branch of the Royal Asiatic Society, No.6), pp. 91-107.

—— (1983). Bali: Slavery and Slave Trade. In *Slavery, Bondage, and Dependency in Southeast Asia*, ed. A. Reid (St. Lucia and London: University of Queensland Press), pp. 315-40.

Lanman, C.R. (1884). *A Sanskrit Reader*. Cambridge, Mass.: Harvard University Press.

Leendertz, C.J. (1894). *De Débâcle van Lombok*. Leiden: J.O. Huysman Jr.

Leenhardt, M. (1979). *Do Kamo. Person and Myth in the Melanesian World*, translated from the French by Basia Miller Gulati. Chicago and London: University of Chicago Press.

Lekkerkerker, C. (1926). De Kastenmaatschappij in Britisch-Indië en op Bali. *Mens and Maatschappij* 2, 175-213, 300-34.

Lévi, S. (1926). *L'Inde et le monde*. Paris: Champion.

Lintgensz, A., ed. V.A. Leupe (1856). Copy van't gheene ick aen Jan Jansz. *Bijdragen tot de Taal-, Land- en Volkenkunde* 5, 203-34.

Mershon, K.E. (1971). *Seven Plus Seven. Mysterious Life Rituals in Bali*. New York: Vantage Books.

Needham, Rodney (1980). *Reconnaissances*. Toronto: University of Toronto Press.

—— (1983). *Against the "Tranquility" of Axioms*. Berkeley, Los Angeles, and London: University of California Press.

—— (1984). The Transformation of Prescriptive Systems in Eastern Indonesia. In *Unity in Diversity: Indonesia as a Field of Anthropological Study*, ed. with an introduction by P.E. de Josselin de Jong (Dordrecht, Holland, and Cinnaminson, USA: Foris Publications), pp. 221-33.

—— (1985). *Exemplars*. Berkeley, Los Angeles, and London: University of California Press.

Pudja, Gdé (1976). *Wedaparikrama*. Jakarta: Lembaga Penyelenggara Penterjemah Kitab Suci Weda.

Raglan, Lord (1945). *Death and Rebirth. A Study in Comparative Religion*. London: Watts & Co.

—— (1949). *The Origins of Religion*. London: Watts & Co.

Rimbaud, J-N-A. (1964). Royauté. In *Rimbaud: Oeuvres poétiques*, chronologie et préface par M. Décaudin (Paris: Garnier-Flammarion), p. 153.

Robson, S.O. (1978). The Ancient Capital of Bali. *Archipel* 16, 75-89.

Schärer, Hans (1963). *Ngaju Religion. The Conception of God among a South Borneo People*, translated from the German by Rodney Needham. The Hague:

Martinus Nijhoff.

Sneeuwjagt, R.J.C. (1926). De legende van het Anstaan der heilige bronnen te Soeranadi. *Tijdschrift voor Indische Taal-, Land- en Volkenkunde* 66, 549-51.

Stutterheim, W.F. (1931). The Meaning of the Hindu-Javanese Candi. *Journal of the American Oriental Society* 51, 1-15.

Swellengrebel, J.L. (1960). Introduction. *Bali: Studies in Life, Thought, and Ritual*, ed. Wertheim, pp. 3-76.

Teeuw, A. (1958). *Lombok: Een Dialect-Geografische Studie.* 's-Gravenhage: Martinus Nijhoff.

Valeri, V. (1980). Notes on the Meaning of Marriage Prestations among the Huaulu of Seram. In *The Flow of Life: Essays on Eastern Indonesia*, ed. James J. Fox (Cambridge, Mass., and London: Harvard University Press), pp. 178-92.

Warna, I Wayan (1978). *Kamus Bali-Indonesia.* Denpasar, Bali: Dinas Pengajaran Propinsi Daerah Tingkat I Bali.

Wertheim, W.F., ed. (1960). *Bali: Studies in Life, Thought, and Ritual.* The Hague and Bandung: Van Hoeve.

Widengren, G. and others, eds. (1959). *The Sacral Kingship.* Leiden: E.J. Brill.

Wirz, P. (1928). *Der Totenkult auf Bali.* Stuttgart: Strecker und Schröder.

Worsley, P.J. (1972). *Babad Buléléng. A Balinese Dynastic Genealogy.* The Hague: Martinus Nijhoff.

# NOTES ON CONTRIBUTORS

PRISCILLA BAWCUTT, formerly a lecturer at the Universities of London and Durham, is an independent scholar resident in Liverpool. She is author of *Gavin Douglas: a Critical Study* (1976) and editor of his *Shorter Poems* for the Scottish Text Society (1967). She is co-editor of *Longer Scottish Poems 1375-1650* (1987), and is currently engaged on a new edition of Dunbar's poems, and a critical study, *Dunbar the Maker*.

SANDRA BILLINGTON is lecturer in Renaissance Drama at the University of Glasgow. Her research interests are those areas where folk customs and games inform the characters and plots of scripted dramas, and she is particularly interested in trying to piece together evidence for popular customs frequently ignored by literate contemporaries. She published *A Social History of the Fool* in 1984 and is at present working on *Mock Kings in Medieval Society and Renaissance Drama*.

JOHN DRAKAKIS is a lecturer in English Studies at the University of Stirling. He is editor of *British Radio Drama* (1981) and *Alternative Shakespeares* (1985) and has published articles, book chapters and reviews on the subjects of Shakespeare, Critical Theory, and Media Studies. He is General Editor of the Methuen English Texts series, and currently engaged on an edition of Marlowe's *Dr. Faustus* for that series.

ANDREW DUFF-COOPER is a visiting lecturer at the Institute of Cultural and Linguistic Studies, Keio University, Tokyo, and an assistant professor at Seitoku Gakuen Tanki Daigaku, Chiba. Since completing his doctoral thesis in Social Anthropology at the University of Oxford in 1983 he has been working on the description and analysis of Balinese life in Pagutan, Western Lombok, Indonesia, where he did his field research, and recently he has also been engaged in the study of Japan. He has published extensively in journals and is writing a book about classification by partition and analogous aspects of Balinese life.

ROBERT HILLENBRAND is reader in Fine Art at the University of Edinburgh, where he has been teaching since 1971. He was educated at the Universities of Cambridge and Oxford, and has held visiting professorships at Princeton and UCLA. He has published widely on Islamic architecture, painting and iconography, with a particular interest in early Islamic art and in the Iranian world. Edinburgh University Press is currently publishing his book *Islamic Architecture*.

EMILY LYLE is an honorary fellow at the School of Scottish Studies, University of Edinburgh. She has been visiting lecturer at the University of Stirling and visiting professor at UCLA, and has held fellowships at Harvard University and The Australian National University. Her publications include editions of folksong collections and articles on literature and on oral tradition. She is now working on two books with the tentative titles *Studies in Western Cosmology* and *Myth, Custom, and Cosmos: The view from Scotland*.

GREGORY NAGY is Francis Jones Professor of Classical Greek and professor of Comparative Literature at Harvard University. His books include *Comparative Studies in Greek and Indic Meter* and *The Best of the Achaeans: Concepts of the Hero in Archaic Greek Poetry*, and his articles include explorations in myth and language and a recent study on "The Indo-European Heritage of Tribal Organization: Evidence from the Greek Polis" in *Proto-Indo-European*, ed. S.N. Skomal and E.C. Polome (1987).

ROSEMARY MUIR WRIGHT is a lecturer in the Department of Art History at the University of St Andrews. She worked in Art Galleries in Glasgow (Pollock House) and in Sheffield (Graves) before joining the Open University as Staff Tutor in Art History with responsibility for the West Midlands. In 1972 she took up an appointment at the University of Stirling to set up the new subject of Art History. She is engaged in research on Mediaeval and Renaissance iconography.

NICOLAS WYATT has lectured in Religious Studies in the University of Glasgow since 1970. His main interests are the religions of the ancient Near East, and in particular the interconnections between them. His published work has appeared mainly in *Ugarit Forschungen*, *Vetus Testamentum*, and *Zeitschrift für die alttestamentliche Wissenschaft*.

COSMOS: The Yearbook of the Traditional Cosmology Society
Volume 2   1986   Kingship

The Traditional Cosmology Society exists for the international study of myth, religion, and cosmology. It aims to provide a forum for discussion and to promote interdisciplinary exchange. The annual subscriptions are as follows:

| | |
|---|---|
| Institutional | £12 |
| Individual | £ 7.50 |
| Joint (two members at the same address receiving only one copy of the publications) | £10 |
| Student (receiving only the newsletter) | £ 3 |

Overseas members. Add £2 to the above rates.
Overseas rates in U.S. dollars are: Institutional $20, Individual $15, Joint $18, and Student $8.

Cheques should be made payable to "Traditional Cosmology Society", and subscriptions should be sent to The Membership Secretary, Traditional Cosmology Society, School of Scottish Studies, University of Edinburgh, 27 George Square, Edinburgh EH8 9LD, Scotland.

Members receive annually two issues of the newsletter, *Shadow*, which is a substantial publication that includes articles and book notices as well as news, and the yearbook *Cosmos*.


Future issues of *Cosmos* will be on the following themes:

3   1987   Analogy
4   1988   Amerindian Cosmology
5   1989   Polytheistic Systems

Contributions are welcome and should be sent to The Editor, *Cosmos*, Traditional Cosmology Society, School of Scottish Studies, University of Edinburgh, 27 George Square, Edinburgh EH8 9LD, Scotland, by 1 October in the year preceding the year of issue. Articles submitted should follow the style of *Cosmos*.